Rath Castle, Co Louth

CASTLES AND STRONGHOUSES OF IRELAND

Mike Salter

ACKNOWLEDGEMENTS

The illustrations in this book are mostly the product of the author's own site surveys in 1971, 1980, 1981, 1983, and 1992. The plans have been redrawn from field notes and drawings and are mostly reproduced to scales of 1:400, 1:800, and 1:1250. The other drawings and maps are also by the author, who took the black and white photos. Thanks are due to Max Barfield, who did the driving on the 1992 expedition, took all the colour photographs, checked proofs of the text, and provided computer facilities. Others who need to be thanked are Pennie Gillis-Taylor who did the driving on the 1983 expedition and Peter Presford who provided the old postcard of Ross Castle. Several owners kindly allowed access to buildings on their lands, and Chris Murphy, the restorer and occupant of Carraigin Castle, was particularly helpful.

AUTHOR'S NOTES

The 350 buildings which feature in this book are a personal choice from the 2,500 or so fortified buildings of the period 1180-1680 known to have existed in Ireland, selection being to some degree determined by what information and illustrations were available. The most notable buildings are all included plus a selection of others, some of which are very ruined but still display interesting features.

Deciding what boundaries to use was difficult especially in view of Ireland's sensitive political state. Using the ancient provinces gives gazetteers of manageable lengths, and to some degree emphasises regional architectural styles. It also means that material for what is now Northern Ireland plus Donegal (Cavan and Monaghan have few castles of interest) is conveniently grouped together in the last section.

Each of the main levels of a building is called a storey in this book, the basement or ground level room being the first storey. Sleeping lofts squeezed under vaults are usually treated as separate storeys. Attics entirely within roof spaces are generally mentioned separately, a building being thus of so many storeys plus an attic.

It is recommended that visitors use the Ordnance Survey 1:126,720 scale maps to find monuments. Grid References are given in the gazetteers. Where A.M. follows the grid reference the castle is maintained in a reasonable state as an ancient monument. An additional * indicates that there are set opening hours and/or an admission fee payable. The other maintained ruins can be freely visited at any time. Most of the unmaintained sites can be visited but some are in a dangerous condition so take care. Ask permission where appropriate (it will rarely be refused) and remember to close gates, keep dogs on leads, and leave the monuments in the condition you find them.

All measurements quoted in the text and the scales on the plans are metric as the buildings have been measured in metres. Additional dimensions and scales in feet and inches would have taken up too much space. Feet are however used in one instance where a medieval statute is being quoted. For those who feel the need to make a conversion 3 metres is fractionally under 10 feet. Unless specifically stated as otherwise all dimensions are external at or near ground level.

I.S.B.N. 1 871731 15 1

Copyright 1993 by Mike Salter. First published July 1993.
Folly Publications, Folly Cottage, 151 West Malvern Rd, Malvern, Worcs, WR14 4AY.

Printed by Severnside Printers, Bridge House, Upton-upon-Severn, Worcs, WR8 OHG

Inchmore Castle, Co Kilkenny

CONTENTS

A map appears at the end of each gazetteer

GLOSSARY OF TERMS

Ashlar	- Masonry of blocks with even faces and square edges.
Bailey	- A defensible space enclosed by a wall or palisade and a ditch.
Barbican	- Porch, tower, or enclosure defending a gateway.
Bartizan	- A turret corbelled out from a wall, usually at the summit.
Bastion	- Flanking projection of the same height as the main wall.
Bawn	- An enclosure, usually modest in size, with a stone wall.
Brattice	- A wooden projection from a wall top providing machicolations.
Caphouse	- Small square gabled space over a staircase or round projection.
Casemate	- A small vaulted chamber providing flanking fire along a wall.
Chancel	- The eastern part of a church containing the altar.
Corbel	- A projecting bracket supporting other stonework or timbers.
Crannog	- A small artificial island occupied as a dwelling.
Cross-Window	- Window with a mullion and a transom but no tracery.
Donjon	- A citadel or ultimate strongpoint. Now usually called a keep.
Four Centred Arch	- A flat arch with each curve drawn from two compass points.
Hall House	- A two storey building containing a hall above a basement.
Harling	- Or Roughcast. Plaster with gravel or other coarse aggregate.
Hoodmould	- Projecting moulding above an arch or lintel to throw off water.
Jamb	- The side of a doorway, window, or other opening.
Keep	- A citadel or ultimate strongpoint. Originally called a donjon.
Light	- A compartment of a window.
Loggia	- Sheltered space behind a colonade.
Loop	- A small opening for light or the discharge of missiles.
Machicolation	- A slot for dropping stones or shooting missiles at assailants.
Moat	- A ditch, water filled or dry, around an enclosure.
Motte	- A steeply sided flat topped mound, usually mostly man-made.
Mullion	- A vertical member dividing the lights of a window.
Murder Hole	- Shooting slot in the roof of an entrance passage.
Nave	- The part of a church or chapel used by the congregation.
Ogival Arch	- Arch of oriental origin with both convex and concave curves.
Oriel	- A bay window projecting out from a wall above ground level.
Parapet	- A wall for protection at any sudden drop.
Pilaster	- A flat buttress. A common feature of 12th-13th century buildings
Plinth	- The projecting base of a wall. May be battered or stepped.
Portcullis	- Wooden gate designed to rise and fall in vertical grooves.
Postern	- A secondary gateway or doorway. A back entrance.
Quoin	- Dressed (i.e. carefully shaped) stone at a corner of a building.
Rath	- Circular enclosure with a rampart and ditch or drystone wall.
Scale-and-Platt Staircase	- Staircase with short straight flights and turns at landings.
Soffit	- The underside of an arch.
Souterrain	- Underground stone lined passage and chamber. A hiding place.
Spandrel	- A surface between an arch and the rectangle containing it.
Stronghouse	- A mansion capable of being defended against an attack.
Squinch	- Arch thrown across an angle between walls to carry walling.
Tower House	- Self contained house with the main rooms stacked vertically.
Tracery	- Intersecting ribwork in upper part of a later Gothic window.
Transom	- A horizontal member dividing the lights of a window.
Trefoiled	- Divided by cusping into three foils or lobes.
Voussoir	- Small wedge shaped stone used to form an arch.
Wall Walk	- A walkway on top of a wall, protected by a parapet.
Ward	- A stone walled defensive enclosure.

INTRODUCTION

Forts built of limestone blocks laid without mortar or of timber with earth ramparts and ditches were common in Ireland in the Dark Ages but only seven castles are mentioned in contemporary annals prior to the Norman invasion of 1169-70. These castles were probably mostly of timber as several are recorded as having been destroyed by fire either maliciously or accidentally. The palace of the King of Leinster at Ferns seems to have been of stone, but nothing remains of it or of any of the others, so there are no means of assessing them in relation to their English and Welsh contemporaries. Thus our story effectively starts with the Norman invasion, and ends with the Cromwellian campaign of 1649-52 after which defences ceased to be fashionable or necessary and the many defensible residences were either modernised or left to decay.

Buildings of mortared stone take several years of relatively peaceful conditions to construct so for several decades after the invasion the numerous castles which the thin veneer of Normans built to maintain their stranglehold on Leinster, Meath, eastern Ulster, and parts of Connacht and Munster were mostly hasty constructions of earth and wood. Commonly earth was dug from a circular ditch and piled within it to form a motte which bore a wooden house or tower forming the lord's residence within a small palisaded enclosure. Usually there was a base court or bailey around the motte or on one side of it. This enclosure would contain a hall, chapel, kitchen, stables, barns, workshops, etc, and was normally defended by a rampart bearing a stockade and a ditch.

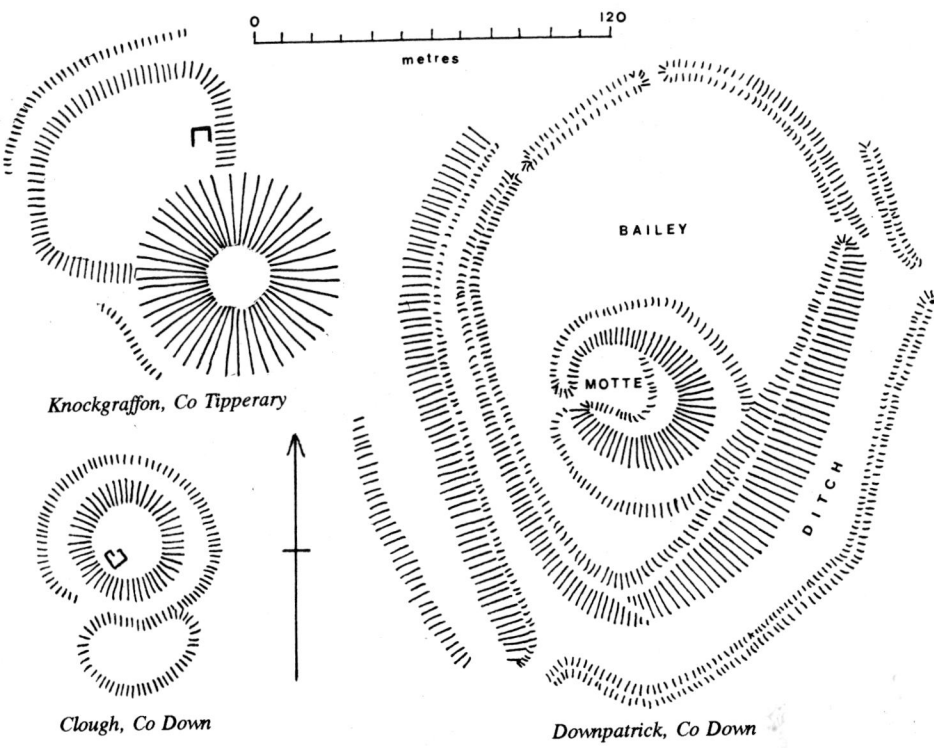

0   120
metres

Knockgraffon, Co Tipperary

BAILEY

MOTTE

DITCH

Clough, Co Down

Downpatrick, Co Down

Plans of Motte and Bailey Castles

Shanid Castle, Co Limerick

Dromore Castle, Co Down

Motte and bailey castles vary greatly in size and shape. Natural features such as promontories or glacial mounds might be used, or even an ancient burial mound as at Knowth. Usually the terrain was allowed to dictate the layout of the defences. On low lying sites the ditches might be water filled permanently or seasonally. There are about 100 mottes in Leinster with particular concentrations in Meath, Westmeath, and Louth. There are a similar number in Ulster, mostly in south Antrim and east Down. Few of the Ulster mottes have baileys, many probably only being temporary observation posts.

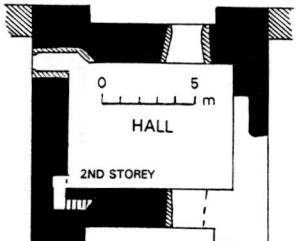

Plan of The Keep at Adare

The ringwork is a fairly common hybrid type between the motte and the bailey, being less high than the former but smaller and with a higher rampart than is normal for the latter. There may be an accompanying bailey or other outworks. Sometimes a ringwork was built first and then the hollow later filled in to make a motte as at Dunsilly, Co Antrim. Ringworks first appeared in Ireland at the time of the Norman invasion although they are similar to the raths of the native rulers. They were still being erected in Henry III's reign (1216-72) but the mottes are probably all pre-1216.

Gerald of Wales and other contemporary writers recorded the construction of a few of the early motte and bailey castles and noted attacks upon them by the Irish, but not many have any subsequent recorded history although some seem to have still had habitable wooden buildings as late as the 15th century. Except for a few of the largest and most important sites and a small number later refortified in stone the earthwork castles are not individually described in the gazetteers.

There are very few medieval buildings in Ireland where the evidence of surviving structures, contemporary records, and archaeological excavation can be tied together to give a precise undisputed dating for the whole or a significant part of a structure. This is partly because Ireland's chaotic history has seen the destruction of many old documents. So guesswork and analogies with similar buildings in England and Wales are required to put the fairly modest amount of surviving early stone castle works into some sort of order of development. Probably the oldest Irish castles with mortared stone walls are the polygonal courts on rocky sites at Carrickfergus (p138), Dundrum (p146), and Carlingford (p50), all on the east coast and generally accepted as being of c1185-1200. The last is the smallest but had a gateway passage between two rectangular towers and two or three other flanking towers, the one which has survived being square at the base but with the outer angles chamfered off above. The other two courts were very plain as first built but by the 1190s a four storey square tower of some size was being built into a corner of the court at Carrickfergus. Turrets are raised above two projecting corners containing the latrines and a spiral staircase respectively. Shanid (p128) also has remains of an early ovoid court on a motte.

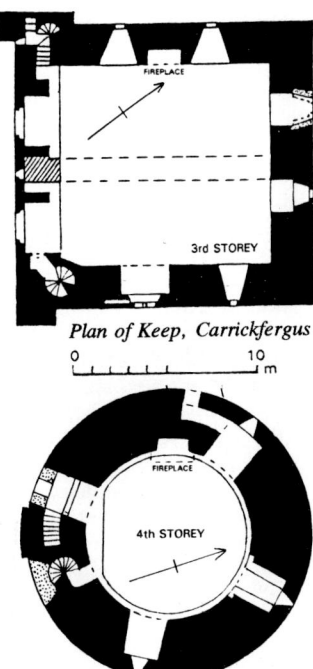

Plan of Keep, Carrickfergus

0   10
          m

Plan of Keep, Nenagh

The Keep, Maynooth, Co Kildare

Medieval writers would call a tower like that at Carrickfergus a great tower (magnum turris) or donjon, but since the 18th century the word keep has been in general use. There is another square four storey keep of c1200 at Adare (p89), where there is also an early hall standing just outside the ringwork containing the keep. Trim (p77) and Maynooth (p70) have large nearly square keeps of c1200-10 originally designed to contain just two storeys with the lord's presence or audience chamber and private living room cum bedroom set side by side on the upper storey instead of with a private room above the public room as in the tower keeps. A forebuilding protecting the entrance at Maynooth has been destroyed. At Trim the entrance was in one of four wings projecting from the middle of each wall, and the corners of the main building were carried up as turrets. This keep lies isolated within a spacious D-shaped bailey with a square NW gatehouse perhaps of c1200-10. The landward wall of c1220-40 has five fairly evenly spaced D-shaped towers originally open at the back and a unique gatehouse which is a full round in plan and has a narrow barbican in front. The largest and most massive Irish keep is that probably of c1200-20 at Dunamase (p59).

The corners of square towers are vulnerable to attack by mining and require cut stones (quoins) of reasonable quality, so round and polygonal forms were occasionally used instead. The much altered multi-sided keep at Athlone (p46) can be fairly securely dated to c1215-20, and other polygonal keeps at Castleknock (p52) and Shanid (p128) were probably of the same decade. The latter was round internally. The circular keeps at Dundrum (p146), Inchiquin (p114), and Nenagh (p123) may also be as early as c1215. To the latter was later added a small court with four round flanking towers, between two of which was the gateway. Other round keeps at Ardfinnan (p90), Parkavonear (p124) and Clougoughter (p142) of later in the 13th century.

Dublin (p58), Kilkenny, (p66), and Limerick (p118) are three of the earliest stone castles in Ireland, dating c1205-30. Each had a quadrangular court with large round corner towers and a twin round towered gatehouse. The inner bailey walls at Adare, with one round tower and a square gatehouse may be as early as c1210-40. Probably of c1260-80 are Liscarroll (p118), a rectangle with round corner towers and a rectangular gatehouse, Roscrea (p127), with the same elements but a D-shaped ward, and Castle Roche (p53), where the triangular ward surrounds the stump of a possibly earlier square tower and has a twin round towered gatehouse and one round flanking tower. Quadrangular courts with rectangular gatehouses at Cahir (p100) and Glanworth (p111) were originally built at about this time but were much altered and rebuilt subsequently. The rectangular court with large D-shaped towers flanking the gateway and at each corner at Roscommon (p42) was built by Edward I in the 1280s and shows similarities to the castle he built at Harlech in North Wales at the same time. D-shaped corner towers, but no gatehouse, appear in the bailey wall of about the same time around an earlier keep at Greencastle (p150), and they also appear in the gatehouse and in a mid-wall position at Ballymote (p30). There the corner towers were fully round and the overall plan was similar to that of the inner ward of another of Edward I's castles, Beaumaris, of c1295-1310.

Ballintober (p28), has a large square courtyard of c1300-10 with outer faces of the gatehouse towers and corner towers made polygonal. The polygonal form is also seen in the outer faces of the gatehouse towers and a large tower at the other end of the courtyard of Greencastle (p151) in Donegal, built c1305-15. Three Limerick castles, Brittas (p97), Carrigogunnell (p103), and Castle Connell (p105), all originally had quadrangular courts of modest size with round corner towers, the latter two being set on rocks. There were similar castles at Dunluce (p147), Granagh (p63), Kiltinane, and Quin (p125), all much altered subsequently. At Castle Grace (p105) two of the corner towers were square. Fragments of other 13th century courtyard castles remain at Ardea (p90) and Askeaton (p91), set on rocks, and Clonmore. Ballymoon (p48) has a square court of c1310 with latrine turrets giving rudimentary flanking fire along three sides but no proper towers.

Corner tower at Greencastle, Co Down

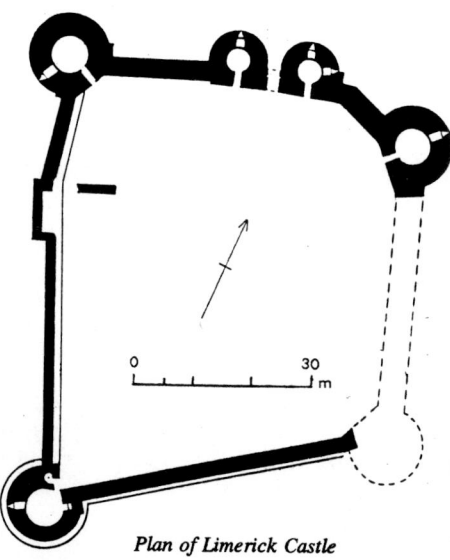

Plan of Limerick Castle

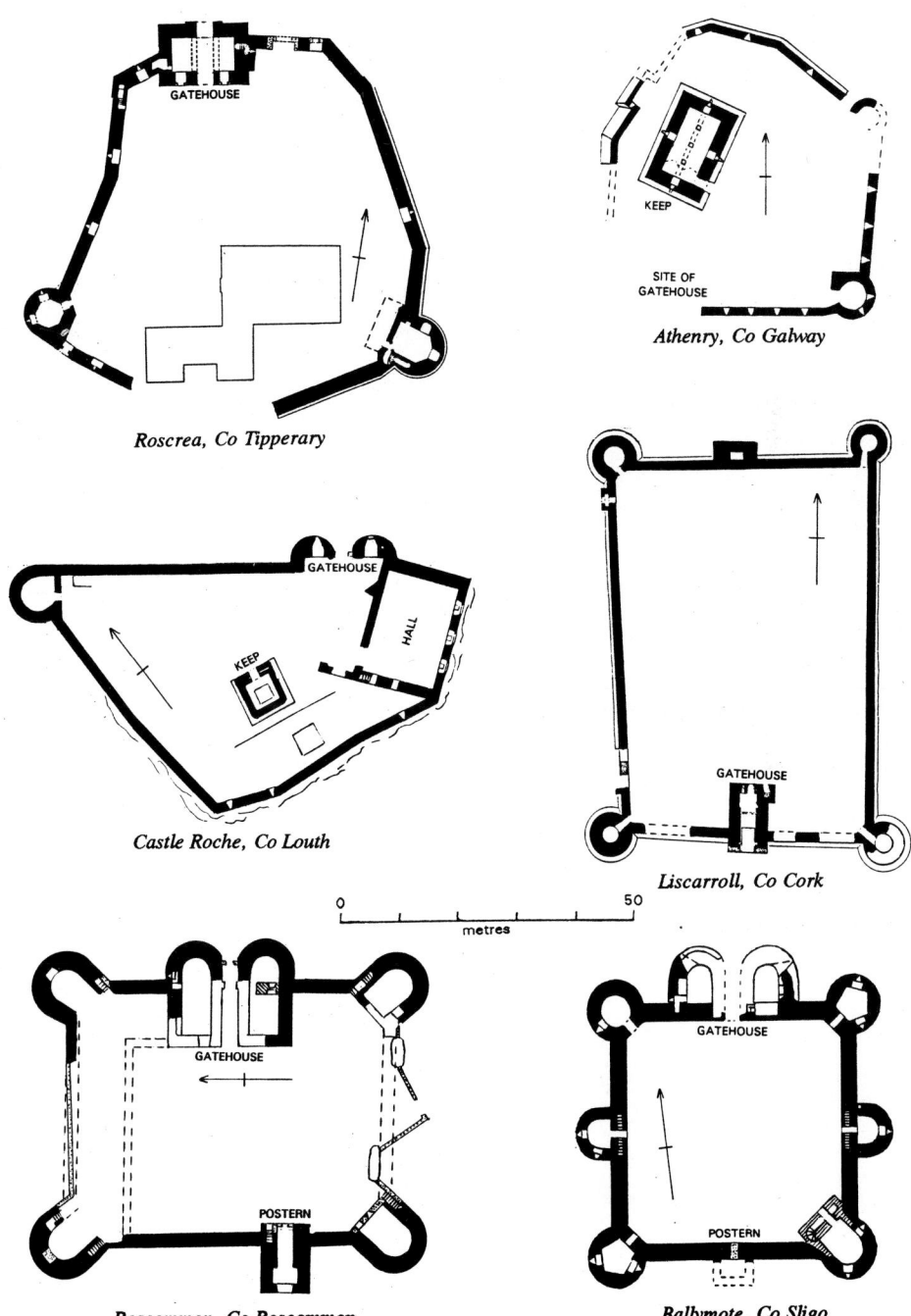

Roscrea, Co Tipperary

Athenry, Co Galway

Castle Roche, Co Louth

Liscarroll, Co Cork

Roscommon, Co Roscommon

Ballymote, Co Sligo

Plans of six 13th century courtyard castles.

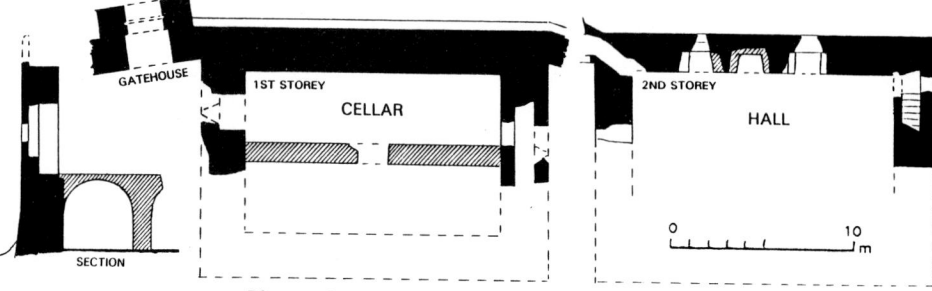

Plans and Section of Keep, Rinndown, Co Roscommon

There are remains of rectangular keeps which contained just a hall over a basement in their original form dating from c1225-65 at Athenry (p26), Ballylahan (p28), Castle Connor (p32), Clonmacnois (p55), Dunmore (p35), Greencastle (p150), and Rinndown (p42). At the latter the keep lies on the most vulnerable side of the bailey. The keeps at Athenry, Ballylahan, and Greencastle all stand isolated within baileys with twin towered gatehouses or round flanking towers. Ballinamantain (p28) has a nearly square keep in a corner of a large bailey with a twin towered gatehouse. Annaghkeen (p25), Carraigin (p30-31), and Castlecarra (p31), all in the parts of Connacht conquered by the de Burgos in the late 13th century, are hall houses, i.e hall keeps intended as modest self contained residences lacking outer defences of stone, earth or wood. There are less well preserved remains of similar buildings at Castle More (p106) in Munster, and Kindlestown (p67) in Leinster. All these buildings had their main entrance at hall level, although some also had a separate entrance to the basement. Only Clonmacnois has a spiral stair in a corner although some of the others have straight stairways in end walls. At the others communication between hall and basement can only have been by a ladder and trap-door. In most of them the basements were provided with crosswalls or arcades to carry vaults in later in the medieval period. Some halls may have had a private room partitioned off at one end and Carraigin and Annaghkeen have tiny wings to contain latrines. Originally the walls rose high above the roofs to protect them. Later on this was realised to be a waste of space and a third storey would be created in the old roof space, and an attic for servants to sleep in would be provided in a new gabled roof within the wall-walk.

Hall House at Annaghkeen, Co Galway

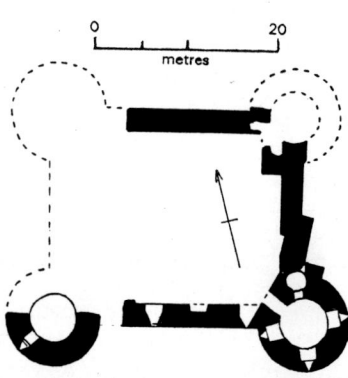

Plan of Ferns Castle, Co Wexford

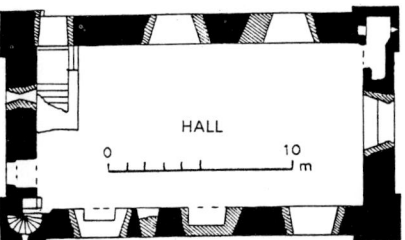

Plan of Keep, Greencastle, Co Down

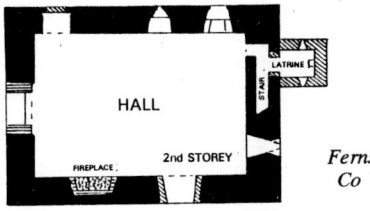

Hall House, Castlecarra, Co Mayo

Ferns Castle, Co Wexford

By 1260 Henry III had walled in a spacious outer bailey at Carrickfergus with a gateway between twin round towers. The outer bailey at Adare is perhaps a little later and contains a second very ruined hall with service rooms at one end. Another hall of c1260-80 adjoins the gatehouse at Roche, whilst the foundations of halls remaining at Trim and in the inner ward at Carrickfergus are somewhat earlier, and there are footings of four ranges of c1310 at Ballymoon. Otherwise little is known of the domestic buildings of these castles apart from the occasional documentary reference.

Peculiar to Ireland is a small group of large and impressive keeps of three or four storeys with round corner towers. That at Carlow (p52) may be of c1220; those at Lea (p68) and Ferns (p62) are more likely to be of c1245-60 as they have windows with trefoiled heads to the lights. All of these keeps had straight mural stairs running up and down from entrances at the level of the hall on the second storey. Terryglass (p130) is smaller and perhaps later and has corner towers of differing sizes, the smallest containing a wide spiral stair. The tower at Delvin (p57) may also belong to this series. Only Lea retains outer defences comprising an oval court with round bastions around the keep and a spacious outer bailey with a gatehouse with twin U-shaped towers added by Edward I in the 1290s. Ferns has a rock-cut ditch around the keep and one tower contains a remarkable rib-vaulted chapel.

There is very little work in Irish Castles which can be dated with certainty to the period 1310-1430. The country was generally in a poor state because of the devastation caused by the invasion by Edward Bruce in 1350 and the Black Death of 1350. The Gaelic Irish chiefs gradually recovered much of the territory taken by the Normans and eventually only the English Pale centred on Dublin and a few isolated towns like Galway and Limerick remained under direct English control. One or two plain towers like Buncrana (p136) and Roslee, Co Sligo may have been built by Gaelic chiefs in the 14th century, but in this period such lords were normally more intent on destroying the castles built by the Normans than building castles of their own. A notable exception is Harry Avery's Castle (p152), a court with a tower house on one side with twin rounded towers facing the field like the late 13th century gatehouses. The keep of three low unvaulted storeys without mural chambers at Moylough (p38) is perhaps 14th century and at Rathumney (p74) is a long, low and rather domestic looking building of two storeys with multiple ground floor entrances.

Much of the Archbishop of Dublin's castle at Swords (p76), which has a chapel and adjacent gateway at one end of a large court with a big tower at the other end, may be 14th century, and at Ballyloughan (p48) is a quadrangular court with rectangular corner towers of differing sizes. A gatehouse in the middle of one side is rectangular with round towers on the outer corners, like several English gatehouses of c1370-85. In Limerick parts of the domestic buildings at Carrigogunnell (p103), including a hexagonal room are late 14th century, and at Glenogra (p112) there are remains of a thickly walled court of c1400 with two large polygonal corner towers.

During the late 13th and 14th centuries many minor landowners lived in timber framed buildings set within a small moated enclosure, usually rectangular in shape and representing a more domestic and much less defensible development of the motte. Recent research has shown that more of these sort of sites exist in Ireland than was previously thought. The moats served as status symbols, provided a barrier to keep vagrants and wild animals out and domestic animals, children, and servants in, and also provided a habitat for waterfowl and fish which were an important part of the diet of the people living on the platforms within the moats.

Before moving onto the tower houses of the 15th century and later we should now make a few comments generally about castles as they appeared before that period. Walls were often whitewashed both inside and out, traces of it surviving occasionally. Carraigin as restored in the 1970s gives an idea of what they may have looked like originally although it should be noted that glass was virtually unknown in medieval castles and windows were closed with wooden shutters so the rooms would be dark, another reason for the liberal use of whitewash. The more important public and private rooms might have wall paintings of biblical or allegorical scenes, tapestries or other hangings, or a modest amount of wainscoting. Latrines are commonly formed in the wall thickness but mural chambers big enough to serve as private rooms rarely occur in Ireland prior to the 15th century. The sort of privacy we now take for granted simply did not exist in a medieval castle. Even lords and ladies usually had servants sleeping in the same room although the lordly bed might be screened off or curtained. Many of the occupants bedded down in the main hall where there would be a central hearth with the smoke from the fire escaping through a hole or louvre in the roof. Others might sleep in the warmth of the kitchen. Otherwise only by several people huddling together in a bed or amongst the rushes that often covered the floors was it possible to keep warm. Furniture was sparse and of the simplest kind. Only the lord and his family were likely to have individual chairs in their room or in the hall, but the latter would contain tables and benches, and there would be several chests in which clothes, plate, utensils, and valuables would be kept.

Swords Castle, Co Dublin

Dating the many hundreds of surviving but mostly ruined tower houses in Ireland is a major problem. Only for about a tenth of the 200 or so towers mentioned in this book is there firm evidence for fixing the construction date within a particular decade. Some are hard to assign even to a particular century as late 16th and 17th century builders often retained or reverted to features thought to have first appeared in the mid 15th century. It is not easy to say why the native Irish and the Anglo-Norman families who had intermarried with them and adopted many of their customs suddenly started building towers in large numbers. But once a few families had transferred from a moated timber house, crannog, or drystone fort to a much more impressive, secure, and comfortable tower house then naturally their neighbours would eventually imitate them, building to whatever scale they could afford.

A handful of towers in Munster may be as early as the 1430s, and on the eastern coast we have an obvious starting point with the Irish parliament's statute of 1429 granting a £10 subsidy to those landowners in the counties of Dublin, Meath, Kildare, and Louth (The English Pale) who in the next ten years built themselves an embattled stone tower at least forty feet high by twenty feet long and sixteen feet wide. Later on it was ordained that the towers built in Meath were to be at least fifteen feet by twelve feet internally. By 1449 sufficient towers had been built for a limit on new construction to be considered. The majority of other towers are the product of a fairly evenly paced building period beginning c1470 and lasting until the 1620s. In Galway Derryhivenny (p33) was dated 1643 on the roughly contemporary bawn wall whilst Castle ffrench is thought to have had a tower house built as late as the 1680s.

In the English Pale, and the counties of Down, Wicklow, and Wexford where English influence was strong many of the towers are not much bigger than the modest dimensions stipulated in the 1429 statute. The majority are probably mid to late 15th century but some are certainly later, Athgoe (p46) being dated 1579, and Castle Ward (p141) being as late as c1620. Towers in these areas generally conform to the layout of towers of the 14th, 15th, and 16th centuries in Scotland, Cumbria, and Northumbria, but have features peculiar to Ireland such as double stepped battlements, machicolations at parapet level over the entrance, and murder holes commanding entrance lobbies. There is no evidence that the basement loops in these towers, commonly splayed both inward and out from a narrow mid-wall opening, were for the discharge of firearms and few of these towers have pistol-loops. Except in Wexford where fine bawns survive at Rathmacknee (p74) and Kiliane (p66) and elsewhere, and some more fragmentary remains in Co Down, the bawns accompanying these towers have been destroyed. On the whole they seem to have been lightly built. At Howth (p64), Monkstown (p72), and Rathcoffey (p73) bawn gatehouses remain although in each case the thin bawn walls have mostly or entirely been destroyed or replaced.

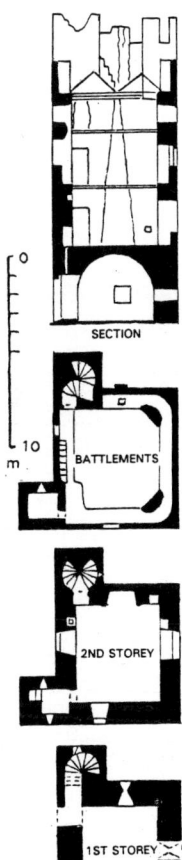

Plans and Section of Dunmahon Castle, Co Louth

Donore Castle, Co Meath

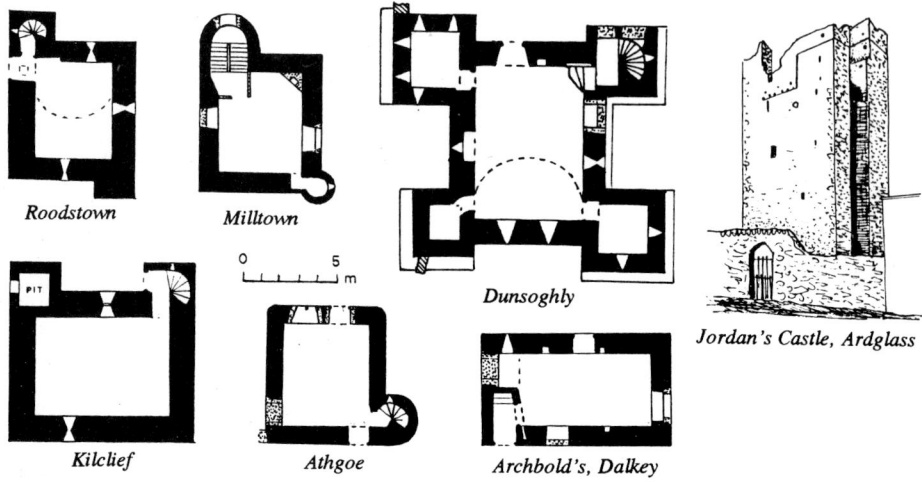

Roodstown   Milltown

Dunsoghly

Jordan's Castle, Ardglass

Kilclief   Athgoe   Archbold's, Dalkey

Tower Houses in the English Pale

The internal layout of these towers tends to comprise a cellar, hall or main living room above, and one or two storeys of bedrooms on top. Over the cellar is usually a vault, sometimes with a sleeping loft squeezed underneath it, providing a solid floor for the hall. Few of these towers have walling over about 1.3m thick above the vault and consequently they lack mural chambers and to accommodate the staircase and tiers of latrines small wings or turrets are provided. At Dunmahon (p60) the square turrets project from adjacent walls whilst at Roodstown (p75) they are set at diagonally opposite corners. In these cases the turrets each only flank one wall but at Castle Dexter (p57) each turret flanks two walls. This also occurs at Lisclogher (p69), where the turrets are round and the stair turret is larger than its twin. It should be noted that these towers are considerably earlier than the so-called Z-plan castles in Scotland. Kilclief (p153), built c1430, was the prototype for a number of towers in Co Down where there are two square turrets on the same face with an arch between them high up to provide a machicolation defending the entrance. Many of the towers had additional corner turrets at the top, usually with their innermost corner carried on a squinch arch between the thin upper walls. Such top turrets are always square, even on a tower such as Milltown (p71), probably late 16th century, where the stair turret is D-shaped, and the latrine turret is a tiny full round.

Athlumney (p46) and Dunsoghly (p60), both probably of c1450, are larger versions of the towers described above with square turrets of differing sizes and degrees of projection at all four corners. Kilsallagan has the last remains of another tower of this type, and at Liscartan (p69) are two standing next to each other. Still larger buildings with round corner towers are Enniscorthy (p61) as rebuilt in the 1580s, and Dunmoe (p60), which is probably 15th century. Bunratty (p98), built c1450, has a large three storey main block with many staircases and passages in the walls and four square corner towers all of the same size and degree of projection. The much altered and also still habitable tower at Dunmahon in Co Roscommon has the same plan, and one end of another castle of this type survives at Listowell (p119). Two of the largest tower houses in Ireland are the MacCarthy seats of Ballycarbury (p94) and Blarney (p97), both probably of c1440-60. Each has a small wing at one corner. At Blarney the wing stood as a tower on its own before the massive main body was added on. Other exceptionally large tower houses built by the native Irish in the late 15th century are those of Greencastle (p151) and Donegal (p145).

Until remodelled in the 1620s the Donegal tower conformed to a standard internal layout for towers in Connacht and Munster with the hall moved up to the top storey and one end wall thickened substantially to contain a spiral staircase and tiers of bedrooms above the entrance lobby and guard room at ground level. Towers with this layout are peculiar to Ireland. It allows the hall to be the biggest room, with thinner walls and larger windows than would be safe further down and, as there is usually a vault immediately below permits a central hearth with a smoke hole in the roof. Later on mural fireplaces became the norm and the roof-space within the wall-walk could then be used as an attic. The wall-walks usually slope outwards and have wide gullies draining through holes in the base of the parapet. Sometimes there is a sleeping loft over the basement which may be covered with a vault. Between this space and the thick end wall a passage carried on an arch over one end of the cellar would sometimes be partitioned off to give access from the staircase to a latrine in the far side wall. The next level would be a suite for the lord, the main room forming his living room and the smaller room in the end wall his bedroom and above that a sleeping loft under the main vault. The haunches of the vaults were sometimes left hollow, allowing the squeezing in of extra sleeping chambers or a prison or secret room.

Towers in Connacht and Munster are nearly always plain rectangles in plan and usually have a battered base rising at least one storey high and then are very gracefully battered at a shallower angle to the summit. The towers are often faced with finely wrought ashlar blocks fitted with great skill. Doorway arches are commonly made of just two large stones instead of numerous voussoirs. Windows are single lights with square, round, or ogival heads, except at the uppermost levels where tall narrow two-light windows with transoms occur. A feature peculiar to Ireland is the use of angle loops serving the staircases, passages, and mural chambers of the middle storeys. The rooms would, however, have been very dark, even when all the shutters (glass was rarely used) were open. Wickerwork mats were used to form vaults and the imprint of these can sometimes be seen on the mortar bed on the underside of a vault.

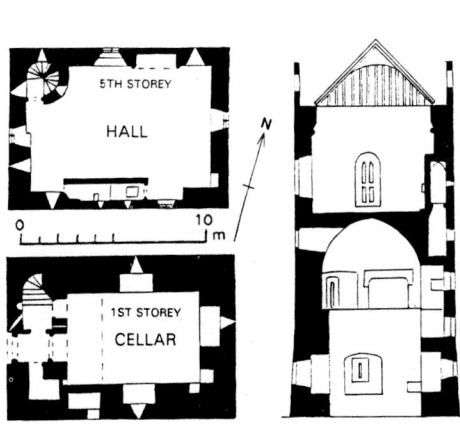

Plans and Section of Tower at Aughnanure, Co Galway

Garraunboy Castle, Co Limerick. Part of the thick end wall containing chambers has fallen.

Brackloon Castle, Co Galway

Plan of Leamaneh Castle,
Co Clare

0   10
⌐_ _ _ _ _ _ _ _ _ _ ⌐ m

SECTION

BATTLEMENTS

Brackloon,
Plan & Section

Mannin,
Co Galway

Bourchiers' Castle, Co Limerick

The towers generally have roof gables set within a continuous wall-walk off which there may be machicolations as at Dunguaire (p34) where there is one in the middle of each face. At Burnchurch (p49), Foulksrath (p62), Twomileborris (p131), Tudbridbritain (p78), and other towers in Kilkenny and Tipperary one or both walls is raised up to form higher fighting platforms reached from the main wall-walk by narrow external stairs. Bartizans or projecting fighting platforms, never common in England and Wales, and mostly only found in a roofed over "pepperpot" form from c1560 onwards in Scotland, are commonly found on the corners of Irish buildings from the end of the 15th century until the 1640s. Round bartizans tend to be supported on the double stepped type of corbel found throughout Britain. Square bartizans are carried on the tall inverted pyramid shaped corbels peculiar to Ireland. In both cases there are machicolation slots between the corbels and there may be shot holes in the parapet. Clonburren (p54) has corbels for both corner bartizans and mid wall machicolations. The continuous machicolated parapet at Blarney was probably added c1600. Where the roof gables stand directly above the outer wall face it is a sign of a late construction date or, as at Anbally, Athenry, and Dunmore, evidence of alteration after c1580. A late tower at Danganbrack (p108) with four roof gables set above the outer wallfaces has open bartizans despite the lack of wall-walks. In some towers square projections like bartizans (for convenience they are called bartizans in this book) are provided at the level of the lord's suite half way up the tower instead of at parapet level, as at Aughnanure (p27), where there are two at the entrance end, and Ballymalis (p95), Fiddaun (p35), and Srah (p76) where a pair are set on diagonally opposite corners giving all round flanking fire and cover for the wall base.

Some towers in Limerick, Clare, and Galway have clear indications that the thick end wall containing the staircase and small chambers was partially or wholly erected before the main body. The joins can be clearly see at Ballinalacken (p92), Seefin (p43), and Bourchiers (p97). At Mannin (p37) and Cratloekeel (p108) the main body was either never added or has been entirely dismantled to provide materials for the much later and slighter farm buildings now adjoining. At Leamaneh (p117) an L-planned stronghouse was later added instead of the intended more modestly sized main body.

Round tower house at Grantstown, Co Kilkenny

0   5
⌞ ⌞ ⌞ ⌞ ⌞ ⌞ m

1ST STOREY   3RD STOREY   5TH STOREY

Plans of Ballynahow Castle

Raheen Castle, Co Cork

Straight flights of steps, especially if in conjunction with a lack of fireplaces as at Carrigaphooca (p103) and Cashel (p103), are thought to indicate an early date. Many towers have a straight flight of steps from the entrance lobby to the foot of a spiral staircase starting in a corner at second or third storey level as at Anbally (p24). Until the mid 16th century at least one level would be vaulted but some of the later towers lack vaults over the main rooms, although the tier of rooms in the end wall might still have at least one vault. Later towers tend to have their upper rooms better lighted with mullion and transom windows of the usual Elizabethan type, sometimes with hoodmoulds. Occasionally, as at Knockkelly (p117), these are set in vertical tiers. The first record of native Irishmen using handguns is as late as 1487 so it can be assumed that pistol-loops only began to be introduced in the towers c1500. The towers were not intended to stand up to long sieges by well equipped armies using cannon and were quickly reduced by such in the campaigns of 1535-6, the 1580s, and 1641-52. Few Irish lords possessed artillery, which was difficult to transport around a country with few good roads, and the towers were quite adequate as a defence against raids by feuding neighbours or for a new landlord to overawe an unruly native peasantry.

Of particular interest are a series of about sixteen round tower houses most of which are in Munster. Amongst the finest of these are Ballynahow (p96) which has four machicolations at regular intervals at the summit, and Newtown (p124), which stands on a pyramidal square base. Recesses where the pyramid dies into the cylinder have shot holes in the sills of third storey windows commanding the whole of the base. A similar idea is used at the rectangular towers of Ballymona and Raheen (p125) in Co Cork where there are gable shaped recesses in the lower parts of the walls with shot holes in each apex, immediately above which are third storey windows.

Many of the towers in Connacht and Munster still retain a bawn wall of about the same date or a little later despite these slighter works having been more prone to collapse and stone robbing in later centuries. The walls are sometimes placed on low rock outcrops but rarely had ditches outside them. They tend to be between 1 and 1.6m thick and are not normally more than 4.5m high to the wall-walk. Doe (p144) has several bartizans providing all round flanking fire, plus one round turret or flanker. Termon (p159) and Pallas (p39) have round flankers at each end of the entrance front with the tower at or near the other end of the bawn. The bawn at Aghalard (p24) is an irregular polygon with square turrets flanking the entrance front and an outbuilding in the far corner. That at Dunguaire (p34) is also polygonal with one square turret beside the gate. Aughnanure (p27) has inner and outer bawns with round and square flankers. This castle also has remains of a large banquetting hall. Other halls remain at Askeaton (p91), Dromahair (p34), and Newcastle West (p124), the latter retaining its original roof. Otherwise outbuildings rarely survive, probably because most of them were modest lean-to buildings of perishable materials like timber and thatch.

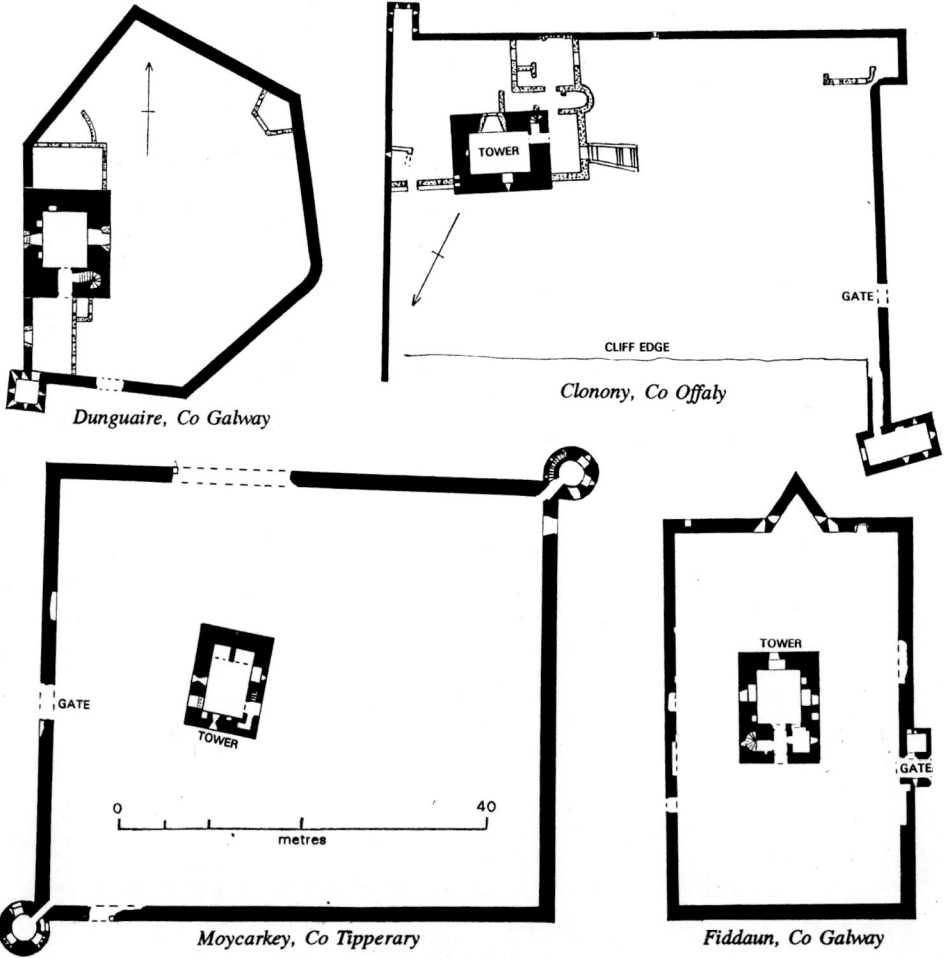

Dunguaire, Co Galway

Clonony, Co Offaly

Moycarkey, Co Tipperary

Fiddaun, Co Galway

Plans of Tower Houses with Bawns

Moygara (p38) has square two storey flankers at three corners of a rectangular bawn and a tower house higher but not larger than the flankers at the fourth. There is a two storey gatehouse in the middle of one side, a feature also found at Pallas and Fiddaun (p35). The bawns at Knockkelly (p117) and Ballynakill (p96) are exceptionally large. Rectangular bawns at Caheravoley (p30) and Moycarkey (p123) have round flankers with shot holes at diagonally opposite corners and the house or tower standing in the middle. The thinly walled bawn at Clonony (p55) has large rectangular flankers. The one round flanker remaining of the bawn at Burnchurch (p49) contained three storeys of living rooms over a basement but generally flankers were military posts only not normally having more than two storeys below the wall-walk. The bawn at Carrigafoyle (p102) beside the Shannon estuary contained a dock for small vessels. There was a similar arrangement at Galey, Co Roscommon, and the rectangular ditch or pit at Aughnanure may have served a similar purpose. In Co Down two towers by Strangford Lough each had part of the basement closed off to contain a boat.

A few instances of 15th and 16th century remodellings of earlier courtyard castles need to be noted. Substantial parts of the large Limerick castles of Askeaton (p91) and Carrigogunnell (p103) are of this period. Castlemartyr (p106) and Carrick-on-Suir (p101) have mid 15th century bawns with a second tower of some size in addition to the main tower house. At Cahir (p100) and Glanworth (p111) the original gatehouses were converted into tower houses and their courtyards with corner towers mostly rebuilt. A tower house was provided in place of a former round flanking tower at Granagh (p63), and then a hall built alongside it. At both Ballymote (p30) and Ballintober (p28) corner towers were remodelled c1600-30 to serve as tower houses, while many new windows were inserted in the outer walls at Roscommon (p42) in the 1580s when a new range of apartments was erected and some of the tower floor levels changed. In the 1560s Carrickfergus (p138) was remodelled for mounting heavy artillery, and much of Dunluce (p147) as it now stands dates from c1580-1635. We have already noted the tendency for older keeps to be provided with dividing walls and vaults in the basements during this period. At Castlecarra (p31) a hall house was also provided with a small surrounding bawn with one round flanker and an outbuilding.

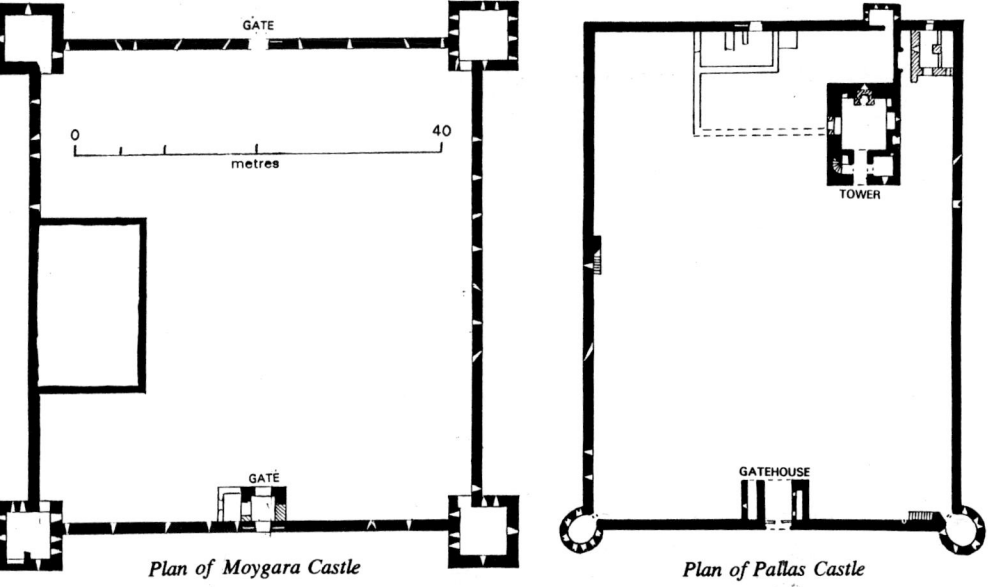

Plan of Moygara Castle   *Plan of Pallas Castle*

Monea Castle,
Co Fermanagh

Mongavelin Castle,
Co Donegal

The totally unfortified type of Elizabethan and Jacobean manor house so common in England and Wales is rare in Ireland. Apart from the occasional town house buildings of that period either had defensive features or were associated with fortifications like the house that stood within Charlemont Fort (p141), the timber framed house that stood just outside the moated bawn with a remodelled tower house at Enniskillen (p149), or the mansion at Carrick-on-Suir (p101) lying immediately in front of a 15th century castle which continued to provide much of the accommodation. Some of the new settlers of the Munster plantations of the 1580s, and the Ulster plantations from 1607 onwards built tower houses or made use of ones already existing. Others, plus a few of the Irish and Anglo-Irish families requiring more space than was available in a tower house, built stronghouses, i.e. mansions similar to the usual Elizabethan and Jacobean types but with pistol-loops below the main windows and in wings arranged to allow flanking fire, open wall-walks, machicolations and bartizans, and/or a defensible bawn wall usually with round or rectangular flankers.

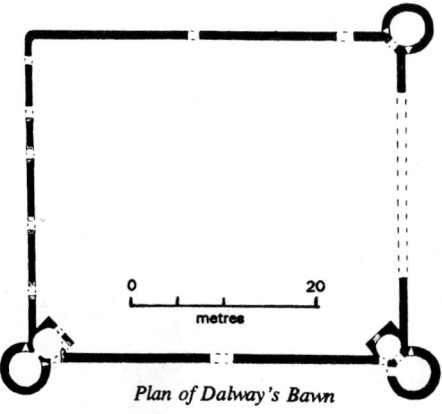

Plan of Dalway's Bawn

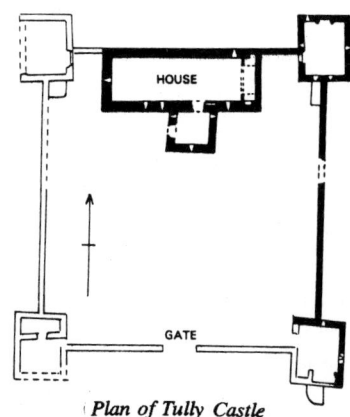

Plan of Tully Castle

Many of the Ulster planters came from Scotland and naturally built in the style then fashionable in their mother country with dormer windows in roofs to light attic rooms, moulded corbelled courses carrying pepper pot roofed corner turrets and narrow upper staircases overhanging re-entrant angles. Ballygalley (p135) is an L-planned tower house with the wing containing the staircase, and Roughan (p158) is a small square building with four round corner towers, but most of the others are larger mansions with the emphasis on length rather than height and with the basement divided partly into separate cellars for the storage of food and wine, the remainder being used for a spacious kitchen (a feature generally lacking in Irish tower houses) with a big fireplace. Mongavlin (p154) and Mountcastle were plain rectangles, whilst Aughentaine (p135) and Tully (p159) were T-planned with staircase wings near the middle of one side. Ruthmullan (p157), Balfour (p140) and Derrywoone (p143) are L-planned, the latter additionally having a round tower on the outermost angle. Monea has two round towers with square caphouses at one end of a long main block. Other Ulster castles of this period built by English or Anglo-Irish landowners are the small eight pointed stair planned tower at Augher (p135), T-planned Castle Archdale (p139), and rectangular mansions at Crevenish (p142) and Caldwell (p140). These all originally had rectangular bawns up to about 40m long and 30m wide in front of them and round or square flankers on two or four of the corners. At Faugher (p149) the house was modest and thinly walled and reliance for defence was placed on the bawn, and this was true of Dalway's Bawn (p143), with round flankers, and of several bawns built by London companies to defend the modest houses of their agents, as at Ballykelly (p135), Brackfield (p136), Dungiven (p147), and Salterstown (p158). At Dungiven the bawn walls were 4.5m high and had upper firing loopholes served by a platform. The others had rather lower walls flanked by round bastions with musket loops.

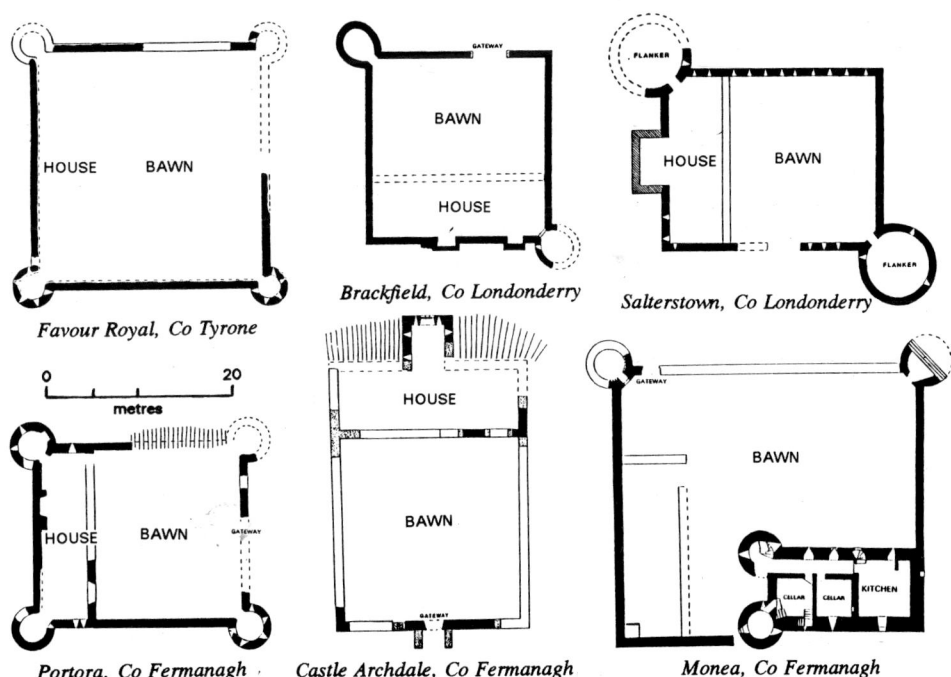

Favour Royal, Co Tyrone

Brackfield, Co Londonderry

Salterstown, Co Londonderry

Portora, Co Fermanagh

Castle Archdale, Co Fermanagh

Monea, Co Fermanagh

Plans of Six Plantation Period Bawns in Ulster

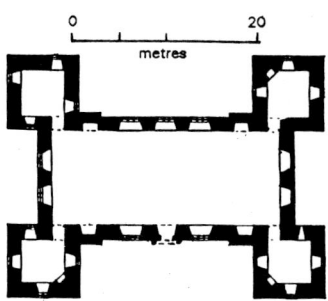

Plan of Kanturk Castle, Co Cork

Ardtermon Castle, Co Sligo

Rathfarnham (p74), Portumna (p41), Raphoe (p156), Kanturk (p115), Burncourt (p99), and Manorhamilton (p38) are all substantial semi-fortified houses of c1590-1645 with square or spear-shaped towers at all four corners. The first three have main blocks two rooms in width. The others are narrower although Manorhamilton has square wings on one side with two of the towers being on the wing outer corners. It has a twin without the corner towers not far away at Dromahair (p34). Otherwise these houses had internal divisions only of wood or lath and plaster (only Rathfarnham is still roofed). Burncourt has numerous pistol loops and Kanturk was intended to have a continuous machicolated parapet although these were perhaps as much for show as defence. Two castles in Co Cork, Monkstown (p122), and Mount Long (p123), have smaller main blocks with four square corner towers, and Mountjoy Fort (p155) in Ulster was similar but with more gunloops. Killenure (p115) has a long low main block with four round corner towers, Iniscrone (p36) was a shorter version of the same plan, whilst Tully (p44) has them only on the side assumed to faced away from the bawn, and at Ballyannan (p93) and Knocklyon in Co Dublin there are two at diagonally opposite corners like the numerous Scottish "Z-plan" castles of c1540-1640.

Coppingers Court (p107) has two square wings facing the main approach through the bawn and a third to contain a wide staircase in the middle of the other side. Ardtermon (p26) and Mallow (p121) have similar layouts with round and polygonal towers respectively although in these cases the staircase wing faced the bawn. Mallow has a second mid-wall projection containing the entrance lobby making a variant on a straightforward cross plain with porch at the front and staircase at the rear found at Ballyduff (p95) and Ightermurragh (p114). The latter is a lofty and strongly built house with a continuous wall-walk, and Coppingers has impressive sections of machicolated parapets on pyramidal corbels. The others are lower and more domestic in aspect. Glinsk (p35) has two wings facing the bawn, bartizans, and numerous pistol loops. The four storey mansion at Leamaneh (p117) has at the opposite end from the thick end wall type tower built earlier (p16), a wing on one corner and a bartizan below the wall summit on the other. The larger mansion at Loughmoe (p120) has a porch wing on one side near the older tower and a large wing clasping a far corner so that every side except the furthest side of the massive old tower is flanked, whilst from one side the house has a semi-symetrical layout. There is indeed an increasing use of regular patterns for windows and other features during this period. Donegal (p145) is another instance of a mansion being added to an older tower, whilst at Parke's Castle (p40) the older tower was destroyed and replaced by a house incorporating the bawn gateway and having one round corner tower. Ballycowen (p47) is a impressive tower-like structure with a wing on one side containing the entrance and a scale-and-platt staircase.

A report on the furnishings damaged or plundered from Castletown in Co Limerick when it was captured by the Irish in 1642 gives us an idea of the furnishings of a tower or stronghouse at that time. The owner, Hardress Waller, lists: "Eleven downe and feather beds, six flocke beds, with boulsters, pillowes, blancketts, rugs, and caddoes (rough woollen coverings) to the said beds. Candlesticks, chamberpotts, stills (5) and such like thinges of pewter and brasse. Hangings for a large dyning room, and two chambers, of tapestrie, and divers other hangings and curtaynes for windows. Two very rich Turkey carpetts. A clocke (brought out of England). A chest of books."

L-planned Castle Baldwin (p31) is distinguished as a stronghouse only by having a continuous wall-walk with a machicolation over the entrance doorway. Tinnehinch, Co Carlow, has a regular pattern of windows on the side away from the doorway which has a machicolation above it. Derrin and West Cloncourse in Co Laois are T plan buildings without wall-walks although the latter has a loopholed bawn wall of 1636. Ballyspurge on the Ards Peninsular in Co Down also has a loopholed bawn wall entered through a small gatehouse. From these minor semi-fortified houses it is but an easy step to the purely domestic farm house of the mid to late 17th century. From the 1650s until James II lost the throne of England and Scotland in 1688 there was comparative peace in Ireland. Cromwell introduced more new settlers but these seem to have either used already existing buildings or have managed without fortifications. Many older towers suffered minor modifications and/or were extended by adding a house on one side in the late 17th century. The majority of these are as ruined as the towers most of which were abandoned for newer and often more modest houses during the 18th and 19th centuries. Only a few castles remain habitable although quite a number of the ruined ones have since the 1920s gradually been made safe and accessible to the public. The 20th century has seen a few ruins restored into a habitable state, notably Ardtermon, Ballylee, Carraigin, Dunguire, and Parke's Castle, whilst work is currently proceeding at Donegal. The 19th century mock castles are not discussed in this book which deals only with defensible buildings.

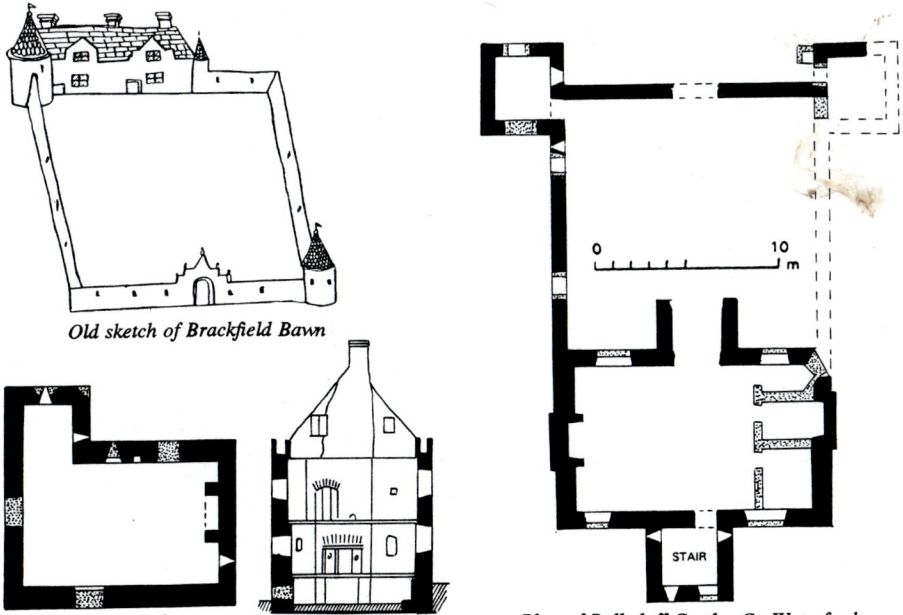

Old sketch of Brackfield Bawn

Plan and Section of Castle Baldwin, Co Sligo

Plan of Ballyduff Castle, Co Waterford

GAZETTEER OF CASTLES OF CONNACHT

AGHALARD *Mayo* M1457

There remain the western half of the tower 11.8m by 8.6m formerly with a spiral stair in the NE corner, and a vault over the third storey, with a thinly walled fourth storey above, plus most of the 1.5m thick wall of the irregularly hexagonal bawn about 30m across with an outbuilding on the east and small square turrets flanking the entrance front towards the NW. The bawn lies on a low rocky platform and there are traces of an outer bawn to the south. In 1596 the castle was captured by the Earl of Clanrickard in collaboration with the English commanders D'Arcy and Brabazon. They evacuated the castle when Red Hugh O'Donnell approached it. The MacDonnells, who were originally mercenaries serving the Burkes, probably built the castle c1500 and held it until it was sold to Sir Benjamin Guinness in the 19th century.

ANBALLY *Galway* M4242

This low lying Burke tower of three storeys with mural chambers in the south wall measures 12m by 12.6m. The entrance is protected by two murder holes and a gunport opening off the straight flight of stairs leading to the base of the spiral stair in the SE corner. The second storey is vaulted. There was a fourth storey within the roof which had gables flush with the outer walls, perhaps a later alteration. The tower lies in a corner of a fragmentary bawn 31m by 35m on a platform above flood levels.

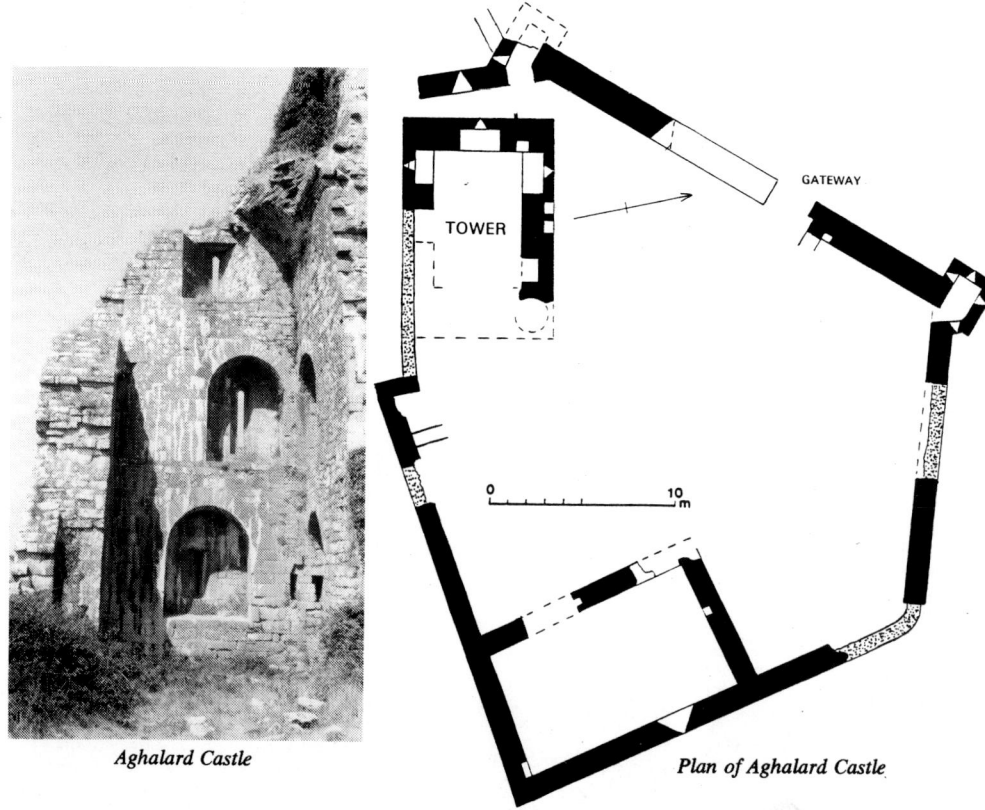

Aghalard Castle

Plan of Aghalard Castle

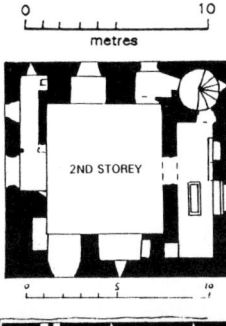

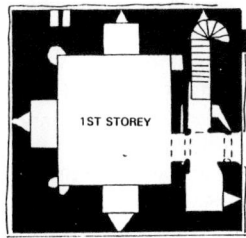

Plans of Anbally Castle

Anbally Castle

ANNAGHDOWN *Galway* M2828

The tower measures 11.2m by 10.1m and has the entrance and mural chambers in a side wall. A straight stair leads to the spiral stair in a far corner. This corner has a bartizan and there are signs of another on the diagonally opposite corner. The fourth storey has a fireplace in each end wall and was probably divided into two bedrooms. Above was an attic within gables flush with the end walls.

ANNAGHKEEN *Galway* M2244

Despite the north corner having fallen and some lower openings being blocked this is a fairly complete and unaltered late 13th century hall house. There were two undivided storeys each with an entrance in the SE wall adjacent to the straight flights of steps in the NE end wall. A square turret at the west corner contains a latrine with a pit below and a small room above reached from the hall SW window embrasure. See p10.

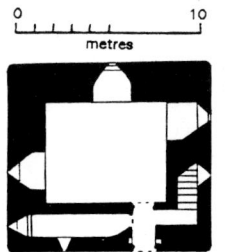

Plan of Annaghdown Castle

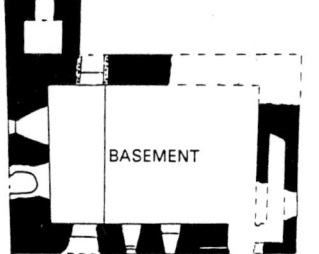

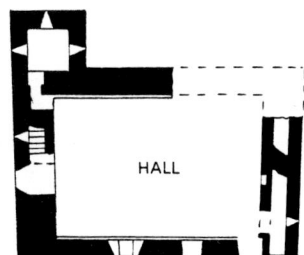

Plans of Annaghkeen Castle

ARDNAMULLIVAN *Galway* R4595

The five storey 16th century tower has vaults over the first and third levels, the latter retaining traces of the wickerwork mat upon which it was constructed. Two mullioned windows and a fireplace are later insertions. An original window embrasure has carved floral motifs. In 1579 Dermot O'Shaughnessy (who favoured the English) and his nephew John killed each other in a fight over possession of the castle.

ARDRAHAN *Galway* M4612

Recent collapse has still further reduced the last remnants of a 13th century hall house which measured about 17m by 12.5m over walls 1.9m thick. The basement crosswall and the blocked upper storey doorway facing a relic of a bawn wall are 15th century.

ARDTERMON *Sligo* G5844

The early 17th century stronghouse of three storeys plus attics built by Sir Nathaniel Gore has recently been restored and reoccupied. It is 35m long by 8m wide and has round flankers 5.2m in diameter with gunloops on the east corners. A fragmentary bawn with a round NW flanker and a range on the south side extends for 25m to the west. From the entrance covered by a gunloop on the east a passage ran through the main block to a stair in a round tower 6.5m in diameter on the west side. See p22.

ATHENRY *Galway* M5127

Meiler de Birmingham's castle of c1235-50 consists of a well preserved hall keep 16.5m by 10.5m above a deeply battered plinth standing free within a D-shaped bailey about 42m across. The loopholed bailey wall has a round tower at the SE corner, traces of a second at the NE, a rectangular projection on the west, and there was once a gatehouse at the SW corner. In the 15th century the keep basement was given a central row of piers and vaults, the old roof space below the wall-walk was converted into a third storey, and gables for a new roof containing an attic were raised above the end parapets. The basement and hall each have a narrow window in the middle of each wall, an odd instance of early symmetry giving rather poor lighting. See p9.

Ardtermon Castle

Flanker at Aughnanure

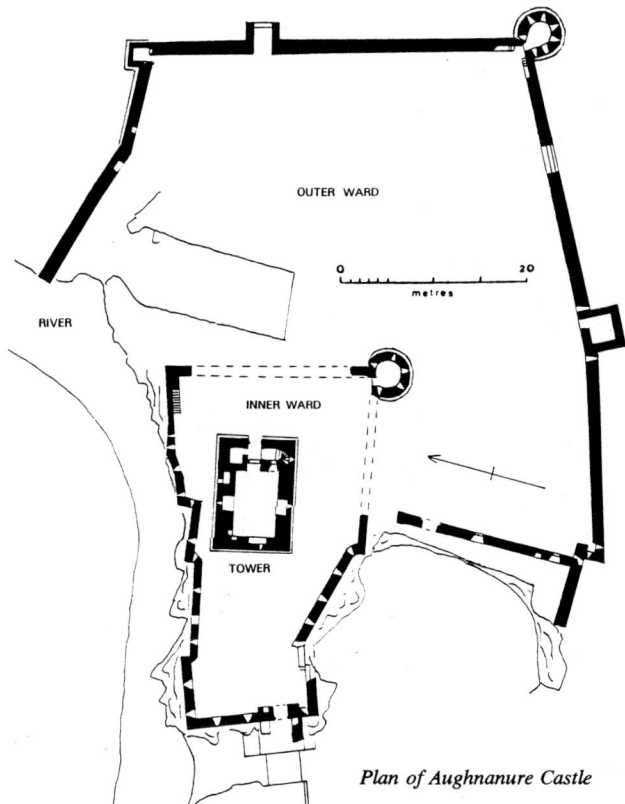

OUTER WARD

RIVER

INNER WARD

TOWER

Plan of Aughnanure Castle

Tower House, Aughnanure

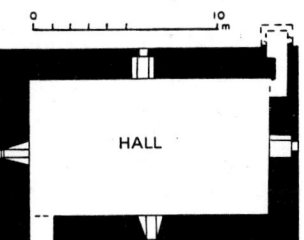

HALL

Plan of Keep, Athenry

AUGHNANURE   *Galway*   M1544   A.M.*

Beside the Drimneen River is one of the best preserved larger strongholds of the Irish chieftains. A modern hipped roof covers the six storey tower, 12.5m by 8.6m at the base, and 16.4m high to the wall walk. The east wall contains the entrance with an external machicolation high above, the spiral stair, and mural chambers, and has square bartizans on the corners at the level of the lord's suite on the third storey. The fifth storey was the hall, and the second, fourth, and sixth storeys formed sleeping spaces for the family and servants. Much of the wall of the irregularly shaped bawn 36m by 21m around the tower stands on low cliffs. The vulnerable east and SE walls facing flat ground have been destroyed, leaving the stone roofed SE flanker with gunports now standing isolated. These sides were protected by an outer bawn roughly 50m square with three square turrets and a round flanker at the SE corner. The west side of this bawn was filled with a banquetting hall of which there remains the inner wall with carvings on the window embrasure soffits. The outer wall has been entirely destroyed by undermining by a tributary river. In 1572 the castle was captured from the descendants of the chief of the O'Flahertys by Sir Edward Fitton, Governor of Connacht, and was handed over to Morogh O'Flaherty, a member of a junior branch of the clan who had been enticed over to the English side. Although granted to the Earl of Clanrickard in the 17th century Aughnanure remained with the O'Flahertys until the early 18th century when it passed to Lord St George on the foreclosure of a mortgage. See p15.

BALLINAFAD   *Sligo*   G7808

Captain St John Barbe built the castle in c1590-1610 and installed a garrison of ten men under a constable. After a stout resistance it surrendered to the Irish in 1641 through lack of water. The three storey main block 10.6m by 8m is dwarfed by four 6m diameter corner towers with high chimneys. One contained a timber staircase next to which is the second storey entrance, and the others had tiers of rectangular private rooms. A secondary doorway in a tower outer face is defended by a machicolation.

BALLINAMANTAIN   *Galway*   M4505

Also called Kiltartan, this is a very ruinous 13th century de Burgo castle with a wedge shaped bailey extending 60m from a front wall with traces of a substantial tower of uncertain shape at one end and a gatehouse 13m wide with twin round fronted towers in the middle. The acute angle at the far end, overlooking a steep drop, is filled with a keep about 12m square. In the 15th century the basement and the storey above were both subdivided and provided with pointed vaults and the third storey added or entirely rebuilt. One wall is thickened to contain the straight main stair. A second narrower stair in the opposite wall is blocked by a flue of a later basement fireplace.

BALLINASLOE   *Galway*   M8632

The 19th century Ivy Castle partly hides a towered bawn of the O'Kellys above the River Suck. In 1572 the castle was held by the Burke Earl of Clanrickard but in 1579 it was taken over and refortified by the English Crown and used as a residence by Sir Anthony Brabazon, Governor of Connacht. It was held against Ireton in 1651-2.

BALLINTOBER   *Roscommon*   M7375   A.M.

This spacious courtyard castle of c1300 measures 80m by 73m inside a wall 1.7m thick which formerly had a moat in front. The twin towered gatehouse 13.4m wide on the south side is now very fragmentary but much of the curtain stands together with four polygonal corner towers averaging 8.4m wide. The northern towers stand highest, having been rebuilt as tower houses in 1627. One was then given a thick new end wall towards the court containing the entrance with protecting machicolation, staircase, and chambers, whilst at the other the stair and chambers were tacked on at either side of the rectangular part projecting into the court. The castle was built either by William de Burgo or the O'Connors. A junior branch of that family captured the castle in 1315, and from 1385 to 1657 it was the seat of the chiefs known as O'Connor Don. The castle suffered several sieges in the 15th century and in 1579 Hugh O'Connor Don was formed to ally himself with Red Hugh O'Donnell against the English after the former breached the walls with the aid of Spanish cannon. Ballintober was a centre of Catholic resistance in the 17th century and held out against Lord Raneleagh and Sir Charles Coote in 1642. Although confiscated by Cromwell it was recovered by O'Connor Don in 1677. The two rebuilt towers are said to have been occupied until the 19th century.

BALLYLAHAN   *Mayo*   M2798

The fragmentary remains of a twin round towered gatehouse 15m wide on the east side of the polygonal court 40m by 34m and the footings of what appears to have been a freestanding hall keep about 14m by 11m are relics of a castle built by Jordan de Exeter in the mid 13th century. His descendants were known as the Mac Jordans. The fragments that remain of the thin curtain wall appear to be a patchwork of various periods. There were buildings on the west side of the court.

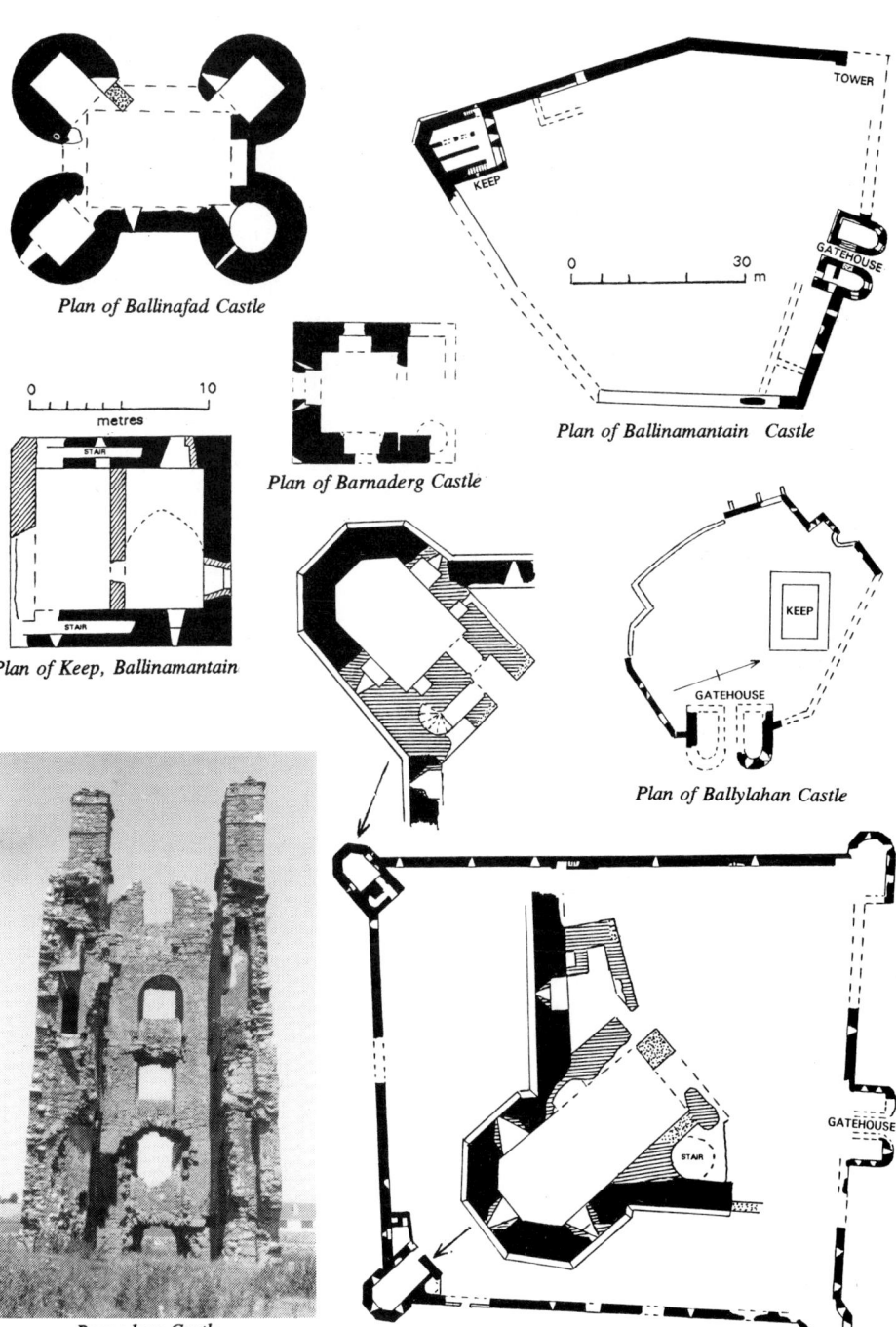

Plan of Ballinafad Castle

Plan of Ballinamantain Castle

Plan of Barnaderg Castle

Plan of Keep, Ballinamantain

Plan of Ballylahan Castle

Barnaderg Castle

Plan of Ballintober Castle

BALLYLEE   *Galway*   N4806   A.M.*

This 16th century tower beside a lake is best known because it was restored and inhabited by the poet Yeats in the 1920s. Original windows survive in the upper part but larger new windows have been introduced in the lower storeys. By the 1930s the tower was derelict again but it was later restored to serve as a Yeats museum.

BALLYMOTE   *Sligo*   G6715

Richard de Burgo's castle of c1300 has 2.8m thick curtain walls surviving around a court about 38m square. A twin towered gatehouse 23m wide filled much of the north front, there was a square lesser gateway on the south side, the corners have large drum towers and there are D-shaped towers in the middle of the east and west sides. In the early 14th century the castle fell to the O'Connors and then to the MacDiarmadas. Although claimed by O'Connor Sligo as his and surrendered by him to the English in 1571 it was mostly held by the MacDonaghs between 1380 and the 1560s. Richard Bigham captured the castle in 1584 and the O'Connors burnt it in 1588. It was recaptured by the MacDonaghs in 1598 and sold to the O'Donnells, who surrendered it to the English in 1602. About this time the SE tower was rebuilt as a tower house with a straight thick wall containing an entrance and stair towards the court. The Taaffes held Ballymote from at least the 1630s until 1652. Lord Granard captured the castle from Captain Terence MacDonagh in 1690 and the outer parts of the two gatehouses were then destroyed to the ground and the moat filled in. See p9.

BARNADERG   *Galway*   M5248

The south end wall containing the entrance, stair, and mural chambers of this late 16th century O'Kelly tower measuring 9.2m by 7.8m has fallen. The surviving walls have corbels for mid-wall machicolations. Including an attic in the roof there were five storeys without vaults or internal offsets to carry floor beams. Gunports flank a basement window embrasure. A fourth storey window has twin ogee-headed lights.

BRACKLOON   *Galway*   M9518

This is a small 16th century tower of four unvaulted main rooms with a fifth within the wall-walk off which open two diagonally opposite square bartizans. Externally it measures 8.3m by 6.3m. An offset carried the third storey room floor. Mural rooms in a thick end wall are vaulted. See plan and section on page 16.

CAHERAVOLEY   *Galway*   M3942

Foundations of a thinly walled house 12m by 6.5m lie in the middle of a rectangular 16th century bawn 48.4m by 36.6m surrounded by a wall 1.5m thick with an entrance on the east side and round flankers 4.4m diameter with gunports at the NW and SE corners. Beside the latter is a latrine shoot.

CARRAIGIN   *Galway*   M2443

In the 1970s this late 13th century hall house was restored from ruin, whitewashed externally, and made into a residence. It was built by the Gaynards and later passed to the Burkes and measures 14.6m by 10.6m over walls 1.9m thick and has a square latrine turret at the east corner. The restored doorway at hall level beside the rebuilt south corner is original. A straight stair in the NW wall leads down from there and another in the SE wall leads up. The subdividing walls, vaults, and doorway of the basement are later insertions. It is unlikely that the hall was originally subdivided to create a private room at one end as it is now.

CARRIGAHOWLEY *Mayo* L9594

The celebrated pirate Grace O'Malley retired to the tower beside an inlet of Clew Bay, also called Rockfleet, with "all her followers and 1,000 head of cows and mares" after the death of her second husband Sir Richard Burke in 1583. She is said to have previously driven off an attacking force sent from Galway to take the tower in 1574. There are four storeys and at the top is a square turret on one corner.

CASTLE BALDWIN *Sligo* G7514

The projecting wing of this thinly walled early 17th century stronghouse measuring 12.7m by 8.7m is thought to have contained a timber staircase. There were two storeys of living rooms, a very low service basement partly below ground level, and at the summit a narrow wall-walk with a machicolation over the entrance and an attic.

CASTLECARRA *Mayo* G1775 A.M.

Beside Lough Carra is a ruined late 13th century hall-house 15m long by 10.5m wide built by the de Stauntons. It had an upper floor entrance facing north. The lower entrance on the south side may not be original but existed by the 14th century when a porch was added in front of it and a turret containing a latrine opening off the staircase to the battlements was added on the east side and a second turret built in front of the other entrance. In the 15th and 16th centuries the MacEvillys (descendants of the de Stauntons) inserted a longitudinal crosswall and vaults in the lower storey and built a small polygonal bawn around the tower with an outbuilding on the SW and gateways on the east and west. They surrendered the castle to the Crown in the 1570s and it was granted to Captain William Bowen who is thought to have added the round flanker with numerous gunloops at the NE corner of the bawn. In the 1660s Castlecarra passed from the Bowens to Sir Henry Lynch, whose descendants held it until the 19th century. See plan on page 11.

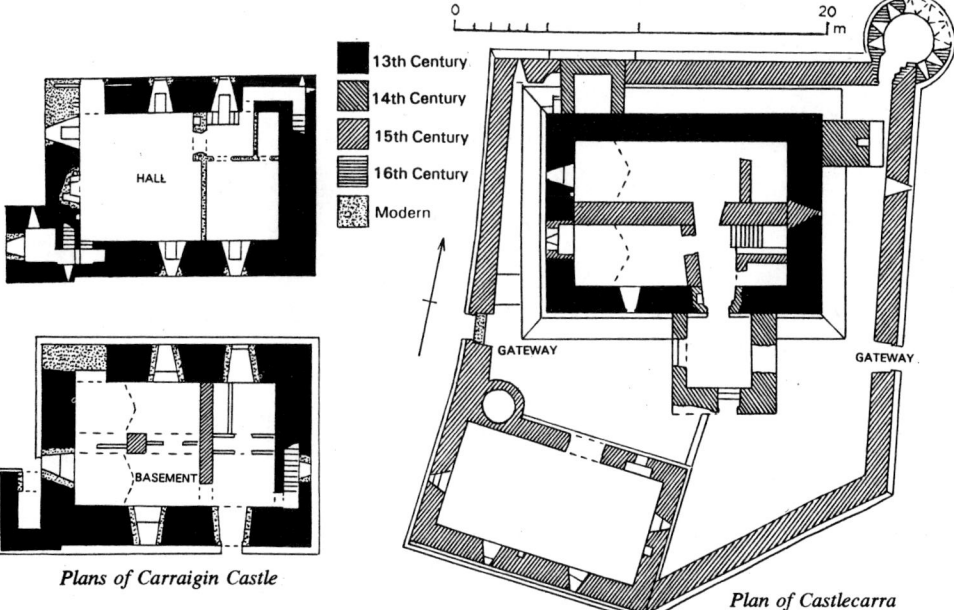

Plans of Carraigin Castle

Plan of Castlecarra

Castle Connor

CASTLE CONNOR *Sligo* G7418

Of a 13th century hall keep 10.6m wide and possibly as much as 18m long only half the west wall with a doorway and most of the north wall with one window embrasure with voussoirs now remain. There are fragments and footings of a bawn wall.

CASTLE DARGAN *Sligo* G7218

On a clifftop site once occupied by an early fort is a 2.1m thick fragment of one side of a tower about 15m long by 11m wide built in the 15th century by Conor MacDonagh. About 28m away is a fragment of a small vaulted turret room with an adjoining stub of the 1.5m thick bawn wall.

CASTLE KIRKE *Galway* L9980

Covering almost all of a small island in Lough Corrib is a rectangular court with square corner towers and a rectangular tower on the south side built in the 1230s by Fedlim, King of Connacht to replace an earlier stronghold taken from the O'Connors by the de Burgos and burnt in 1233. The castle later passed to the O'Flahertys and was wrecked in the Cromwellian invasion.

CLAREGALWAY *Galway* M3833

Beside the bridge is a fine 16th century tower 12.3m by 10.2m at the base rising 17m to the wallwalk where there are corbels for machicolations in the middle of each face. There are gunports, crossloops, corner loops, and bigger windows, and there is a murder hole covering the entrance passage in the thick east wall. The second storey was the lord's suite. Above was a vaulted sleeping loft, with a lofty hall above that.

0   10
metres

SECTION

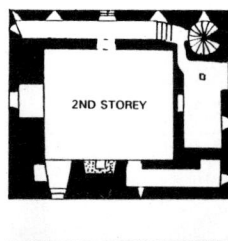

2ND STOREY

4TH STOREY

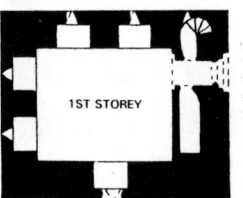

1ST STOREY

3RD STOREY

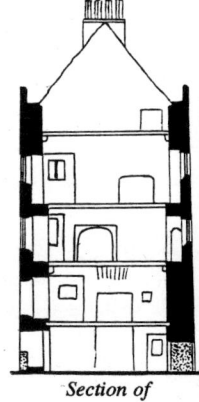

Section of Derryhivenny Castle

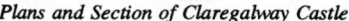

Plans and Section of Claregalway Castle

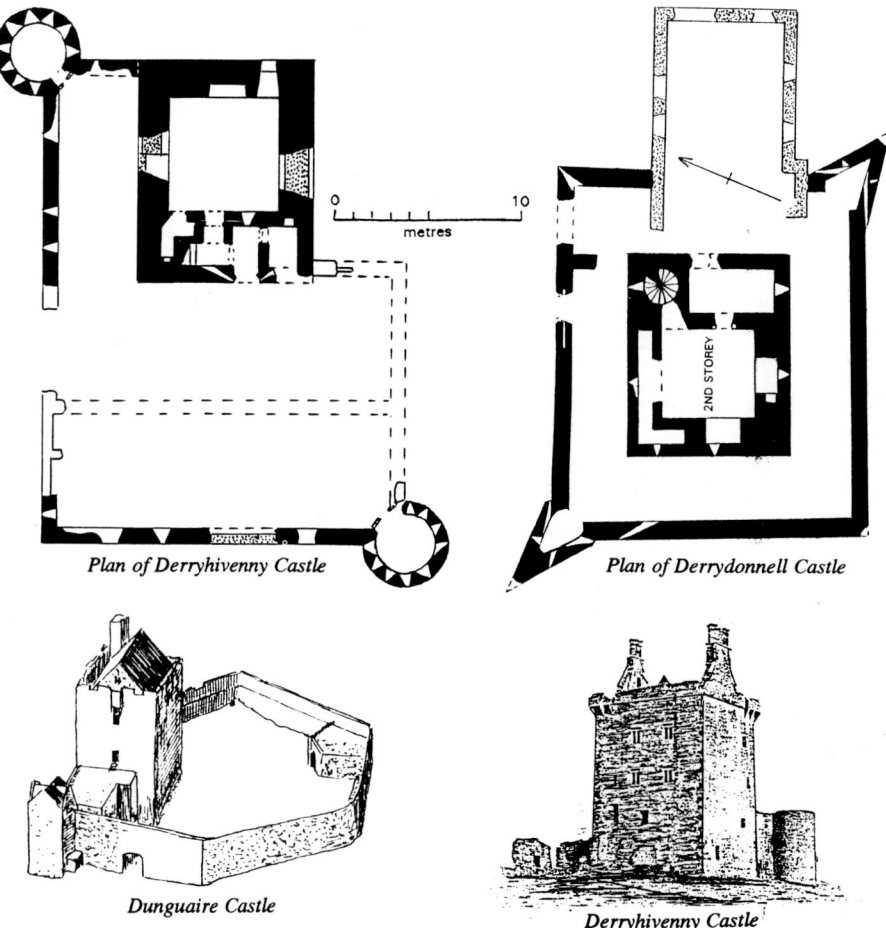

Plan of Derryhivenny Castle

Plan of Derrydonnell Castle

2ND STOREY

Dunguaire Castle

Derryhivenny Castle

DERRYDONNELL *Galway* M4525

Evidence of a late date (c1600-40) is the lack of vaulting in the tower, which measures 10.8m by 8.9m and has main rooms which are longest across the width of the tower because of a thick end wall, and the salient angled flankers at diagonally opposite corners of the 1m thick bawn wall surrounding the tower at a regular distance of 3.3m. A later house adjoins the east side and there is a corbel for a machicolation over the bawn gateway on the north. The ruins are heavily overgrown.

DERRYHIVENNY *Galway* M8708

This is one of the few dated Irish tower houses, a corbel of one of the diagonally opposite square bartizans being inscribed with the year 1643 and the initials of Daniel O'Madden. Signs of late date are the lack of vaults over the five square main chambers, the two and three light mullioned windows, and the profusion of gunports in the two 4.5m diameter flankers set at diagonally opposite corners of the fragmentary bawn measuring 24m by 18m covering just two sides of the tower. The bawn wall is loopholed and has signs of a former large outbuilding opposite the tower.

DROMAHAIR   *Leitrim*   G8031

All that remains of the chief seat of the O'Rourkes is a ruined banquetting hall 22m long by 7.5m wide within ivy covered walls 1.3m thick on a rock by the River Bonet. Nearby is a much altered stronghouse built in 1626 by Sir Edward Villiers to replace the original tower house. It has a main block 21m long by 10.6m wide of which the south wall is much ruined. The north wall is thicked to contain staircases, fireplaces, and latrines, and has two wings each 6.8m wide projecting beyond it.

DRUMHARSNA   *Galway*   M4411

Shane Ballagh held this tower in 1574. It measures 9.6m by 8.3m and has vaults over the basement and third storey. The fourth storey was partly within the roof and there were wallwalks on parts of the side walls only. A machicolation commands the entrance. There are signs of a number of later alterations to the upper parts.

DUNGUAIRE   *Galway*   M3811   A.M.*

The O'Hynes 16th century tower with machicolations in the centre of each face and the hexagonal bawn about 35m across stand on a mound at the head of Kinvarra Bay. The tower measures 11.6m by 9.8m and has four storeys and an attic. As rebuilt in 1642 the bawn wall is 1.2m thick and rises 2.7m to a wallwalk protected by a parapet 2m high with pistol holes. A four-gabled corner turret 4m square flanks the gateway. The castle later passed to the Martins of Tullira. The tower was re-roofed a few years ago and is now used for staging medieval banquets. Two low modern wings adjoin it.

Fireplace, Dromahair

Dunmore Castle

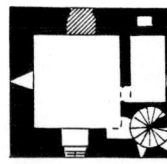

Drumharsna Castle

Plan of Dunmore Castle

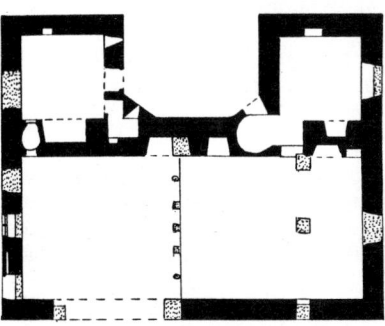

Plan of Stronghouse at Dromahair

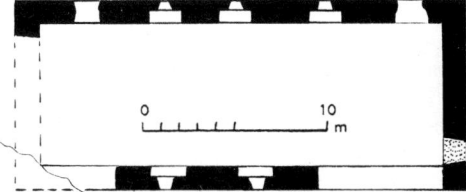

Plan of Banquetting Hall, Dromahair

DUNMORE   *Galway*   M5064

Dunmore was held by the de Birminghams from the 13th century until confiscated by Cromwell in the 1650s. It was captured during Elizabeth's reign by Sir Henry Sidney. The hall keep measuring 16.4m by 11.8m above a tall battered plinth on top of the motte may have been built after the first of several recorded burnings of the castle, by the O'Connors in 1249 and 1315, and by the O'Flynns in 1284. Having been inhabited until the 19th century, the keep shows signs of frequent repair and alteration. It has four unvaulted storeys and gables for an attic within the parapet. As built the keep was probably just of two storeys, so the narrow loop at third storey level may be a relic of the original parapet. The fourth storey mullion and transom window and other openings and fireplaces are of c1560-1620.

FIDDAUN   *Galway*   R4196

Both the tower 11.7m by 8.7m, of five storeys plus an attic, and having square bartizans at third storey level, and the surrounding rectangular bawn 39m by 24m are well preserved. The bawn wall is mostly 1.5m thick and has a salient flanker in the middle of the west side, a rectangular gatehouse on the north, and a postern on the south. There are traces of former lean-to buildings and a latrine shute at the SW corner. Only a gatehouse remains of an outer bawn. The castle was built by the O'Shaughnessys, the last of whom fled to France in 1697. See Plan on Page 18.

GALWAY   *Galway*   M7266

On the outside of the 16th century tower known as Lynch's Castle after one of Galway's leading families are their arms plus those of Henry VII and the Earl of Kildare. There are also gargoyles, a rarity in Ireland, and several fine windows. The tower was much altered in 1966 when it became a branch of the Munster and Leinster bank.

GLINSK   *Galway*   M7266   A.M.

Sir Ulick Burke, created a baronet in 1628, is thought to have built this stronghouse about that time. It measures 22.6m by 13.3m over well preserved walls 1.25 to 1.7m thick. The interior had only timber divisions and is gutted, leaving no trace of a stair. There were three storeys of pleasant living rooms with cross windows over a low basement with gunloops on either side of each narrow window. On the north is a service doorway with a flanking gunloop. The main entrance was at second storey level on the south side where the centre is recessed to give the effect of two wings each of which has a square bartizan on the outer corner, and where there was a bawn of which one round flanker still remains.

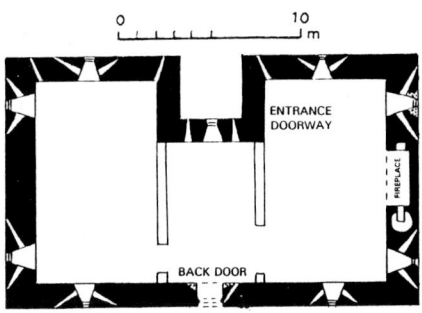

Plan of Glinsk Castle

Glinsk Castle

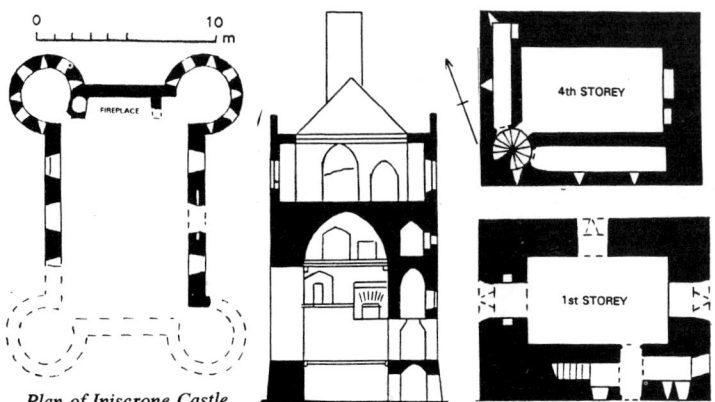

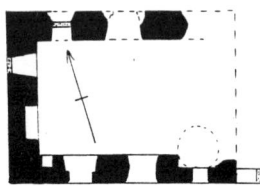

Plan of Lismore Castle

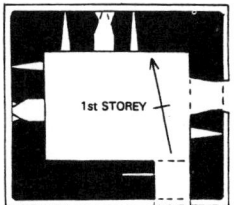

Plan of Kinlough Castle

Plan of Iniscrone Castle

Plans & Section of Kinvoynell Castle

INISCRONE   Sligo   F2930

The east wall and two of the four round corner turrets 4.6m in diameter with numerous gunloops of this early 17th century stronghouse measuring about 14m by 8m have vanished. The basement contained a kitchen at the west end and cellars. The principal roofs were on the next level, and there were attic rooms for the servants.

ISERT KELLY   Galway   M5411

The castle belonged first to the MacHuberts, and then the MacRedmonds, both branches of the Burke clan. There are footings of a square bawn with a 16th century tower in one corner. The third storey room, over a vault, is reached by an unusually tortuous staircase and has a fine fireplace inserted in 1604 with the initials W.H.

JENNING'S   Galway   M3858

The name Jenning's Castle is anglicised from Eoin, the first name of several of the Burke owners. It was confiscated by Cromwell in the 1650s. There are two staircases. The second of four storeys is vaulted. The alternative name is Feartagar Castle.

KINLOUGH   Mayo   M2651

The 16th century tower has walls battered externally so that the four main rooms are all of similar size but the upper walls are much thinner than below. There are corner fireplaces with high stacks at diagonally opposite corners. There are no stairs within the wall thickness so there must have been timber stairs within the rooms. The castle was held by Sir John Fitz Oliver Burke in 1574 (he may have built it), and was later mortgaged to the Blakes, who leased Kinlough to John Darcy in 1668.

KINVOYNELL   Mayo   M1677

This fine five storey tower with narrow mural chambers in a side wall and latrine chambers in an end wall with a spiral stair in the corner between them lies in a farmyard. It measures 12.6m by 9.6m and rises 14.4m to the wallwalk with chimneys on the gables rising a further 6.5m. There are gunports and a vault over the fourth storey to support the hall floor. The alternative name of Castle Burke derives from Miles Burke, 4th Viscount Mayo, who was granted the castle. His successor sold the castle to the Brownes of Westport.

Bawn Gateway, Pallas

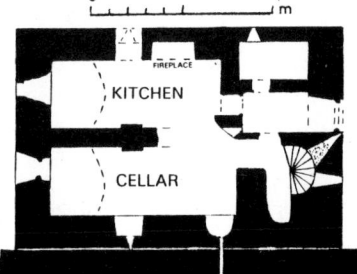

Plan of Loughmask Castle

Loughmask Castle

LISMORE *Galway* M9516

Lismore was an important O'Madden seat, later passing to the Burkes, and then the Dalys of Dunsandle. Three walls of a tower of c1600 measuring 12.5m by 9.2m remain. There is a square bartizan on the SW corner. The thick east wall has fallen or was removed when an extension was added but a square staircase well can be traced.

LOUGHMASK *Mayo* M1560

Among the outbuildings of a later mansion is a large four storey tower house 18m by 12m which is thought to have been built by Sir Thomas Burke, last of the MacWilliam Iochtair Burkes. A fireplace within bears the year 1618 and the initials of Sir William and his wife Elizabeth Butler. The tower adjoins a section of massive bawn walling, relic of a castle of the 1480s or even a 13th century castle of Maurice Fitzgerald. The tower has an end wall 6m thick containing the entrance with a covering gunloop and machicolation, a wide spiral stair, and numerous small rooms. The basement beyond is divided by a crosswall to carry segmental shaped vaults. There were attics within gables flush with the outer walls and the SW. corner has a square bartizan.

MANNIN *Galway* M5417

This is an instance of where a thick end wall 5.3m by 9.6m containing the entrance, spiral stair, and tiers of mural chambers was built in advance of the main tower which was never actually added. Adjoining the tower are outbuildings of much later late, proof of continued use, even if a decline in status. Perhaps the seat was transferred to Newmannin nearby where there are the last traces of a tower on the east side of a polygonal bawn about 45m in diameter. An entrance in the north wall can be traced.

MANORHAMILTON *Leitrim* G8839

Sir Frederick Hamilton's ruined stronghouse of 1638 has two wings 9m wide which projected 8m beyond a destroyed sidewall of a four storey main block 10m wide by 24.5m long. Numerous extra bedrooms were provided in four corner towers roughly 5.5m square but with acute outermost angles. One wing has a big kitchen fireplace. The house was wrecked in 1652 by the forces of the 5th Earl of Clanrickarde.

MOYGARA *Sligo* G6903

The filled in basement of a large rectangular building may be a a a relic of a hall house or keep built by the Cuisins in the 13th century. The O'Garas had taken it over as their chief seat by 1338 and in the 16th century they erected a bawn about 70m square on the south side of the older structure. The bawn has a loopholed wall 1.1m thick with a tower about 7m square at each corner. Three of these are of two storeys, the other is higher and formed a tower house. It had a timber stair in a recess in the south wall. There are no vaults. The bawn west side has a two storey gatehouse in the middle and there is a a secondary entrance on the east. See plan on page 19.

MOYLOUGH *Galway* M6248

The plinth has been mostly ripped off this 13th or 14th century hall house standing on a mound. It measures 17.6m by 11.7m over walls up to 2.5m thick in which are plain window openings with voussoirs. The entrance is in the south side wall at hall level. A stair led up to a low third storey, originally perhaps just a roof space below the battlements. Access to the high basement must have been via trapdoor and ladder.

MOYNE *Mayo* M2549

This is a particularly fine late 15th century tower 14.5m long by 10.2m wide over walls mostly 2.4m thick. The east wall is thickened to 3m to contain chambers opening off the spiral stair in the NE corner. A straight stair leads from the entrance in the north wall to the foot of this stair. The outer corners are rounded.

Moylough Castle

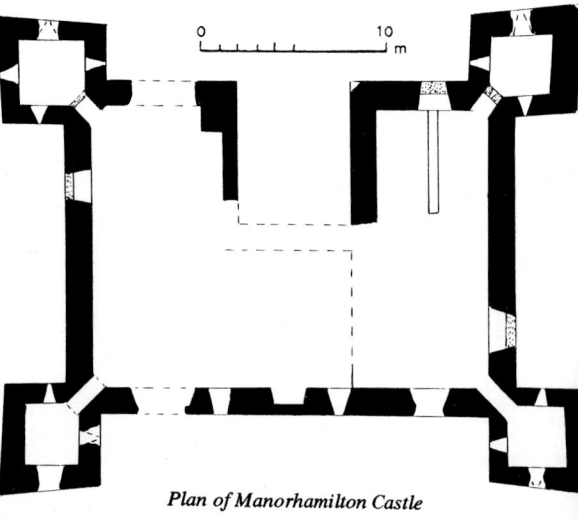

Plan of Manorhamilton Castle

Old print of Moygara Castle

PALLAS *Galway* M7608 A.M.

The fine tower built by the Burkes c1500-40, and later held by the Nugents is still roofed but uninhabited. It has corner loops at the level of the lord's suite on the second storey, square bartizans, and a machicolation over the entrance. It lies beside fragments of a later house near one corner of a bawn with a well preserved wall 1.1m thick with a rectangular flanker near the tower and round flankers 4.7m diameter bristling with gunports at the other end, where there is a two storey gatehouse.

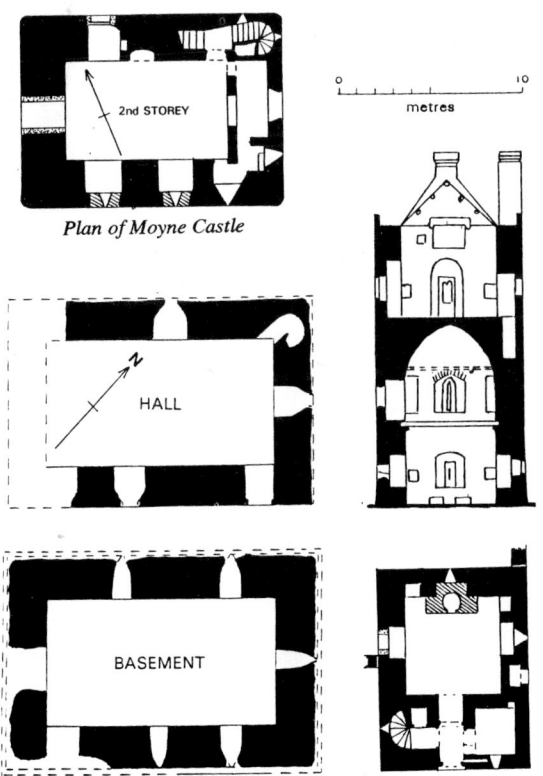

Plan of Moyne Castle

Plans of Moylough Castle

Pallas, Plan & Section

Pallas Castle

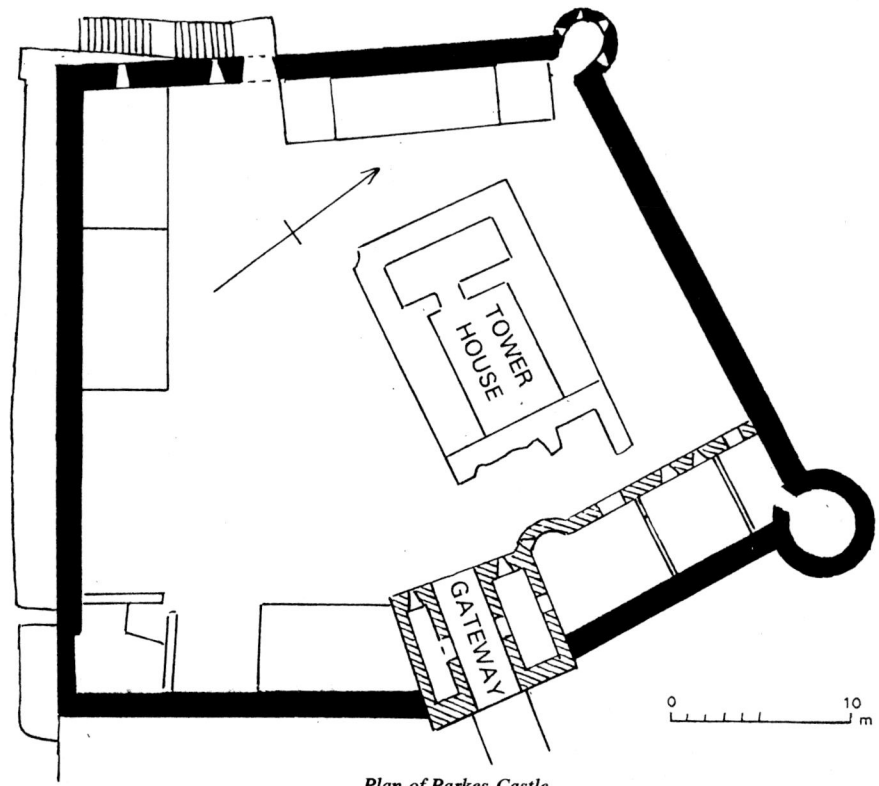

Plan of Parkes Castle

PARKE'S CASTLE *Leitrim* G7835 A.M.*

Francisco de Cuellar, a survivor from an Armada ship, was sheltered here by Sir Brian O'Rourke in 1588. De Cuellar describes his host, who was hanged for treason in London in 1591, as permanently at war with the Protestant English. Excavations in 1974 revealed the base of a 16th century tower 9.5m wide by about 17m long which is assumed to have been destroyed by the English about the time of O'Rourke's execution. It seems to have had thick walls containing chambers at each end, one of them having been built before the rest of the tower. Around the tower was a pentagonal bawn with the longest side 33m long rising from the waters of Lough Gill. Two of the landward corners are flanked by a round tower and a small turret later remodelled to contain a dovecot, and there was a dry moat now mostly filled in. In the 1620s the castle was transferred to Captain Robert Parke after whom it is now named. He built a three storey stronghouse with numerous mullioned windows on the east side, incorporating the round tower and the bawn gatehouse with narrow guard rooms either side of a passage. This building has recently been reroofed by the Office of Works. The pepper-pot roofed turret on the SE corner and footings of various outbuildings also remain from this period. The castle was captured for the Confederate Catholics by the O'Harts and in 1652, then still called Newtown, was surrendered to Sir Charles Coote. The last occupant of the castle was Robert Gore, son of Robert Parke's daughter Anne.

Parke's Castle

PORTUMNA   *Galway*   M8504

The stronghouse built in 1609 by Richard Burke, 4th Earl of Clanrickarde (who lived mostly in England and probably never saw the completed house) was gutted by fire in 1826. It measures 29.7m by 21.2m over walls up to 1.8m thick and has corner towers 6.5m square with gunports. On each storey was a central corridor possibly also containing the stairs off which were many rooms with timber dividing walls. The stone corridor walls contain numerous recesses and fireplaces. The 5th Earl lost Portumna to Henry Cromwell from 1652 to 1661, and the estate was forfeited under William III only to be restored by Queen Anne. Subsequent Earls lived in great state in the house, laying out an elaborate approach from the north with gardens, avenues and three gates. Only minor alterations were made to the house, some ground floor window sills being lowered c1800 when the small round south porch was added.

Shrule Castle

Plan of Rawgordon Castle

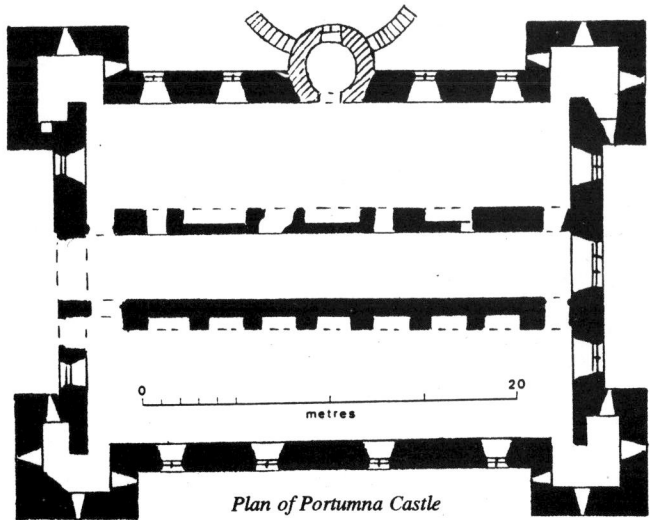
0   20
metres
Plan of Portumna Castle

RAWGORDON   *Galway*   M3230

Only the lower part of the north side wall 10.6m long now remains of a tower probably of the late 16th century. It has a fireplace flanked by windows and at either end are square turrets 3.5m wide containing the flues of second and third storey latrines. Later walling 1.8m thick blocks the space between the turrets.

RINNDOWN   *Roscommon*   N0254

Geoffrey de Marisco erected a ringwork on a promontory on the west side of Lough Ree in 1227. It was stormed and burnt by Felim O'Connor in 1236 and the bailey walls and the hall keep 19m by 13.5m were probably built by Henry III between then and 1260. Further large sums were spent on the castle in 1273-9 and in 1299-1302 Robert of Oxford was in charge of building a new hall at a cost of £113. The ruins of the castle and adjacent town are extensive but much overgrown. The keep north wall stands 10m high to the wallwalk but the south side has vanished. The hall fireplace and the longitudinal crosswall and vaults of the basement are later. Beside the keep is the bailey gatehouse 5.2m by 3.5m with a groove for a portcullis. See plans p10.

ROSCOMMON   *Roscommon*   M8865   A.M.

The castle erected by Robert de Ufford, the Justiciar, in 1269 was soon wrecked by Hugh O'Connor of Connacht although the rectangular secondary gatehouse 11.4m by 8.8m on the west side may be a relic of it. In the 1280s Edward I had the site refortified as a court 52m by 40m with walls 2.5m thick flanked by three storey D-shaped corner towers 10.5m in diameter, and having on the east side a huge gatehouse 22.2m wide with a long passage flanked by round fronted towers. Donogh O'Kelly captured the castle in 1308, and the O'Connors took it in 1340. The latter family held the castle until it was captured by Sir Henry Sidney in 1569 although it was taken by the Earl of Kildare in 1499 and was granted to MacWilliam Burke in 1544. In the 1580s the castle was remodelled as the chief residence of Sir Nicholas Malby, Governor of Connacht, a fine new range being built on the north side to replace the supposed original domestic buildings on the south side, and numerous mullion and transom windows being inserted in the gatehouse and northern corner towers in each of which the floor levels were changed. The Confederate Catholics captured the castle in 1645. The north and south curtains were destroyed by the Cromwellian commander Reynalds after the castle was surrendered to him in 1652. See Pages 9 & 81.

Roscommon Castle

ROSSCLOGHER *Leitrim* G8455

On an islet at the south side of Lough Melvin are remains of the chief seat of the MacClancys. It comprises a roughcast late 15th century round tower surrounded by a thick breastwork with a loopholed bastion facing the nearby shore. Francesco de Cuellar, a survivor from a wrecked Armada galleon, defended the castle against Sir William FitzWilliam, the Lord Deputy of Ireland, in 1588.

SEEFIN *Galway* M5116

The ivy mantled thick east end wall containing the stair, entrance and small rooms with angle loops stands high. Much less survives of the rest of the tower which was added later. A passage to a latrine adjoined the end wall at second storey level, being carried over part of the basement room on an arch.

SHRULE *Mayo* M2753

Commanding the bridge is a 16th century tower which belonged to the chief of the MacWilliam Burke Iochtair family and was relieved by him in 1570 when attacked by The President of Connacht and the Earl of Clanricard. At each of the three unvaulted storeys the tower measures 9.9m by 6.8m inside. The walls are 2.6m thick at the base but are battered so that at the third storey they are only 1.5m thick. At second storey level there are rooms in the western corners, a latrine shoot at the NE corner, and a flight of straight steps leading up around the SE corner. The corners are splayed off above the base and have bartizans with splayed off outer corners at the summit. There is a cross-window in the third storey. There was an attic in the roof.

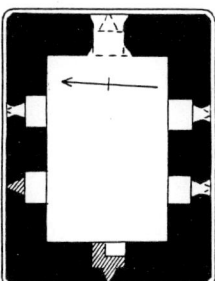
Plan of Shrule Castle

Plan of Seefin Castle

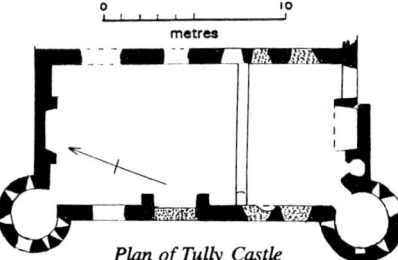
Plan of Tully Castle

Seefin Castle

TERRYLAND .*Galway* M2926

This is a fragmentary early 17th century stronghouse of the Earl of Clanricard. It had three storeys plus attics and there are traces of a quadrangular bawn about 30m by 42m between it and the river. The house was 25m long and was 11m wide at one end, and 10m for the other half it its length. This narrower part stands high and has a big kitchen fireplace, an oven, and corbels for a corner bartizan.

TULLOKYNE *Galway* M2337

The western side wall 10.8m long survives to the full height. Below the large top room was a vault under which were four storeys of main rooms and five levels of smaller rooms in the thick north wall.

TULLY *Roscommon* M9531

Beside a modern house are the ivy mantled ruins of a thinly walled early 17th century stronghouse of two storeys plus attics. On the gables are the high stacks of big fireplaces, that of the kitchen being at the south end. The house measures 17.6m by 9m and has round flankers 4m in diameter with gunloops on the western corners. It is assumed that there was a bawn on the other side. See plan on p43.

MAP OF CASTLES OF CONNACHT

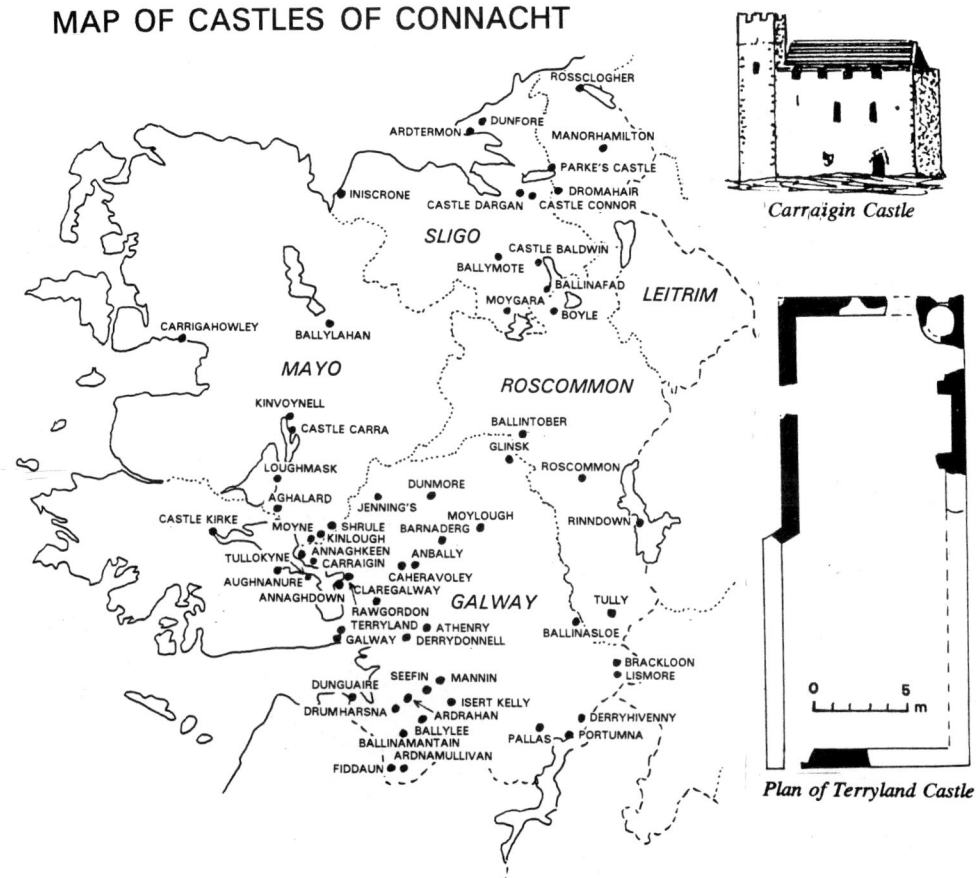

Carraigin Castle

Plan of Terryland Castle

The last remnant of Dunfore Bawn, Co Sligo, (G6245). Other fragmentary bawns in Connacht lacking a tower or stronghouse are Aughrim, which has a small gatehouse, Ardnabrone, Ardnaglass, and Coola.

Boyle Abbey, Co Roscommon, (G8003) was converted into a stronghouse in Elizabeth I's reign. A small gatehouse (in the centre of the picture) was added to the west side of the cloister which was used as a bawn.

GAZETTEER OF CASTLES OF LEINSTER

ARKLOW   *Wicklow*   T2574

Beside the Council Offices is a long curving length of curtain wall, perhaps 13th century, extending from the main road to an ivy mantled round tower above a ravine. The Butlers had a seat here by the 1190s. It was captured in 1331 by the Irish, but recaptured in 1332 by Justiciar Lucy. The MacMurroughs took the castle in 1452 and held it until 1530 when it was returned to the Butlers. The castle was repaired in 1571 and was captured by the Confederate Catholics in 1642. It was burnt by them in 1649 to prevent it being taken and occupied by Cromwell's forces.

ATHGOE   *Dublin*   N9926

Next to a house of 1750 is a round cornered four storey tower 7.3m by 6.5m with a round staircase turret and an original door. It belonged to the Lockes, who also held Colmanstown Castle, and is dated 1579, which may refer to when it was built.

ATHLONE   *Westmeath*   N0442   A.M.*

In 1129 Turlough Mor O'Connor, King of Connacht, built a new bridge over the Shannon and erected a fort to guard it. The same site was probably used for the motte and bailey castle built by Geoffrey de Costentin, which was looted and burnt in 1199 by Cathal Crovderg O'Connor except for the timber keep. The decagonal tower keep 13m in diameter is perhaps the successor of the tower built by John de Grey in 1210 which collapsed in 1211, killing nine of the garrison. Henry III had the castle repaired in 1251 and the curtain walls flanked by D-shaped towers are probably the works recorded in 1273-9. The castle held out for 22 weeks against the Catholics in 1641 but was abandoned to them in 1642. Sir Charles Coote captured Athlone in 1650 after two attempts. The castle was badly damaged in 1691 when it was bombarded and captured by the Williamite General Ginkell, and subsequently the keep, towers and curtain walls were all reduced in height and strengthened for the mounting of heavy cannon. The castle remained in military use until the 1920s and is now a museum.

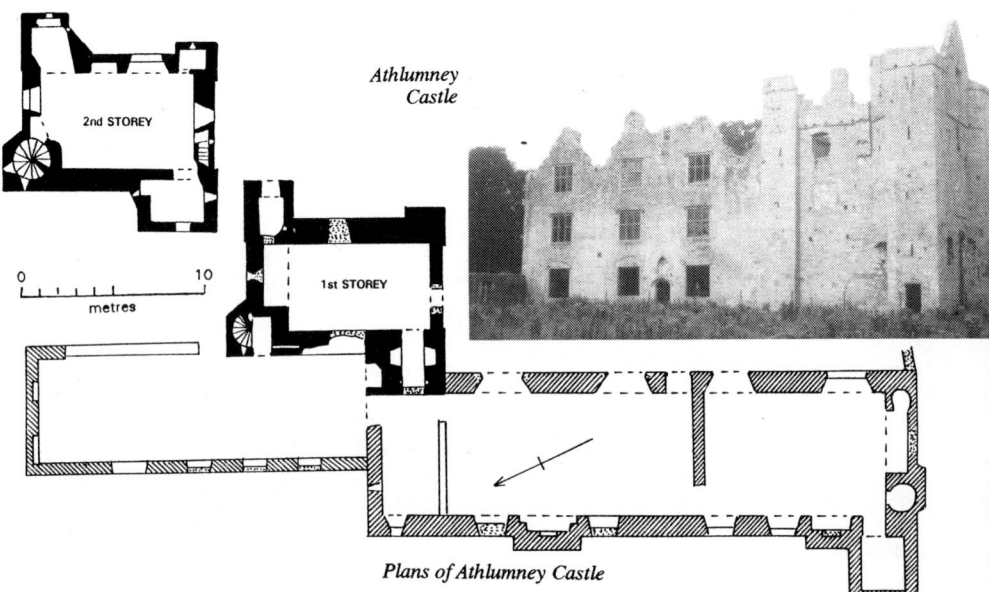

Athlumney Castle

2nd STOREY

1st STOREY

0   10
metres

Plans of Athlumney Castle

Ballycowen Castle

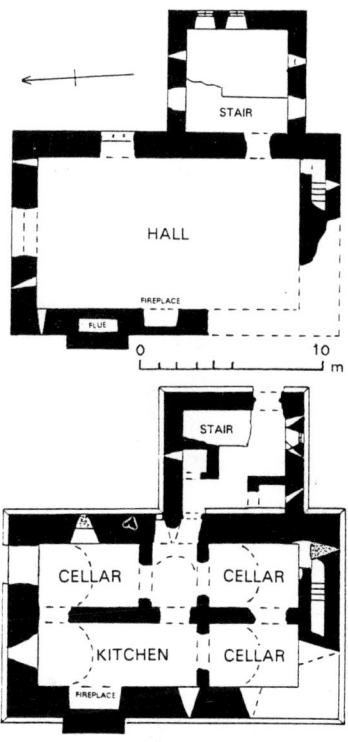

*Plans and Section
of Balief Castle*

Plans of Ballycowen Castle

ATHLUMNEY *Meath* N8966 A.M.

The three storey 30m long mansion of c1600 with mullion and transom windows and a lower kitchen range has a small wing at one end while projecting from the opposite end of the other side wall is the Dowdalls' 15th century tower measuring 10.6m by 7.2m. It has four storeys plus an attic and four rectangular corner turrets of different sizes and degrees of projection. In 1649 the Maguires are said to have set the castle on fire rather than let Cromwell occupy it.

BALIEF *Kilkenny* S3263

The round tower house built in the 16th century by the Shortalls has a diameter of 9m and rises 10m to the wall walk. It contains a cellar, the lord's bedroom, a dome vaulted sleeping loft, and a hall on top, bigger and better lit than the lower rooms.

BALLYCOWEN *Offaly* N2925

An O'Melaghlin castle here was captured by Lord Deputy Grey in 1586 and granted to Thomas Nonnes in 1589 but the present ruin is a tower-like stronghouse of three storeys plus attics built in 1626 by Sir Jasper Herbert. There are numerous gunloops in the wing on the east side which contained a scale-and-platt staircase. The NE corner has a square bartizan and it is assumed there was another on the fallen SW corner. The basement is large enough to warrant subdivision to help carry the vaulting and has a kitchen with a big fireplace and separate cellars for food and wine, the latter having a service stair leading up.

Ballyloughan Castle

Balief Castle

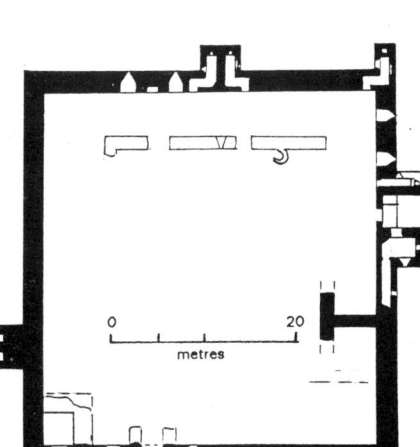

Plan of Ballymoon Castle

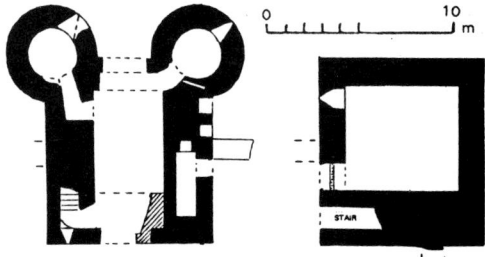

Ballyloughan: Plans of Gatehouse and SW Tower

BALLYLOUGHAN   *Carlow*   N7558

This 14th century castle was held by the Kavanagh MacMurroughs until c1660 when it passed to the Bagenals. It was later sold to the Bruens. Little now remains of the curtain wall 1m thick around a courtyard 47m long by 41m wide and the moat has been filled in, but there are ruins of a three storey gatehouse 10m by 9m with 5m diameter round towers on the southern, or outer, corners. At the SW corner is a two storey tower 9m by 10m with one wall twice the thickness of the others to carry a straight stair to the upper room. Less survives of the NE tower 7.8m by 6.4m and only footings remain of a small turret at the NW corner.

BALLYMOON   *Carlow*   S7362

The castle is thought to have been built by the Bigods or Carews c1290-1310. A curtain wall 2.2m thick surrounds a court 37m square containing vestiges of two storey domestic ranges on each side. The large fireplace on the north belonged to the main hall 6.7m wide. The gateway on the west is a plain arch with portcullis grooves. There are no proper towers but the other three sides are flanked by latrine turrets.

BALLYRAGGET *Kilkenny* N4472

The Butler Earls of Ormond built the still roofed 15th century tower and large well preserved bawn with a surrounding ditch. In the late 16th century it was the chief seat of Viscount Mountgarret, head of a junior branch of the Butler family. His descendants held the castle until it passed to the Kavanaghs of Borris in 1788. It served as a British military post during the Insurrection of 1798.

BARRYSTOWN *Wexford* S8612

The third storey of this 16th century tower measuring 8m by 7.5m lies above a vault and is very overgrown. The entrance passage has a dog-leg arrangement and is covered by two gunloops. A straight stair then leads up to the base of a spiral stair.

BILLESTOWN *Westmeath* N5867

There are traces of earthworks around a ruinous tower of three storeys without vaults measuring 9.7m by 7.4m over walls 1.5m thick at basement level. The entrance is segmental arched and has a narrow stair beside it. See plans on page 78.

BIRR *Offaly* N0505

A motte and bailey castle built in 1186 was destroyed in 1207 but rebuilt in 1212. Birr was later the principal seat of the O'Carrolls of Eile. The castle was rebuilt as a stronghouse, perhaps by Laurence Parsons who was granted Birr in 1620, and was captured by the Catholics in 1642 and Ireton in 1650. James II confiscated the estate but the Parsons regained possession after William III's victory at the Boyne and the castle held out against an attack by Patrick Sarsfield, Earl of Lucan. The Parsons, now Earls of Rosse, still inhabit the much enlarged and remodelled castle.

BOLEYVILLISH *Westmeath* N3050

Three sides remain of a late 16th century tower 9.1m wide over walls 1.4m thick, probably once 11.7m long. The basement has loops either side of a small fireplace and traces of a plinth which has been ripped away. Two more storeys also survive.

BURNCHURCH *Kilkenny* N4747

Of a bawn about 30m long only the 12m high NW flanker survives. It is 5m in diameter and has four storeys linked by stairs curving round in the outer wall, the top three stages being living rooms. The late 15th century tower house of the Burnchurch FitzGeralds in the SW corner of the bawn is roofless but well preserved. It measures 10.2m by 9.5m at the base and has four storeys below a vault and a hall above. The latter has a fireplace with a high chimney. The ends of the tower continue up one more stage to form fighting platforms. There are angle loops at the second and third storeys and latrines in the SW corner. See colour picture on page 82.

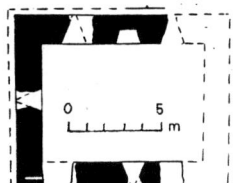
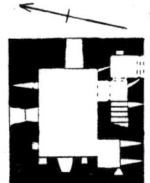
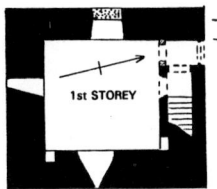
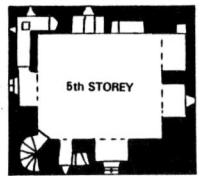

Plan of Boleyvillish Castle   *Plan of Barrystown Castle*   *Plans of Burnchurch Castle*

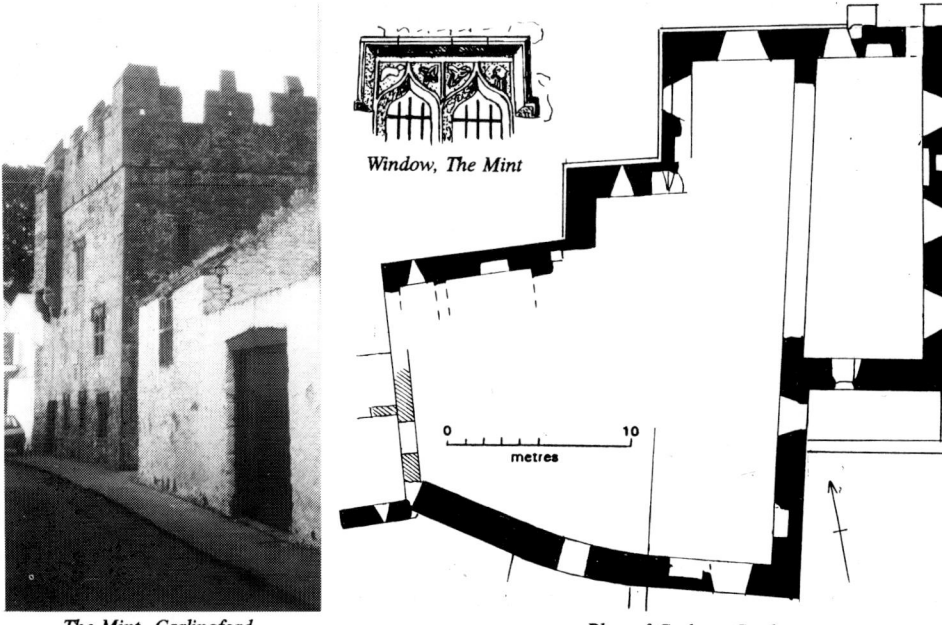

Window, The Mint

The Mint, Carlingford

Plan of Carbury Castle

CARBURY   *Kildare*   N6935

A large and impressive late 16th century stronghouse lies within the earthworks of a Norman castle on a commanding hill. The interior is gutted, buried in debris, and difficult to understand but there seems to have been a staircase wing on the west side of a large block divided longitudinally with vaulted cellars. Another wing, perhaps later, extended south. Later on a small court seems to have been created on the SW. There are many hooded mullioned windows and some fine lofty chimney stacks.

CARLINGFORD   *Louth*   J1812   A.M.

In c1185-1200 Henry de Lacy built a loopholed curtain wall 2.4m thick around an oval court 32m long by 26m wide on a rock near the sea. Only the lower part of one of the two rectangular towers flanking the gate on the west now remains, but a square tower to the SW with the upper corners chamfered is better preserved. King John visited the castle in 1210 and had it repaired in 1211 and 1215. In the mid 13th century Henry III built the hall block on the east side, a plain but impressive structure measuring 25m by 15m with walls up to 2.8m thick. The basement is divided by a set of steps leading down to a vaulted cellars under the southern part and another cellar to the east. A 15th century four storey range beyond to the south containing smaller private rooms is now very ruined. Hugh O'Neill tried to take the castle in a surprise attack in 1596 and it was also attacked in 1642, 1649, and 1650. In the town are two ruined tower houses. Taaffe's Castle is an impressive four storey structure with maximum dimensions of 14.4 by 8.7m. It has angle loops and a machicolation over the entrance. A later two storey block adjoins to the north. The Mint is supposedly the site of the mint of 1467 although it is actually a thinly walled building roughly 8.5m square more likely to be at least a century later. There are three unvaulted storeys. The openings towards the street are wide and have carvings in the spandrels. See picture page 84.

Plan of Carlingford Mint

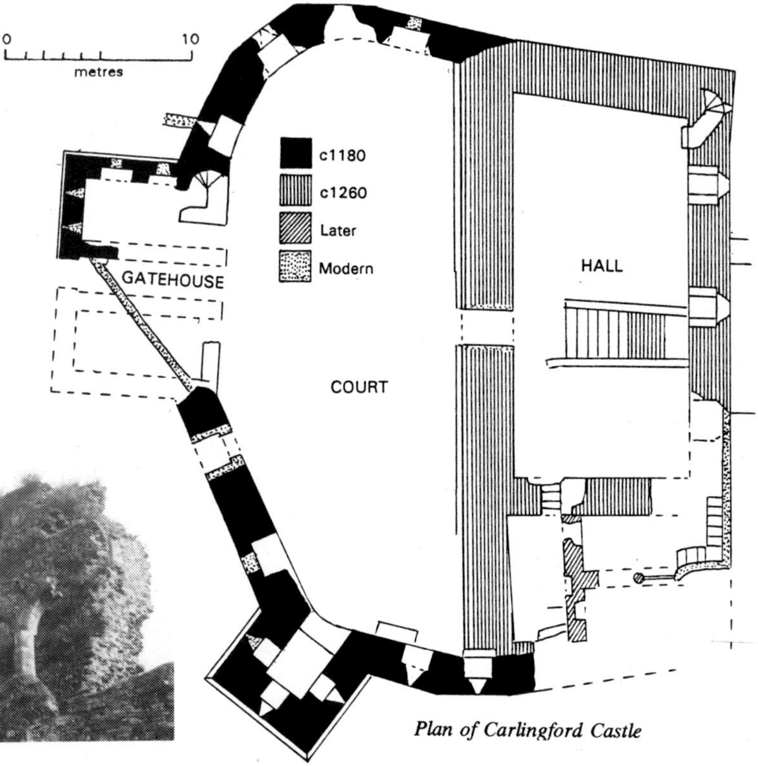

0 — 10
metres

■ c1180
▨ c1260
▧ Later
▨ Modern

GATEHOUSE

HALL

COURT

Carlingford Castle

Plan of Carlingford Castle

Taaffe's Castle, Carlingford

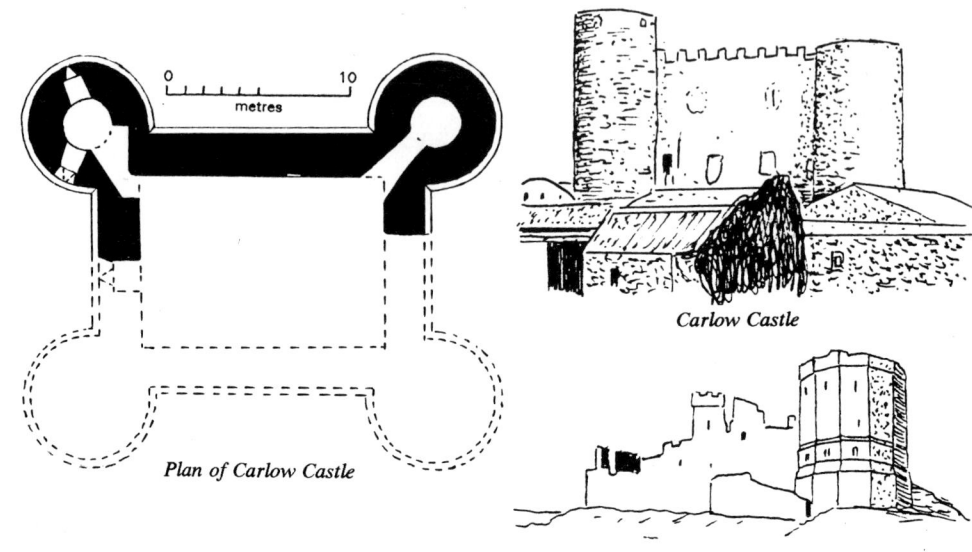

Plan of Carlow Castle

Carlow Castle

Old sketch of Castleknock

CARLOW *Carlow* S7376

Within the grounds of a factory are parts of a keep remaining from an extensive castle mostly demolished in the early 19th century to build a lunatic asylum. Hugh de Lacy is thought to have built a motte here c1180, and the keep was probably built by William Marshall in c1208-13. It was later held by the Bigod Earls of Norfolk and their successors the Howards until confiscation in the 1530s. The castle was captured and briefly held by James FitzGerald in 1494 and again by Silken Thomas in 1535. It was granted to Edward Randolf in 1552, to Robert Hartpole in 1577, and was sold to Donough, Earl of Thomond in 1616. The castle was captured by the Confederate Catholics in the 1640s and surrendered to Ireton in 1650, and later returned to the Earl of Thomond. It was later held by the Hamiltons. Only the 2.7m thick west wall containing straight staircases up and down from the hall on the second storey remains of the keep which was 21m long by 14m wide above a battered plinth. A stub of the north wall contains the entrance doorway at hall level. Two of the four corner towers 8m in diameter survive, that to the NW having a top stage of the 16th century when mullioned windows were inserted to give more light to the state rooms.

CASTLE KEVIN *Wicklow* T1898

A rectangular stone revetted motte and a bailey to the east with traces of a gatehouse and NE tower remain of a castle built c1214 by Henry de Londres, Archbishop of Dublin. It was repeatedly destroyed by the Irish and eventually became an O'Toole seat until it was taken from Felim O'Toole by Lord Deputy Mountjoy in 1597. Red Hugh O'Donnell was recaptured here after his escape from Dublin Castle in 1591.

CASTLEKNOCK *Dublin* O0827

Beside the college are the earthworks of a castle built c1180 by Hugh Tyrell. Fragments remain of the extensive bailey buildings shown on a drawing of 1689 by Francis Place. Only footings survive of the three storey polygonal keep he shows on the motte. Castleknock was captured by Edward Bruce in 1317, and the Confederate Catholic garrison was butchered after it was taken by General Monck in 1642.

Castle Roche

CASTLE ROCHE   *Louth*   H9913

On a rock is a kite shaped court 60m long by 40m wide with a fairly complete curtain wall 1.4m thick. Towards the east end of the long NE front facing the site of an outer bailey beyond a rock cut ditch is a twin towered gatehouse of which only the outer part survives. South of the gateway, at a lower level, and having large windows with seats in the embrasures, is a block containing an upper floor hall 17.6m long by 12.8m wide reached from the court by steps in a porch. The basement must have had timber subdividing walls to allow the flooring of such a span. At the NW corner is the vaulted basement of a round tower about 8m in diameter. All these works are attributed to John de Verdon, who died in 1274, but in the middle of the court is a square building around a pit, perhaps the castle recorded as built by his mother Rohesia before 1236. See plan on page 9.

Clara Castle

CLARA   *Kilkenny*   N5747

The late 15th century tower of the Shortalls is unusually well preserved as a result of continued occupation, and, although now empty, retains some original floor beams. There are five storeys, the uppermost being a hall above a vaulted sleeping loft. Angle loops open off the lord's suite on the third storey. The tiny forecourt with gunloops outside the entrance is an early 17th century addition.

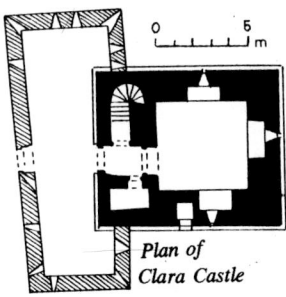

Plan of Clara Castle

Clonburren Castle

Clonony Castle

CLARE *Westmeath* N2446

On one side of a roughly circular bawn of which traces survive is a tower 12.4m by 8.0m over walls 1.8m thick. The only features remaining are a loop at one end of the basement and a stair from the second storey to a destroyed third storey.

CLONBURREN *Laois* S2574

On a low rock is a tower 14m high to the wall-walk at which level are corbels for former corner and mid-wall machicolations. It measures 12.6m by 9.5m over walls 2.3m thick up to the level of the fourth storey vault. Above the walls are only 1.3m thick and have two light windows. Some of the loops below are roundels or crosses. There are smaller chambers in the thick east wall below a fourth storey vault.

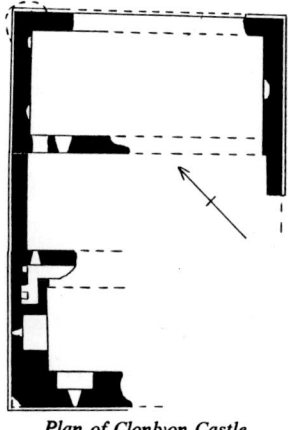

Plan of Clonlyon Castle

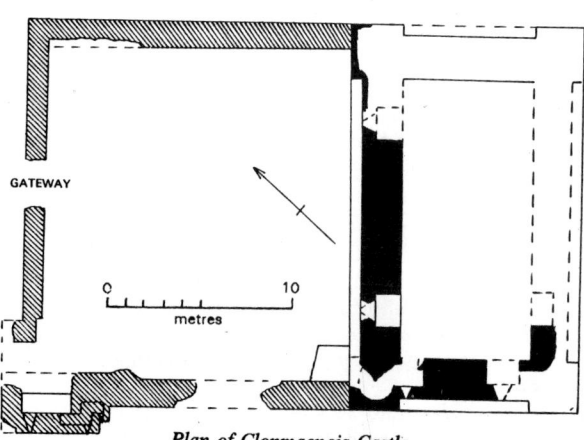

Plan of Clonmacnois Castle

GATEWAY

0   10
metres

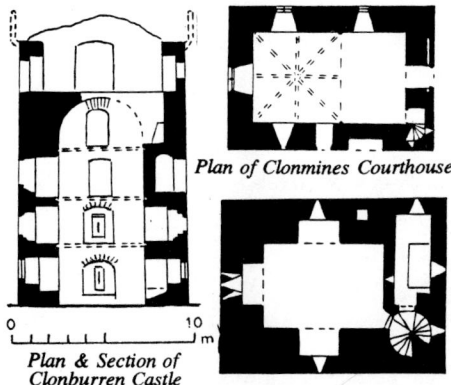

Plan of Clonmines Courthouse

Plan & Section of Clonburren Castle

Clonmacnois Castle

CLONLYON *Offaly* NO726

Most of the space within a bawn 21m by 15m externally with a round bartizan just 2.8m above ground on the north corner was taken up with an outbuilding filling the NE end and the tower 8.3m wide with a vaulted third storey in the west corner.

CLONMACNOIS *Offaly* NO130

The ringwork and bailey between the monastery and the lake were built by King John c1212. Henry III built a hall keep on the ringwork and the bailey bears a 16th century bawn about 17m square with a NW entrance and a square west turret. The keep, which was blown up c1650, measured 19m by 11.4m above a battered plinth from which rose clasping corner turrets, of which only one, containing the stair, survives.

CLONMINES *Wexford* S8413

The embattled court house of c1400 measures 11.4m by 7.7m. The lower level is a courtroom with a rib vault over the main space but a barrel vault at one end where there was a gallery. The main entrance below the gallery is protected by a machicolation on tall pyramidal corbels, and there is also a side entrance. Two of the corners rise up at turrets. Nearby is a four storey tower house built by the Suttons or FitzHenrys measuring 9.3m by 7.5m with straight staircases and a vault over the second storey. A third tower is incorporated into a nearby house. See page 78.

CLONMORE *Carlow* S9676

The crossloops and windows with pairs of trefoil headed lights indicate a late 13th century date although the castle is not mentioned until later. It comprises a nearly square court with rectangular towers on the southern corners and turrets on the other two, and traces of domestic apartments on the east. The castle was captured by the Earl of Kildare in 1516, the Earl of Ormond in 1598, and Colonel Hewson in 1650.

CLONONY *Offaly* NO521 A.M.

The ruined four storey tower measuring 10.6m by 8.2m appears to be well preserved, although it has been somewhat altered, having been occupied until the 19th century. It lies in a small court of mostly 18th or 19th century buildings which in turn lie in the east corner of a bawn 52m by 37m within a thin but high embattled wall with rectangular flankers of 17th century type at the east, south and west corners. No wall survives on the NW side where there is a low natural fall of the ground level.

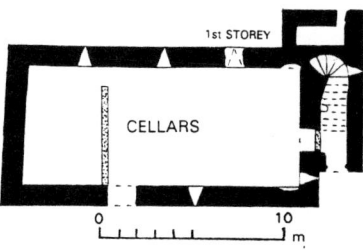
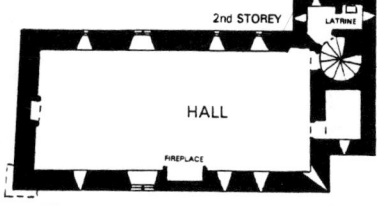
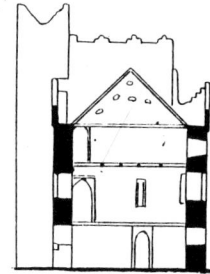

Plans and Section of Coolhull Castle

SECTION

COOLHULL *Wexford* S8810

The late 16th century stronghouse has double stepped battlements and upper windows of twin round headed lights. It has a main block of three low storeys 17.6m long by 8.6m wide. One end wall is thickened outwards for most of its length and rises one storey higher. It contains the entrance, staircase, small rooms, and latrines.

DALKEY *Dublin* O2827

Out of seven fortified houses in and around the town three, all of three storeys, still remain. One, measuring 12.4m by 8.7m, is thought to have been a town hall or court house and has been renovated to serve as the Rates Office. On the other side of the road is Archbold's Castle, a ruin measuring 10.3m by 6m with a cellar and sleeping loft below a vault and a living room above. The entrance has a machicolation and leads onto the foot of a straight stair rising up over a recess in an end wall. Bulloch's Castle overlooks the nearby harbour and has a turret at one end of a long main block and at the other an added second turret with below it an arched entrance for a former bawn.

Town Hall, Dalkey   *Archbold's Castle, Dalkey*

*Bulloch's
Castle,
Dalkey*

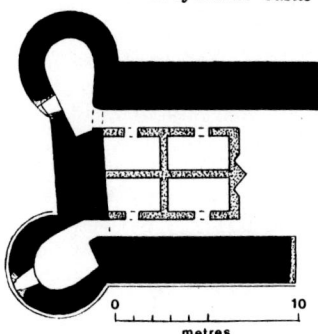

Plan of Dexter Castle

DELVIN *Westmeath* N6064

The scrub covered motte was erected in 1181 by Hugh de Lacy for his brother-in-law Sir Gilbert de Nangle, who later built another castle nearby at Clonyn. His descendants the Nugents built a stone keep at Devlin probably in the late 13th century. It was 11.7m wide over walls 2.5m thick with round corner turrets 5.5m in diameter. The building was probably about 20m long (the east end is missing) and contained a basement (subdivided in modern times), a hall above, and a private chamber on the third storey. The attic was probably a later addition.

Plan of Delvin Castle

DEXTER *Meath* N9473

Near the River Boyne far from any road is a four storey 15th century tower measuring 9m by 6.6m and an adjoining L-shaped house probably of the late 17th century. The tower has turrets 2.8m square for the stairs and latrines boldly clasping two diagonally opposite corners.

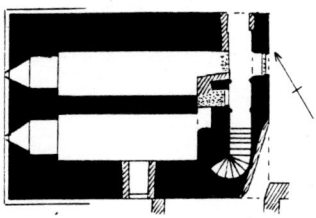

Plan of Donadea Castle

DONADEA *Kildare* N8433

This four storey tower may be as late as 1624, the year given on a date-stone over the entrance. The basement has narrow cellars with loops at one end either side of a longitudunal crosswall, an uncommon layout. A house, now ruined, was added later.

DONORE *Meath* N7149

The tower has rounded corners, double splayed basement loops, a round turret to contain the spiral stair next to the entrance, and vaults over the first and third of four storeys. Above a plinth it measures 8.1m by 6.4m. James, son of Niall Mageoghegan, and over 40 other members of his clan, including women and children, were executed after the castle was captured in 1650 by Commissary-General John Reynolds.

DROGHEDA   *Louth*   O 0975

Hugh de Lacy probably built the motte and bailey south of the river in the 1180s. The motte bears a modern round tower within a much reduced and patched shell wall of uncertain date. Walls in a similar condition surround the bailey now occupied by a military barracks. When Cromwell's troops stormed Drogheda in 1649 the castle was the first part of the defences to be taken so it must have then been very decayed. Of the town walls on the north bank there is one notable relic, the 13th or 14th century barbican which stood in front of St Laurence's Gate. It is a lofty square structure with two round turrets facing the field.

DUBLIN   *Dublin*   O1534

King John ordered the construction of a strong tower at Dublin in 1204 and there may have been a fortress on the rise above the Poddle in the 1170s, but the main defences are thought to have been built during the period 1213-1228 when Henry de Londres was Justiciar. It seems to have only ever endured one siege, Silken Thomas making an unsuccessful attempt to take it in 1534. A Confederate Catholic plot to seize it in 1641 was betrayed. Until 1922 Dublin Castle was the centre of English authority in Ireland and was the official residence of the Lord Deputy or Lord Lieutenant. Some Parliaments and law courts were held within it. The buildings were almost entirely rebuilt during the 18th century but old records and fragments revealed in 1961 make clear the outline of the walls, which were surrounded by a moat. The nearly rectangular bailey was 120m long from east to west by 70m wide and had a twin round towered north gate, and corner towers up to 16m in diameter, except on the SW where there was a smaller square tower, perhaps earlier work. The 14th century Birmingham Tower close to this corner was rebuilt on the old base in 1775, but the Record Tower at the SE corner still has massive 13th century work two storeys high. The octagonal tower on the south side replaces a small original D-shaped tower.

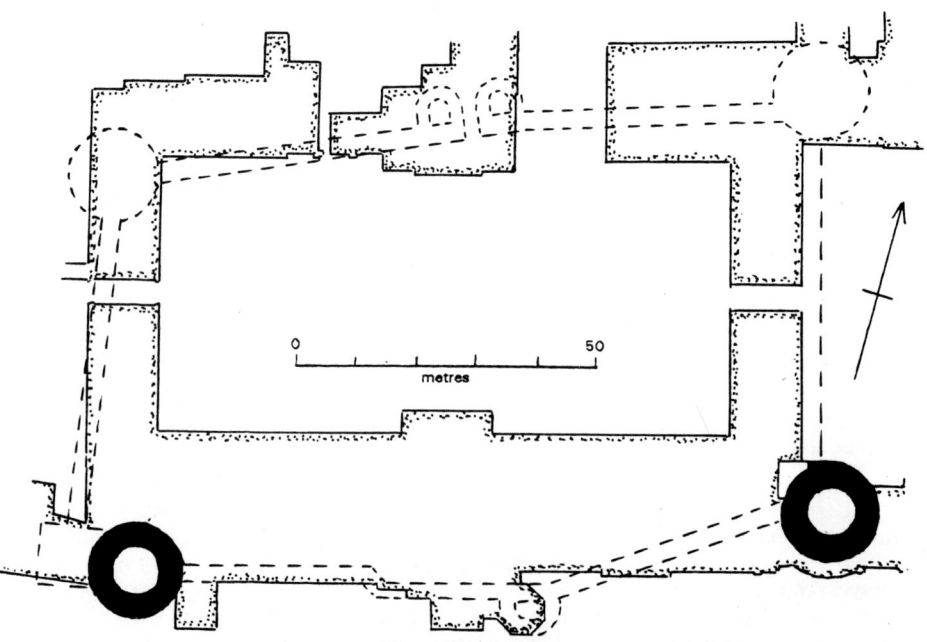

Plan of Dublin Castle

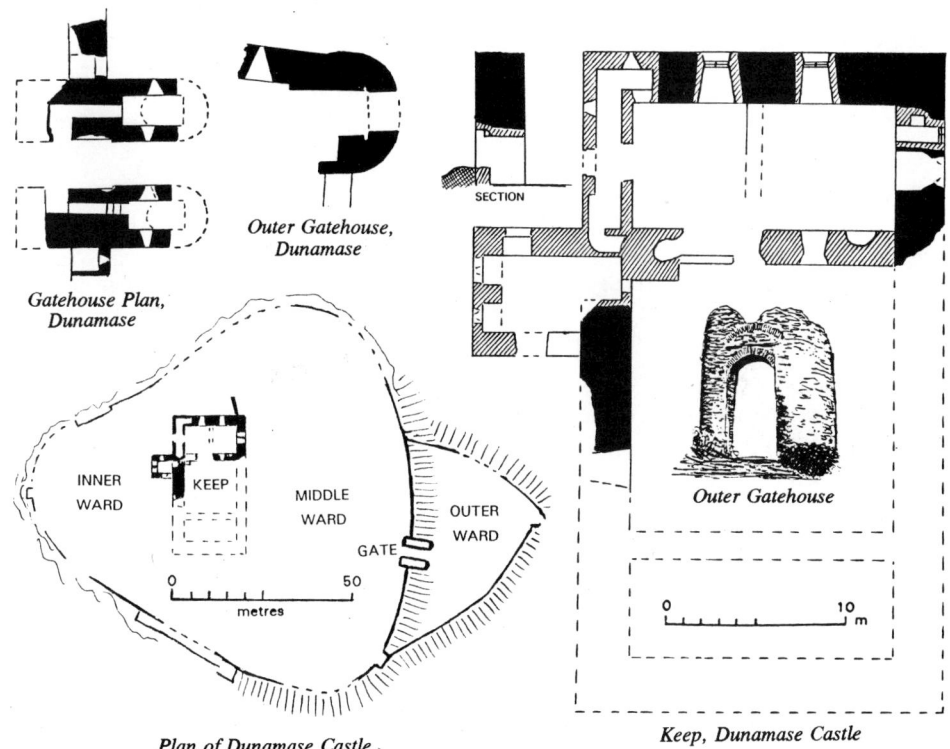

Gatehouse Plan,
Dunamase

Outer Gatehouse,
Dunamase

SECTION

INNER
WARD

KEEP

MIDDLE
WARD

OUTER
WARD

GATE

0   50

metres

Plan of Dunamase Castle

Outer Gatehouse

0   10
m

Keep, Dunamase Castle

DUNAMASE   *Laois*   S5397

A fort on the rock of Dunamase was plundered by Vikings in 944. It was given to Strongbow by Dermot MacMurrough as part of the dowry of his daughter Aoife. William Marshall may have built the keep and the surrounding walls are probably the work of his son-in-law William de Braose c1250, with later additions by the Mortimers. The castle was later held by the O'Mores, from whom it was taken by Sir Charles Coote for Parliament in 1641. The castle was captured by Eoghan Rua O'Neill in 1646 and occupied by Confederate Catholic forces until capture and destruction by Hewson and Reynolds in 1650. It was partly restored by Sir John Parnell but soon allowed to decay. The heart shaped summit of the rock about 100m across has fragments of a wall 1.9m thick with square towers on the more vulnerable east side. A thinner wall crowned the western cliff edge. In the middle are remains of a huge keep 20m wide over walls 2.8m thick and perhaps as much as 35m long (the south end is missing). It is uncertain whether it formed a court or a roofed building. In the 17th century the northern third was closed off and remodelled to form a stronghouse with a tower on the west side flanking the doorway. Walls seem to have joined the keep to the main wall to close off the area to the west as an inner ward. A postern approached by a ramp within a barbican lies on the south side of the main court. The outer part of the twin round fronted gatehouse on the east has fallen. Beyond is a triangular outer court about 30m across with its own round fronted gatehouse facing another enclosure.

DUNCANNON   *Wexford*   S7408

A Norman castle replaced an early fort on the promontory above Waterford harbour. In 1588 Elizabeth I had it replaced with a new fort which was captured by the Confederate Catholics in 1645 after a two month siege. They successfully held it against Ireton in 1649 until Waterford surrendered. It was subsequently rebuilt and remained in use until the 19th century.

DUNMAHON   *Louth*   J0605

An internal machicolation protects the doorway of this late 15th century tower measuring 7.4m by 7m and rising through four storeys to a wall-walk 12m above ground. A square turret contains a spiral stair beside the entrance, and another on an adjacent corner contains latrines. The other corners have top turrets. Here in 1641 some 200 people were slaughtered during a surprise attack whilst they were at mass. See plans and section on p13.

DUNMOE   *Meath*   N9070

Above the Boyne lies the ruin of the D'Arcys' 15th century tower measuring 18.5m by 9m. There were 4.6m diameter turrets containing square chambers at one end and solid 3.6m diameter turrets at the other. One turret of each size and the landward facing wall between them has been destroyed. Cromwell is said to have bombarded the castle in 1649 but the thinly walled two storey extension at one end shows that it remained in use well beyond that date.

DUNSOGHLY   *Dublin*   O1245   A.M.*

This castle has a lofty four storey tower with four square corner turrets of differing sizes and degrees of projection which was built c1450 by Sir Thomas Plunkett, Chief Justice of the King's Bench. It has the last original roof of its kind left in Ireland. The chapel adjoining on the south is a nave now lacking a chancel. It bears the year 1573, the Instruments of The Passion, and the initials of Sir John Plunkett and his third wife Genet Sarsfield. A thin wall encloses a bawn 26m by 15m to the north, and around the whole are earthwork defences of the 1640s when this was an important outpost. See plan on page 14.

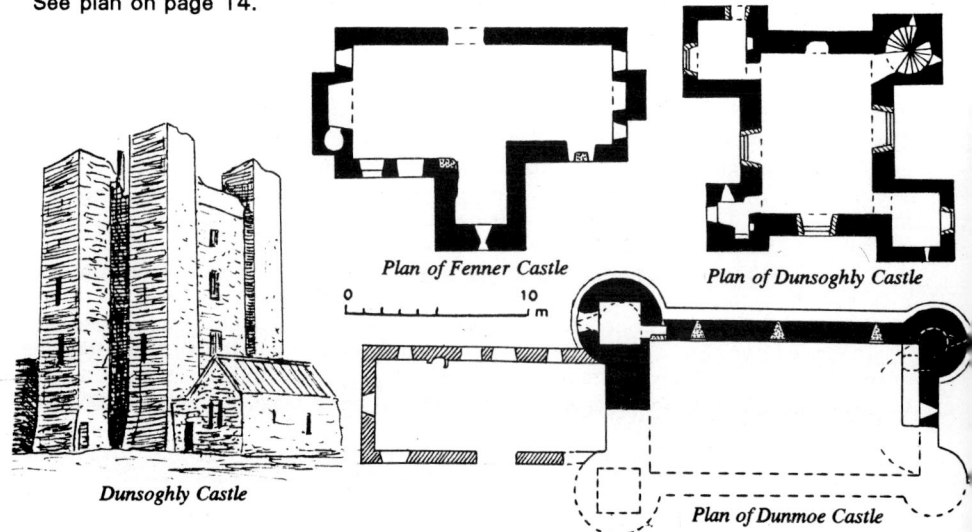

Plan of Fenner Castle

0   10
                     m

Plan of Dunsoghly Castle

Dunsoghly Castle

Plan of Dunmoe Castle

Plan of Enniscorthy Castle

Old Print of Dunmoe Castle

ENNISCORTHY *Wexford* S9840 A.M.*

The 13th century castle of the Prendergasts was long held by the MacMurroughs Kavanagh. The present building, now a museum, is a rebuilding perhaps on the original plan by Sir Henry Wallop in 1586. It measures 14.4m long by 11.6m wide and has an entrance on the west side flanked by round corner towers 5m in diameter one of which contains the staircase. The other corners have smaller round turrets, one of which starts above ground level. The castle was captured by Cromwell in 1649 and served as a prison during the revolt of 1798. It was later restored for the Earl of Plymouth, and was repaired again c1900. There is a modern extension at the back.

FENNER *Meath* N9674

This early 17th century stronghouse is 16m long by 8m wide and has three storeys and an attic. Chimney breasts project beyond the end walls, the larger fireplace with the oven marking the position of the ground floor kitchen. The wing in the middle of one side contained a timber scale-and-platt staircase.

Enniscorthy Castle

Tower House, Granagh Castle

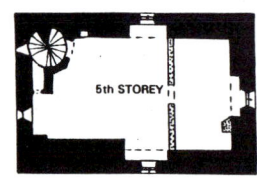

Plans of Foulksrath Castle

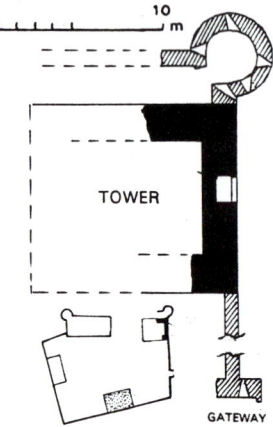

Plans of Garry Castle

FERNS *Wexford* T0350 A.M.

William Marshall had a castle here but the trefoil headed windows of the present building suggest a mid 13th century date when Ferns was held by William de Valance, husband of a Marshall heiress. It is a much ruined keep 27m long by 23m wide over walls 2.4m thick above a battered base outside which was a rock-cut ditch, now partly re-exposed. Of the four corner towers 10.6m in diameter one has vanished, little remains of another, and only half remains of a third, which has a cistern or well in its base. The fourth is still complete and contains a vaulted chapel on the third of four storeys connected by a spiral staircase. The castle was captured by the O'Tooles in 1331 but was retaken by Bishop Charnell. It was later held by the MacMurroughs until taken over for the English Crown by John Travers in 1550. Lord Grey captured it during the rebellion of 1536. The Mastersons held the castle from 1583 until 1649, and in the 1660s it was sold to Thomas Kiernan of Dublin, from whom it passed to the Donovans, owners until it became a state monument. See pages 10, 11 and 84.

FOULKSRATH *Kilkenny* S4666

On a low moated mound lie a 16th century polygonal bawn with a loopholed wall and a tower house of five storeys with the end walls carried up one more stage. The tower has suffered a few alterations and remains in use as a youth hostel.

Plan of Granagh Castle

Drum Tower by the River, Granagh

GARRY *Offaly* N0314

The large 16th century bawn has a gateway on the north and round flankers 4.4m in diameter with gunloops on the western corners. It appears to have been extended southwards later and contains a house and two other outbuildings, all ruined, and the north end wall of a tower house 11m by 10m near the NW corner.

GRANAGH *Kilkenny* S5815 A.M.

In the late 13th century the Le Poer family built beside the River Suir a square court about 30m square with walls up to 2.2m thick with round corner towers. Those on the landward or northern side have gone, but that at the SW corner survives, although much altered later when the rooms inside were converted from rounds to squares, and a fragment of that at the SE corner remains. In the south curtain wall adjoining each tower were latrines draining into the river. The west of another riverside tower is the only relic of an outer court to the west. In 1375 the castle was granted to James, Earl of Ormond and then or later on a tower house was built in the NE corner. This seems to have been truncated later and a two storey hall block over 8m wide was built against it in the 16th century, whilst an oriel was added to the tower south side in the 17th century. The castle was captured by the Cromwellian commander Axtell in 1650.

GRANARD *Longford* N3382

There are traces of the footings of a round keep and curtain wall on the summit of the motte of 1199 within which vaulted rooms of square mortared masonry are reported to have been found. There is a bailey on one side of the motte.

GRANGE *Kildare* N6236

This small tower measuring just 8.5m by 6.6m is probably early 17th century, the third storey fireplace being of that date. The thick end wall is only big enough to contain a latrine rather than the usual bedchamber at this level.

HEYNESTOWN *Louth* J0504

Some of the four round turrets of various sizes set at the corners of the main block measuring just 7.2m by 5.4m may be later additions. One turret contains a staircase and another diagonally opposite contains latrines. A blocked arch suggests that the larger of the two vaulted cellars was originally a gateway passage. Yet there is no sign of an arch on the other side. Altogether this is a very peculiar and puzzling building.

HOOK *Wexford* X7496

The lighthouse on the headland near which Raymond le Gros landed in 1169 is very massively built and contains three vaulted storeys. It may be as old as the 13th century and certainly existed by 1657 when it was whitewashed as a landmark.

HOWTH *Dublin* O2839

This castle has been the seat of the St Lawrence family since c1180. An early 19th century martello tower has replaced the motte. The mid 16th century keep with stepped battlements at the SW corner and the square NE gatehouse have survived the rebuilding of 1738 and the many 19th and 20th century alterations.

Plans of Grange Castle

Kildare Castle

Kilbline Castle

0   10
⌊_ _ _ _ _ _ _ _ _⌋ m

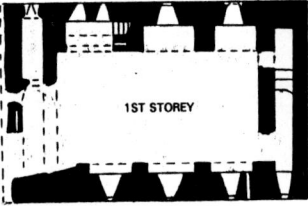

1ST STOREY

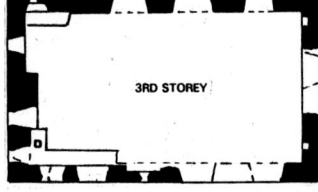

3RD STOREY

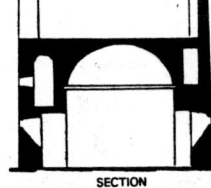

SECTION

Plans and Section of Kilbreedy Castle

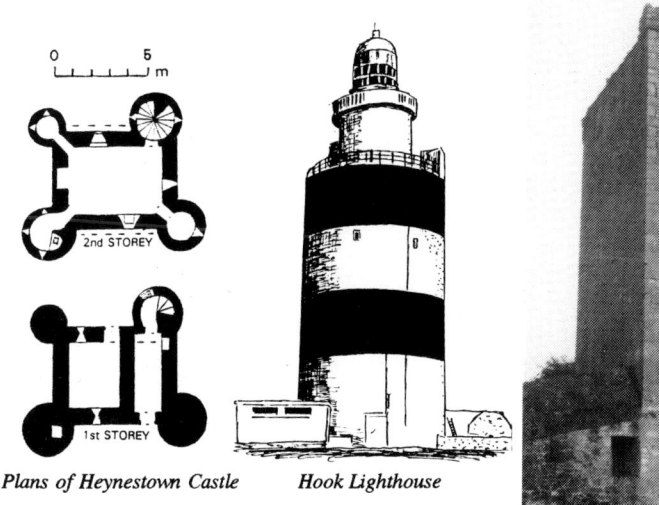

Plans of Heynestown Castle   *Hook Lighthouse*

Tower House in outer courtyard at Kells Priory

KELLS *Kilkenny* S5043 A.M.

A motte in the village bears fragments of a much later heptagonal bawn. To the east is the priory, famous for its high outer precinct wall on the line of which are four independent tower houses, mostly of four unvaulted storeys, for the use of lay officials. Other towers lie beside the inner precinct gateway and by the church.

KILBLINE *Kilkenny* S5647

On the second storey of the well preserved tower house is a chimney piece dated 1580. Shortly after this date Kilbline passed from the Comerfords to the Shortalls, who added the still inhabited two storey adjoining house in the late 17th century. The castle later passed to Ralph Gore and was subsequently held by the Candlers and Ryans. The latter still use two storeys of the tower as storerooms.

KILBREEDY *Laois* S3080

This is a 16th century building of unusual design. On either side of the basement are loops contained in deep embrasures like an arcade. Squeezed under the vault was a large sleeping loft. The storey above has much thinner walls with big windows.

KILDARE *Kildare* N7313

William Marshall's castle here later passed to the de Vescis, and in 1316 was granted to John Fitzgerald, 6th Baron Offaly and 1st Earl of Kildare. The small four storey inhabited tower still remaining is much later and may even post-date the destruction of the castle by Elizabeth I's officials in the 1580s.

KILKEA *Kildare* S7588

The original L-shaped tower was later extended and then heavily altered in a restoration of 1849 after being wrecked in the revolt of 1798. It was given to the Jesuits in 1634 and in 1646 the papal nuncio Rinuccini stayed here for the Confederation of Kilkenny. The castle was captured by Colonel Hewson in 1650.

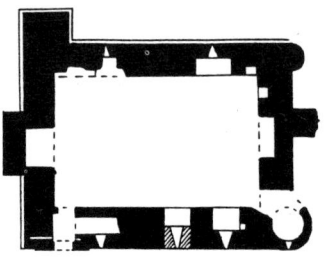

Plan of Kyle Castle

Kilkenny Castle

KILIANE   *Wexford*   T0616

A still inhabited house has replaced one side of a quadrangular bawn 35m long by 26m wide. The 1.4m thick wall is otherwise complete and has a machicolation over the gateway and a round turret at one corner. The diagonally opposite corner contains a ruined five storey tower house measuring 12m by 8.3m. The second storey is vaulted. Straight stairs are contained in an end wall. The basement loops have recess-like embrasures. This was a Hay seat, later passing to the Cheevers of Ballyhally.

KILKENNY   *Kilkenny*   S5255   A.M.*

Strongbow probably erected a motte here in 1172. William Marshall built a quadrangular courtyard with walls 1.8m thick and round corner towers in c1204-12. Of it there remain parts of the west and south walls, and the SE, SW, and NW towers, 11.2m, 7m, and 8.6m in diameter respectively. The castle passed in 1245 to the de Clares. After the last of the male line was killed at Bannockburn in 1314 Kilkenny went to the Despensers, absentee lords, and then the Straffords. James Butler, 3rd Earl of Ormond purchased the castle in 1391 and it became the principal seat of the earldom. From the later medieval period remain the vaults over the tower basements. In 1650 Cromwell battered with his artillery the lost eastern side of the castle which formerly had a gateway between twin round fronted towers. The building was remodelled in the 1660s by James, 12th Earl and 1st Duke of Ormonde but fell into decay after the attainder of the 2nd Duke for his support of the Jacobite cause in 1715. It was renovated by Walter Butler of Garryricken after he inherited the title in 1766 and the park and a new approach laid out, plus new stables erected. In 1826 the north wing was rebuilt to house a picture gallery and the rest of the castle medievalised. The castle was occupied by the Republicans in May 1922 and besieged by the Free Staters. Most of the original contents were sold in 1935 and the castle was left in a sorry state after military occupation in World War II but it has since been restored and refurnished by Irish Board of Works as an ancient monument.

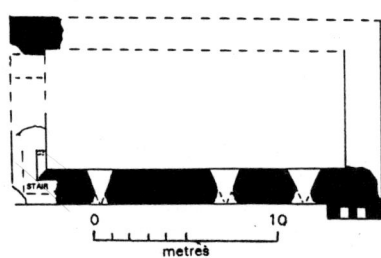

Plan of Kindlestown Castle

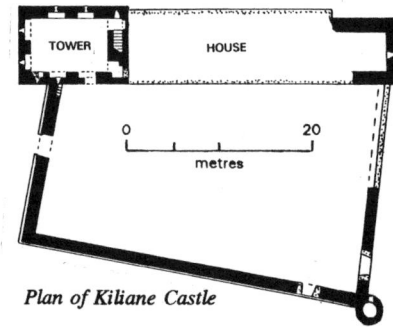

Plan of Kiliane Castle

KINDLESTOWN *Wicklow* O2813

This is a 13th or 14th century hall-house built by the Archbolds. It is 20.6m long by 9.7m wide over walls up to 1.9m thick. The basement was vaulted and has a stair in the NE corner to the hall which was served by latrines in a projection at the NW corner. There was a third storey perhaps formed later in the original roof space. In 1798 the castle was captured from a British garrison by the Insurgent Irish.

KINNEFAD *Kildare* N6235

Most of the thick east wall has collapsed. The room within it at second storey level with one jamb remaining of a fireplace was the lord's bedroom. The third storey was a sleeping loft squeezed under the vault below the hall. There are many pistol loops.

KYLE *Wexford* S9827

The lack of vaults to the four storeys and the projecting chimney breast with a kitchen fireplace at ground level indicate a late date for this tower measuring 14.7m long by 11m wide. A thick side wall contains a straight stair up from the entrance near a corner. The opposite wall has a square turret and there are smaller round turrets, one of which contained a spiral staircase, projecting from the far end wall. The castle lies by the River Slaney and has an alternative name of Deeps' Castle.

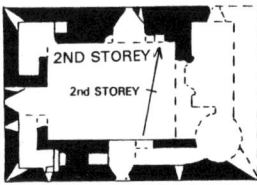

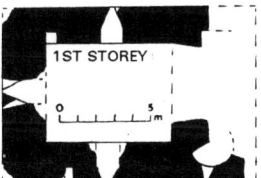

Plans of Kinnefad Castle.

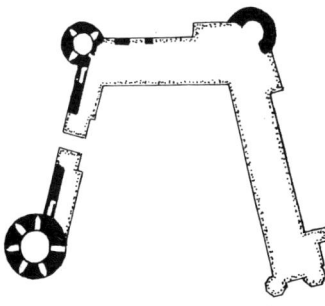

Plan of Kilkenny Castle

Kindlestown Castle

Lea Castle

LEA   *Laois*   N5712

William Marshall had a motte and bailey castle here in 1203. A window with two trefoiled headed lights dates the lofty but very ruined keep to c1250-60, the time of Maurice FitzGerald, 2nd Baron Offaly. The castle was burnt by the O'Connors in 1285 and the gatehouse added by Edward I in the 1290s failed to save it from being wrecked by the O'Mores in 1307 and 1346, and by Edward Bruce in 1315. An adjacent town never recovered from these incursions. In 1422 O'Dempsey captured Lea from the Earl of Kildare only to lose it to the Earl of Ormond in 1452. Silken Thomas retreated to the castle during his rebellion of 1535. The O'Dempseys seized Lea for the Confederate Catholics in 1641 and it was blown up by the Cromwellians in 1650. Only one of the 8.6m diameter corner towers of the four storey keep 21m long by 15m wide over 3m thick walls now survives. From it leads a straight stair in the north wall, and the entrance at second storey level adjoins on the east. The basement vaults and crosswall are 15th or 16th century. Around the keep was an oval court about 55m long by 40m wide with D-shaped bastions. Two of these, on the south, and SE, survive, with adjoining walls and an eastward facing gateway beyond which the wall was arcaded to provide sufficient width for a wall-walk. Immediately beyond the SE bastion is the outer gateway with a passage 3m wide with two portcullis grooves flanked by elongated 6m wide round fronted towers. A latrine turret adjoins the east tower. The gateway was later blocked and the building used as an apartment block. The outer court measures about 60m across and extends towards the River Barrow which was probably used to fill the moats.

LEIGHLINBRIDGE   *Carlow*   S6965

In the garden of a house by the bridge is the western part of a tower built in 1547 by Sir Edward Bellingham. In 1567 the Devonshire knight Peter Carew obtained it by falsely claiming a hereditary title. The castle was damaged by Rory Og O'More in 1577 and was finally dismantled in 1650 after defying the Cromwellian Colonel Hewson.

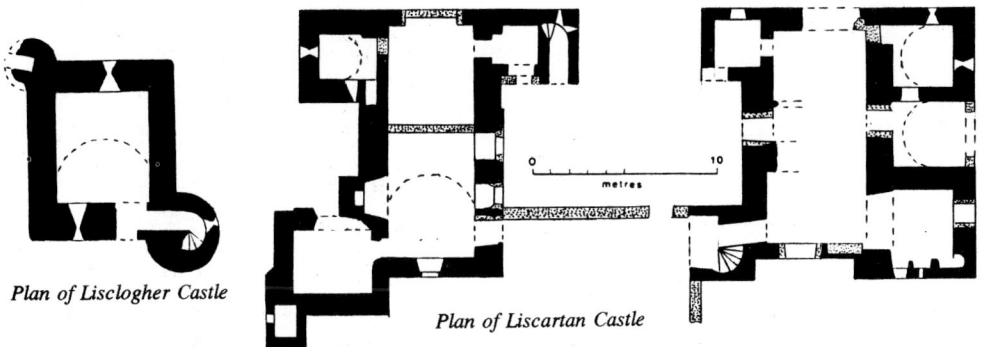

Plan of Lisclogher Castle

0
10
metres

Plan of Liscartan Castle

LISCARTAN *Meath* N8469

Two ruined and iny mantled tower houses lie just 13m apart. One is of three storeys and measures 14.3m by 7.7m. It has a square staircase turret and three other corner turrets or wings containing rooms of various sizes. The other tower, now only two storeys high, has projections at just three of the four corners.

LISCLOGHER *Meath* N6862

Only the vaulted basement with double splayed loops remains of a tower 9.8m by 8m. Set at diagonally opposite corners are a stair turret 4.3m in diameter and a much smaller latrine turret, also round.

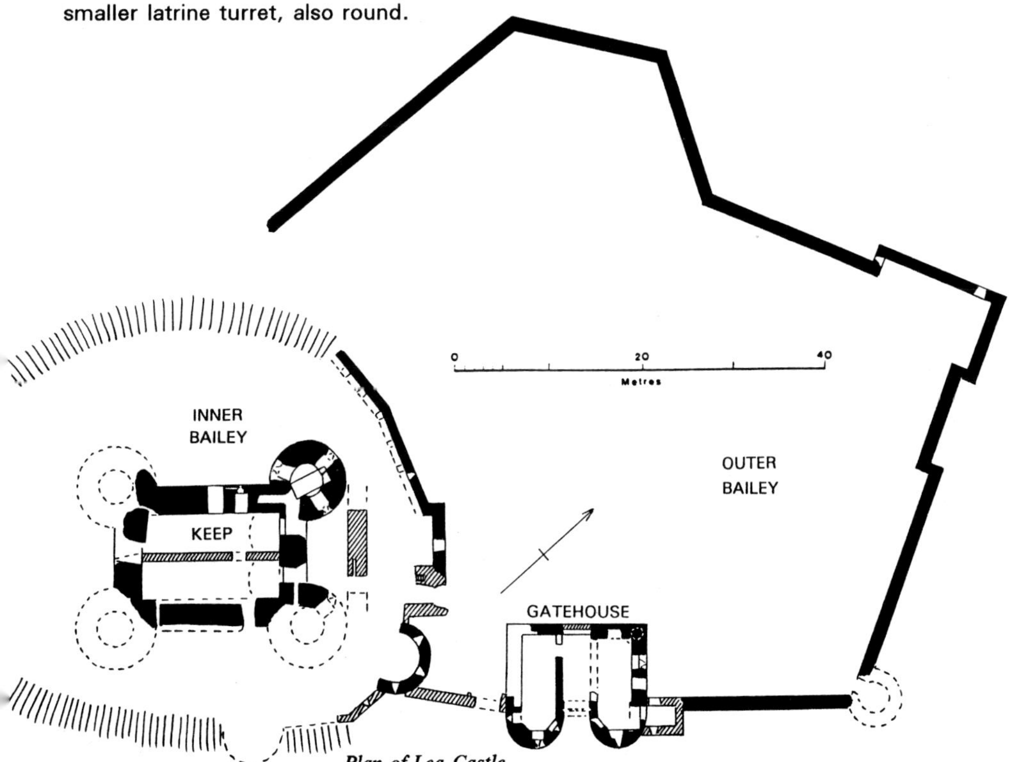

0
20
40
Metres
INNER
BAILEY
KEEP
OUTER
BAILEY
GATEHOUSE

Plan of Lea Castle

LOUGH SEWDY   *Westmeath*   N2350

The O'Melaghlins are thought to have had a fort on a peninsular on the south side of the lough and Hugh de Lacy's motte of 1184 was presumably on the same site. Edward Bruce spent Christmas here in 1315. The site long remained in use, being garrisoned by the English in 1641 and the Jacobites in 1690.

MALAHIDE   *Dublin*   O2446   A.M.*

This is the seat of Lord Talbot de Malahide whose family was here by c1180. It seems to consist of a 16th century stronghouse with round corner towers but has been much rebuilt and extended in later centuries.

MAYNOOTH   *Kildare*   N9437   A.M.

Gerald Fitz-Maurice, 1st Baron Offaly, d1203 is thought to have had a castle here beside the River Lyreen. Beyond the west side of a court about 42m square is a huge keep of c1210 measuring 21.8m by 18.7m over walls 2.8m thick at basement level. It seems that this storey was always subdivided although the present arched crosswall and vaults are 15th century, perhaps the work carried out by the 6th Earl of Kildare in 1426. Low sleeping lofts were squeezed under the vaults. A block of masonry at one end contains a stair to the storey above which contained a hall and private chamber side by side. Another storey was later formed in the original roof space below the wall-walk. Shallow buttresses in the middle of the west, north, and south walls contain mural chambers. The windows were given new outer openings in the late medieval period. Little remains of the courtyard walls but there is a gatehouse measuring about 8.5m by 8m on the south side, there is a rectangular tower in the SE corner, and there is a very mutilated tower projecting diagonally at the NE corner. In 1535 Sir William Skeffington bombarded the castle and executed the garrison when it fell. It was not restored to the Earl until 1552. The castle was repaired in 1630, taken by the Catholics in 1641, and was dismantled by Eoghan Rua O'Neill in 1647 See photographs on pages 7 & 83.

Malahide Castle

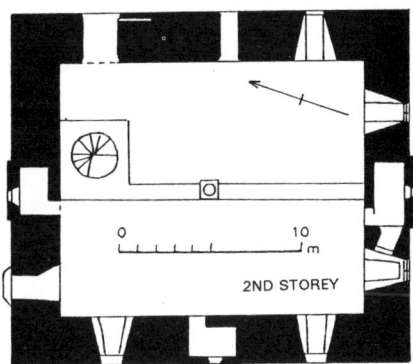

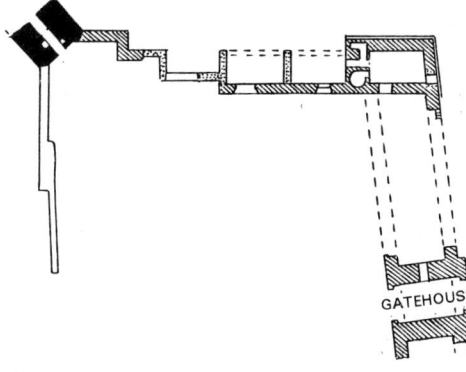

0
10
m
2ND STOREY

GATEHOUSE

Plans of Maynooth Castle

0
40
metres
KEEP
1ST STOREY

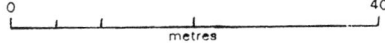

MILLTOWN *Louth* J0503

This 16th century tower measuring 7.5m by 6.6m has a tiny round latrine turret at one corner. On the other side is a larger round turret now containing straight flights of stairs but perhaps originally fitted with a spiral stair. The other two corners have square top turrets. See plan on page 14.

Maynooth Castle

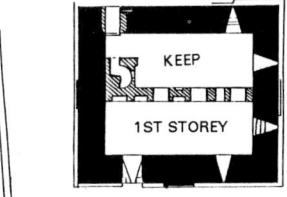

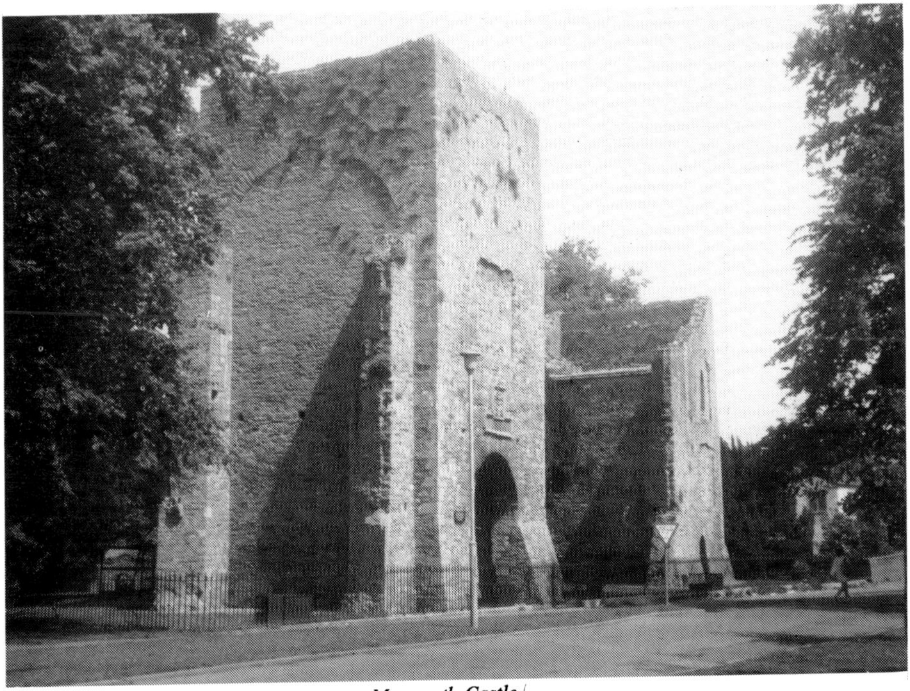

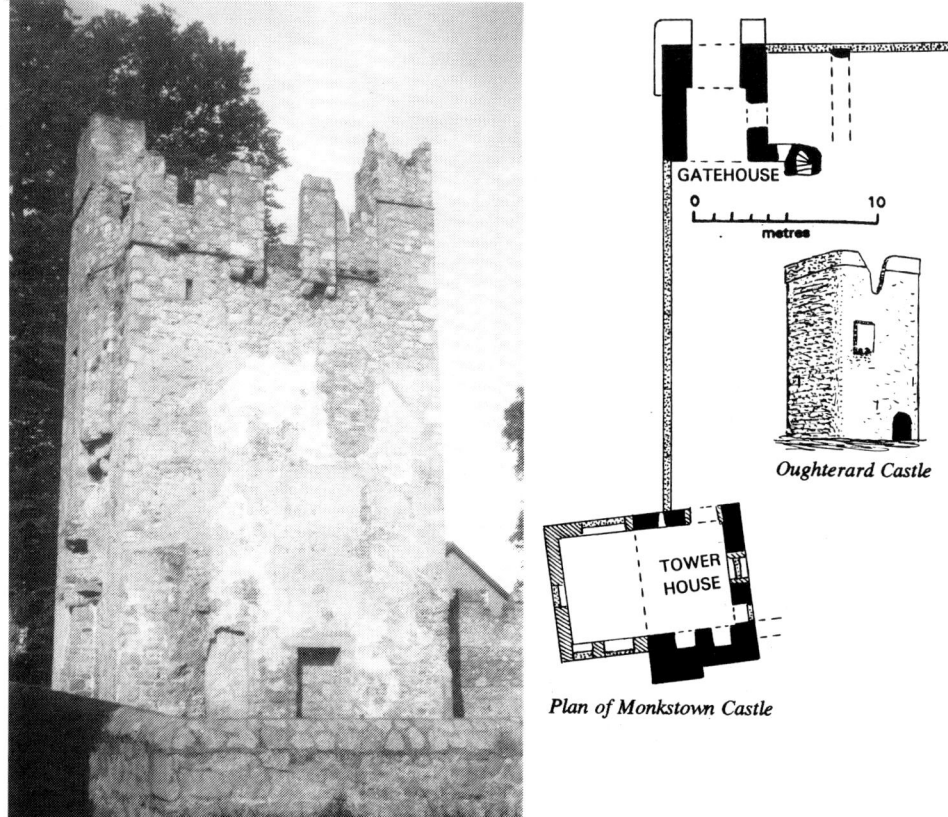

Oughterard Castle

Plan of Monkstown Castle

Monkstown Castle

MONKSTOWN *Dublin* O2428

The Cistercian monks of St Mary's Abbey at Dublin are said to have had a castle here in the 13th or 14th century, but the present much altered and extended four storey tower house and the three storey bawn gatehouse are late 15th or early 16th century. The thin 20m long wall connecting the two, and the walling east of the gateway are 19th century. The castle passed to John Travers and was subsequently held by the Eustaces, Sir Henry Wallop, Henry Cheevers, the Cromwellian commander Ludlow, Archbishop Boyle, and Anthony Upton.

NEWCASTLE *Wicklow* O2904

King John had a castle built here c1200. It was captured several times by the O'Byrnes and finally destroyed in 1405. On the west side of the 60m diameter summit of a mound is a ruined gatehouse of a new castle built after Henry VIII recovered this district from the O'Byrnes in the 1540s. It measured about 14.6m by 8.6m and has basement rooms either side of a vaulted passage. The three storeys above were divided into large northern public rooms with smaller southern withdrawing rooms which were pleasant chambers with large windows and brick fireplaces.

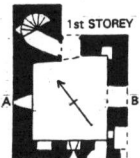  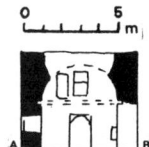 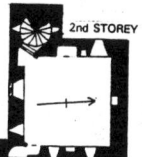 

Plans of Tower Houses at Newcastle, Co Dublin

NEWCASTLE   *Dublin*   OO029

The motte and bailey of an early royal castle lie by the church. The Old Rectory measures 6.8m by 6.4m over walls 1m thick. It has a SW stair turret and a tiny SE latrine projection. A second less well preserved tower lies in an nearby field. In the 16th century there were four other small private tower houses in the village.

OUGHTERARD   *Kildare*   N9526

This tiny round cornered four storey tower measures just 7.1m by 5.5m over walls 1.1m thick. The basement has double splayed loops and recesses. The second storey is vaulted. There is neither a hatch in the vault nor a staircase and the third storey has its own separate entrance.

RATHCOFFEY   *Kildare*   N8932

Rathcoffey was the chief seat of the Wogans and was attacked in 1454 by a junior branch of the same family. In 1800 Archibald Hamilton Rowan replaced most of the castle by a mansion, now ruined, but there survives a mutilated and somewhat altered bawn gatehouse with a passage between a narrow guard room and a cellar.

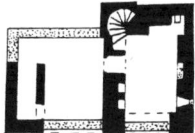

Rathcoffey Gatehouse

Plan of Oughterard Castle

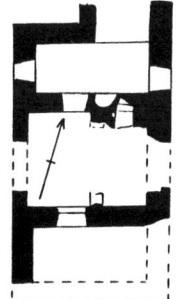

Newcastle, Co Wicklow

Gatehouse, Newcastle, Co Wicklow

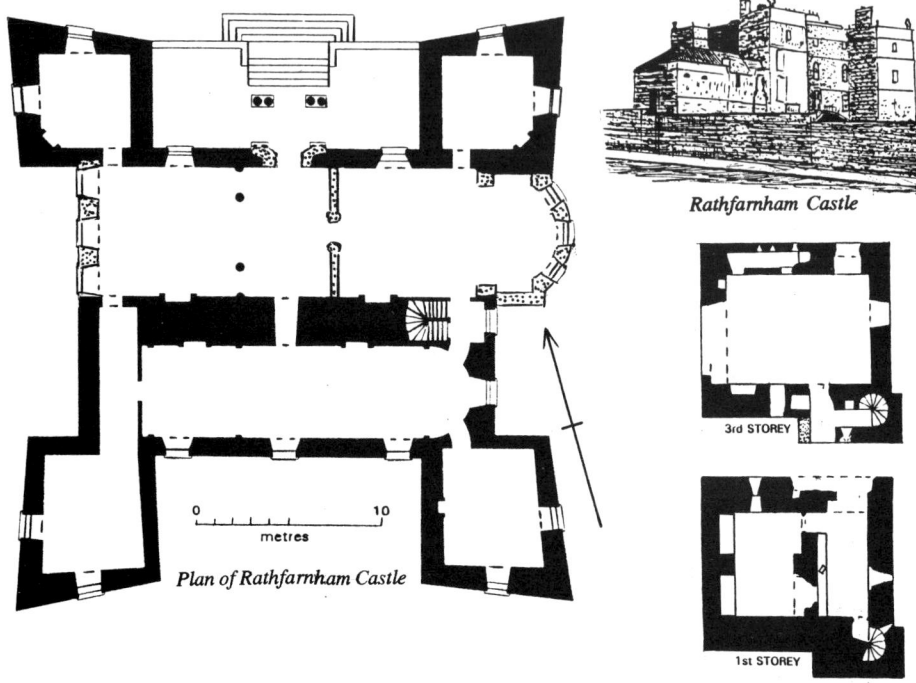

Rathfarnham Castle

3rd STOREY

1st STOREY

Plan of Rathmore Castle

Plan of Rathfarnham Castle

RATHFARNHAM *Dublin* O1529

This large stronghouse with four corner towers with acute outermost angles was built in the 1580s by Archbishop Loftus. It was surrendered to Parliament in 1647 but in 1649 was stormed by Royalists just before the Battle of Rathmines. The Loftus family recovered it and altered it in the 18th century. In 1913 it was taken over by Jesuits.

RATHMACKNEE *Wexford* T0414 A.M.

A five storey tower 12.5m high and measuring 8.2m by 7.6m above the second storey vault occupies one corner of a nearly complete bawn 25m long by 21m wide which contains a modern house occupied by the custodian. The bawn wall is 5.3m high to the wall-walk and is 1.2m thick, increased to 1.6m on the side which contains the entrance beside the tower with a machicolation over it. A round bartizan lies on the other end of this side. The tower has four square turrets at the top. See page 82.

RATHMORE *Meath* N7566

Half of the length of one wall of this four storey tower measuring 10.4m by 9.4m is thickened externally to contain the entrance and spiral staircase. The cellars and the vaulted lofts above are divided by a crosswall. Above are two undivided rooms.

RATHUMNEY *Wexford* S7616

This peculiar structure is thought to be 14th century. It is a hall house 25m long by 8.6m long over walls just 1.2m thick. It contained just two low storeys probably each divided into three rooms. There are several ground floor entrances some of which have slots for drawbars.

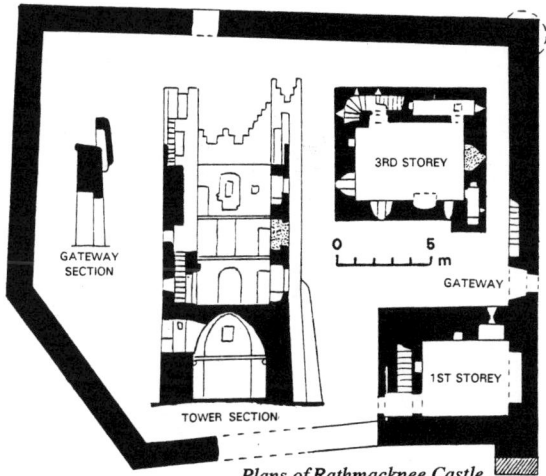

Plans of Rathmacknee Castle

Roodstown Castle

RATHWIRE *Westmeath* N5652

Hugh de Lacy built this motte and bailey castle for his brother Robert. In 1210 King John met Cathal Crovderg O'Connor here although the negotiations failed as Cathal failed to bring his son as a hostage. In the bailey are the extensive foundations of a later stone castle destroyed in 1450 by the Mageoghegans.

ROODSTOWN *Louth* N9993

This is a well preserved (though roofless) example of a £10 subsidy type tower house (see pages 13 & 14) with a vaulted cellar, hall above with two light windows with mullions and transoms, and two further storeys of bedrooms. Diagonally opposite turrets contain the staircase and latrines and the other corners have square top turrets.

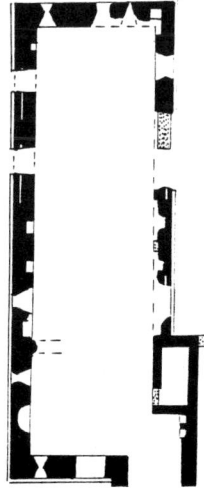

Plan of Rathumney Castle

Bawn Wall, Rathmacknee Castle

SLADE   *Wexford*   X7597

In the late 15th or early 16th century the Laffans built a small tower 17m high to the top of the stair turret. To it was later added an embattled two storey house, to which in turn a small annex with a corbelled roof was subsequently added.

SRAH   *Offaly*   N3325

Built in 1588 by the Elizabethan officer John Briscoe, this tower measuring 8.9m by 7.2m is notable for its numerous gunloops and the square bartizans opening off the fourth storey at the SW and NE corners. The entrance is protected by a machicolation' at the level of the fifth storey in the roof.

SWORDS   *Dublin*   O1847

The castle begun c1200 by the Archbishop of Dublin has a large pentagonal bawn in good condition. The constable resided in the tower house at the north end. There are square east and west towers, a SW turret on squinch arches, and a substantial gatehouse adjoining a fine 14th century chapel. A tower west of the latter provided rooms for the porter and chaplain. The stepped battlements are 15th century. The castle was later held by the Barnewall family as hereditary constables.

THREECASTLES   *Wicklow*   OO105   A.M.

There were once three castles here where in 1547 the English and Brian O'Toole defeated the FitzGeralds. Just half of one tower 9.8m survives to the height of the third storey vault. It has double splayed basement windows, cross loops and hooded two light windows higher up, and was divided throughout its height by a crosswall.

TIMAHOE   *Laois*   S5490

The motte and bailey castle west of the village is mentioned in 1182 by Gerald of Wales. After being granted Timahoe in 1609 Richard Cosby converted a 15th century church into a castle. A tower was built in the east end of the unusually wide nave (10m across inside), the rest of which became the bawn.

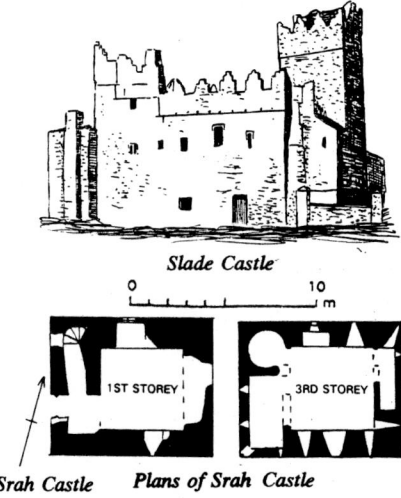

Slade Castle

Srah Castle   *Plans of Srah Castle*

TRIM *Meath* N8056 A.M.

Hugh de Lacy erected a motte beside the Rover Boyne in 1172. Hugh Tyrell abandoned and burnt the wooden buildings before they could be captured by Roderick O'Connor but they were soon rebuilt. A huge stone keep was built on the motte stump c1200-20, and then c1220-40 under William Peppard the wedge shaped bailey 150m by 100m was gradually enclosed by walls up to 2m thick. Around the more vulnerable sides are five D-shaped towers from 6 to 7m in diameter, originally left open on the inside, although some were closed with thin inner walls later. The SE gatehouse is a full round 11m in diameter with half round rooms flanking a central passage. The long barbican in front is a later addition. A rectangular bastion faces the river and has a later vaulted cellar nearby. At the north corner is a tower 13m square and towards the NW is a rectangular gatehouse. The keep measures 19.6m by 19.2m over walls 3.6m thick and contained a hall and private chamber side by side on the main storey. The entrance is within one of four more lightly built wings which project from the middle of each side and has a chapel above it. The wings are the same hight as the main block which has the corners carried up as turrets to a height of 23m. In the late 13th century the castle passed to the Mortimers, created Earls of March in 1328. Richard II visited Trim in 1399 and left behind the future Henry V lodged in the SE gatehouse with Humphrey of Gloucester. Silken Thomas captured the castle in 1537, and it was bombarded and captured in 1648s by Sir Charles Coote for the English Parliament.

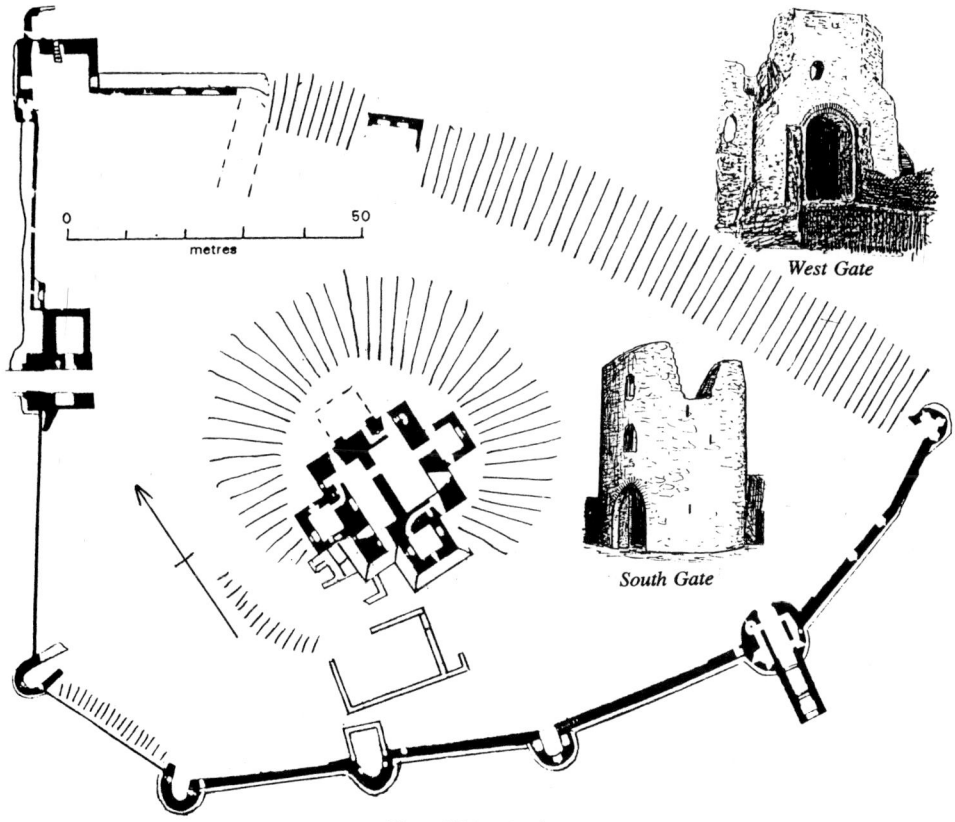

West Gate

South Gate

Plan of Trim Castle

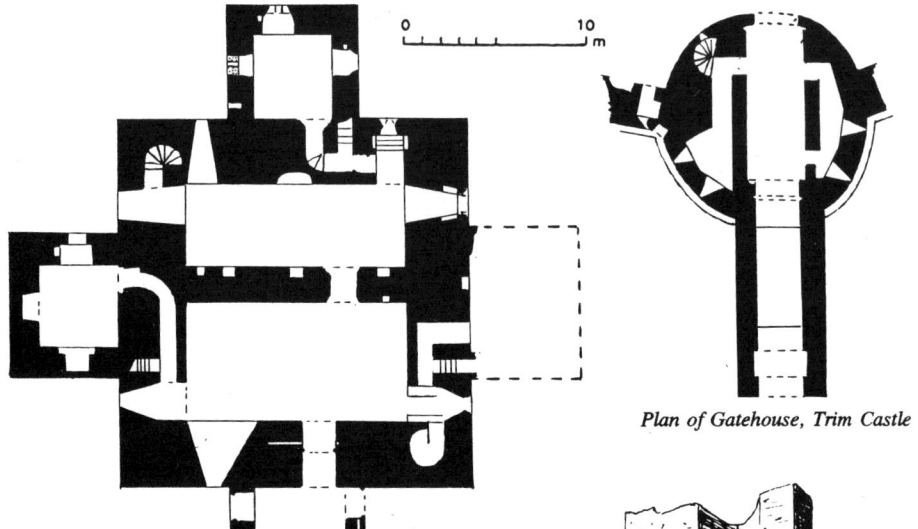

Plan of Keep at Trim Castle

Plan of Gatehouse, Trim Castle

Keep, Trim Castle

TUBBRIDBRITAIN *Kilkenny* S3662

One end of the tower continues up to contain a room at the level of the attic in the main roof and provide a fighting platform over. Below are four storeys connected by straight flights of stairs, the third being vaulted. The tower measures 11.5m by 10.1m.

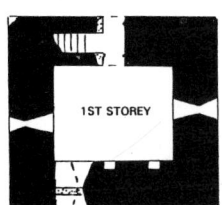

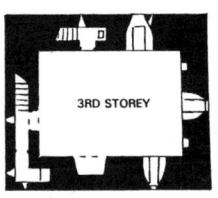

Plans of Tubbridbritain Castle

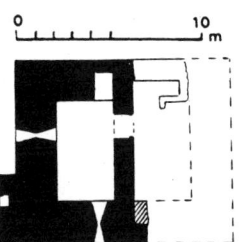

Plan of Threecastles Castle

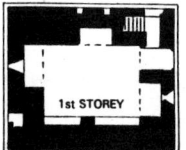

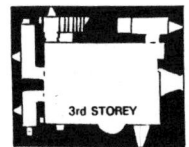

Plans of Clonmines Castle

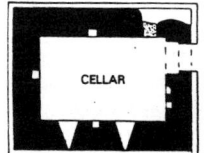

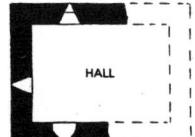

Plans of Billestown Castle

Round flanker of bawn, Burnchurch

Keep, Athlone Castle

Delvin Castle

Hilltown Castle, Co Wexford

MAP OF CASTLES OF LEINSTER

CASTLE ROCHE
CARLINGFORD
HEYNESTOWN • DUNMAHON
MILLTOWN
ROODSTOWN
LOUTH
DROGHEDA
GRANARD
DEXTER
LISCARTAN • FENNER
DUNMOE
ATHLUMNEY
LONGFORD
RATHMORE
WESTMEATH
RATHWIRE LISCLOGHER
TRIM
RATHMORE
DUBLIN
LOUGH SEWDY DELVIN **MEATH**
SWORDS
CLARE • BILLESTOWN DONORE ROBGILLS
BOLEYVILLISH DUNSOGHLY MALAHIDE
ATHLONE GRANGE CASTLEKNOCK HOWTH
KINNEFAD CARBURY MAYNOOTH DUBLIN MONKSTOWN
CLONMACNOIS DONADEA NEWCASTLE
CLONLYON BALLYCOWEN OUGHTERARD RATHFARNAM DALKEY
SRAH RATHCOFFEY ATHGOE
CLONONY **OFFALY**
GARRY KILDARE
KINDLESTOWN
BIRR LEA THREECASTLES
KILDARE NEWCASTLE
KILDARE
LAOIS DUNAMASE CASTLE KEVIN
CLONCOURSE TIMAHOE KILKEA
DERRIN **WICKLOW**
KILBREEDY CARLOW CLONMORE
CLONBURREN ARKLOW
BALLYRAGGET **CARLOW**
BALIEF • FOULKSRATH LEIGHLINBRIDGE
TUBBRIDBRITAIN CLARA BALLYMOON
KILKENNY BALLYLOUGHAN
KILBLINE FERNS
BURNCHURCH TINNAHINCH
KELLS ENNISCORTHY
KILKENNY **WEXFORD**
KYLE
FERRYCARRIG
HILLTOWN
GRANAGH RATHUMNEY KILIANE
BARRYSTOWN RATHMACKNEE
DANE'S BRIDGTOWN
COOLHULL
DUNCANNON CLONMINES
HOOK SLADE

Ferrycarrig Castle, Co Wexford (T0304)

Robgills Castle, Co Dublin (O2545)

Castle near Bridgtown, Co Wexford (S9910)

Danes Castle, Co Wexford (S8612)

Ballymote Castle, Co Sligo

Roscommon Castle, Co Roscommon

Bawn Gateway, Monkstown, Co Dublin

Clonmines Castle, Co Wexford

Burnchurch Castle, Co Kilkenny.

Rathmacknee Castle, Co Wexford

Interior of the Keep, Maynooth, Co Kildare

Ferns Castle, Co Wexford

Kells Priory, Co Kilkenny

The Keep, Lea Castle, Co Laois

Dunmoe Castle, Co Meath

Carlingford Castle, Co Louth

Limerick Castle, Co Limerick

Cahir Castle, Co Tipperary

Round Tower House, Golden, Co Tipperary

Ballinalacken Castle, Co Clare

Knockgraffon Motte, Co Tipperary

Gatehouse, Dundrum, Co Down

Round Keep, Dundrum, Co Down

Quoile Castle, Co Down

Inch Castle, Co Donegal

Loggia, Dunluce Castle, Co Antrim

The fine Hall Keep of Greencastle, Co Down

Greencastle, Co Donegal

GAZETTEER OF CASTLES OF MUNSTER

ADARE *Limerick* R4747

Adare is one of the largest and most impressive castles in Ireland but is now very neglected and overgrown. It belonged to the Earls of Kildare but was confiscated after the rebellion of 1535 and given to the Earl of Desmond. When the Munster Geraldines rebelled in turn in 1579 it was restored to the Earl of Kildare, but is thought to have been dismantled in 1599. The ruins lie neglected and overgrown between the River Maigue and a golf course. It is first mentioned in 1226 when is was held by Geoffrey de Marisco. The wall 1.6m thick with one open-gorged round tower facing west and a gate tower facing south surrounding the D-shaped inner ward 28m across may be of about that time but the tower keep and a hall on the river bank beyond the wet moat of the inner ward are likely to have been begun c1200. The hall is 16.5m long by 9m wide and has windows with two round headed lights with roll mouldings. It lies above a basement, later subdivided, and has a wing contain latrines projecting into the river from the SW corner. The keep measures 13m by 10.8m over walls 2m thick and has corner turrets which project from the side walls only. It was originally of three storeys with the basement only reached from above by a trap-door. In a 15th century remodelling the basement was provided with its own entrance and was subdivided and vaulted. A doorway was provided to new apartments to the north. The upper parts of the south half are destroyed, possibly the result of Cromwellian slighting. The castle was in a poor condition in 1329 and the re-aligning of the SW part of the inner ward wall may be part of repairs of c1340. East of the hall of c1200 are footings of a kitchen and beyond that is a very ruinous aisled hall 22m long by 10.5m wide with a porch facing north and on the east service rooms either side of a passage leading to a detached kitchen. This hall may be late 13th or mid 14th century. A wall up to 1.7m thick and 3.5m high to the well preserved wall-walk surrounds an outer court containing these buildings. This court extends over 50m east of the keep and has traces of its own wet moat. There are plain entrances to the north and east and a square west gate tower close to the hall of c1200, but there were no towers or turrets to flank it. See plan of upper storey of keep on page 6.

Wall of Outer Ward, Adare, from the east.

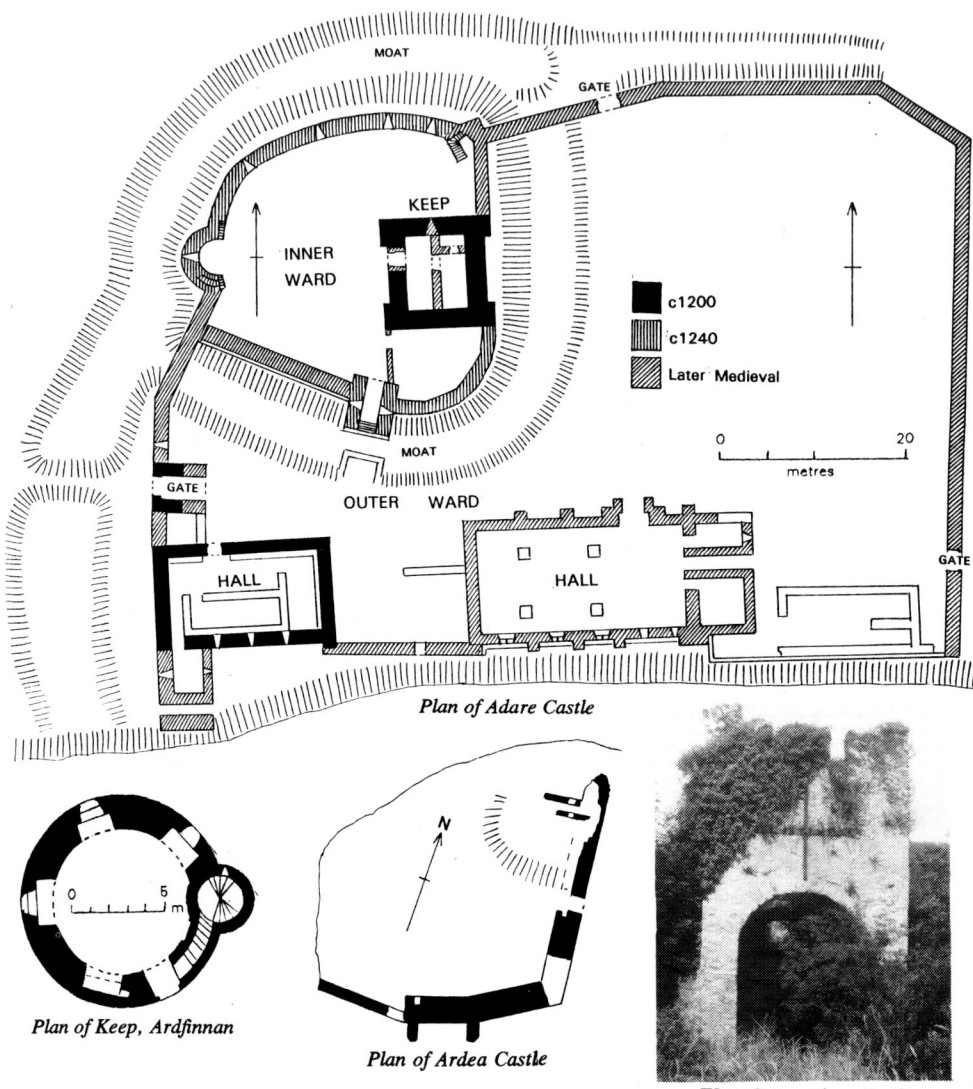

Plan of Adare Castle

Plan of Keep, Ardfinnan

Plan of Ardea Castle

West Gate, Adare Castle

ARDEA *Kerry* V7763

Walls up to 2.8m thick with traces of two towers and on the east a pointed arched gateway suggesting a 13th century date defend the landward sides of a polygonal court 25m across on a rock on the south side of the mouth of the Kenmare River.

ARDFINNAN *Tipperary* S0818

A ruined three storey round keep 11.5m in diameter probably of c1280-1310 lies on top of the motte erected by Prince John in 1185 high above a crossing of the Suir. The keep has a vaulted basement and a round staircase turret. The rest of the castle was rebuilt in the 18th and 19th centuries after being wrecked by Cromwellian troops c1650 although it incorporates some old work including one high 15th century tower.

ASKEATON *Limerick* R3550 A.M.

The castle lies on a rock in the middle of the River Deel and is thought to have been founded c1200 by William de Burgo. It passed to Thomas de Clare in the 1280s and in 1318 was granted by Edward II to Robert de Welle. By 1348 it had passed to the Earls of Desmond and served as one of their main seats until it surrendered to the English commander Pelham in 1580 after a two day bombardment, and was handed over to the Berkeleys. In 1599 the Earl of Essex relieved the castle after it had withstood a 247 day siege by the "Sugan" Earl of Desmond. The castle was surrendered to the Confederate Catholics under Purcell in 1642 and was captured and slighted by Cromwellian forces in 1652.

The upper ward has fragments of a 13th century polygonal wall around a court 40m long by 24m wide with latrine shoots on the west and footings of a gateway on the east. North of the gateway was a hall block about 20m long by 9.2m wide, probably of 13th century origin. In the 15th century the north end was made into a high tower of which little remains although an added west wing containing smaller rooms and latrines still stands high. There is another building on the south side of the court. Surrounding the upper ward was a lower ward of which little remains except the fine hall block on the west side. This has a 13th century basement which was provided with vaults and crosswalls in c1440-60 when the 7th Earl rebuilt the hall above. A bridge or wall connected the upper ward with the hall which two light windows and seats in embrasures in seats on either side and a staircase turret in the west. To the south are remains of a chapel block.

BALLEA *Cork* W7164

The Cogans built the earliest castle on the rock above the Owenboy estuary. It was held by the MacCarthys of Muskerry in the 16th century and in 1604 was granted to Sir George Carew. He sold it to Richard Boyle who in turn sold it to Edward Martel from whom the MacCarthys purchased it back, only to lose it again in the 1650s. One of these families built the present stronghouse which is still inhabited.

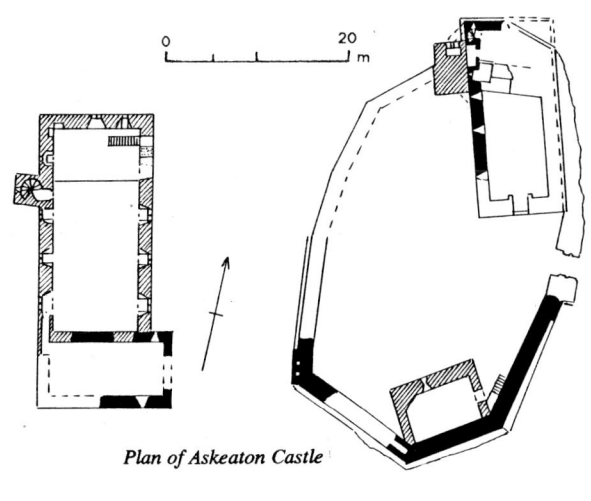

Plan of Askeaton Castle

Askeaton Castle

Fireplace, Ballinalacken

*Bawn Gateway,
Ballinalacken*

BALLINALACKEN   *Clare*   M1001

A high rock above a stream beside a hotel has a roofless but well preserved tower lying within a large bawn which only required much of a wall towards the west where there is a gateway with corbels for a machicolation above. A straight joint shows that the 4.6m thick east wall containing the entrance with a machicolation high above, the staircase, and six storeys of small rooms was built first. The main block has two dark storeys below a vault, two better lighted storeys above, and there was an attic within the wall-walk. Mid-wall projections with machicolations and shot-holes open off the fourth storey which was probably the owner's private suite. The castle was spared dismantling in 1654 and was granted to Captain Hamilton in 1667, although later recovered by the original owners, the descendants of Turlough O'Brien.

BALLINGARRY   *Kerry*   Q7633

Overlooking the mouth of the Shannon are traces of a castle held by the Cantillons from 1280 until their forfeiture for supporting the Desmond rebellion of 1579. Gearold Rua Stack held the castle in 1602-3 against English assaults by land and sea. In 1641 loyal English settlers led by Colonel David Crosbie withdrew into the castle, strengthened it, and held out against the rebel Irish for five years. On the mainland are remains of a turret and Crosbie's two diverging covered ways with earthworks behind, and then there is an isolated inner ward containing traces of numerous houses.

BALLINGARRY   *Limerick*   R4237

The lofty tower measures 11.4m by 8.0m at the level of the hall on the third storey where a large window embrasure has a piscina on one side and has evidently contained an altar. Other embrasures have seats and two-light windows. A spiral stair in a corner leads down to the entrance and basement. The stair to the battlements is squinched out over the re-entrant angle between the end wall and a wing containing a latrine and bedchamber. The tower was repaired in 1821 and served as a hospital.

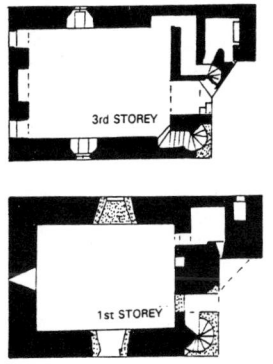

Plans of Ballingarry Castle, Limerick

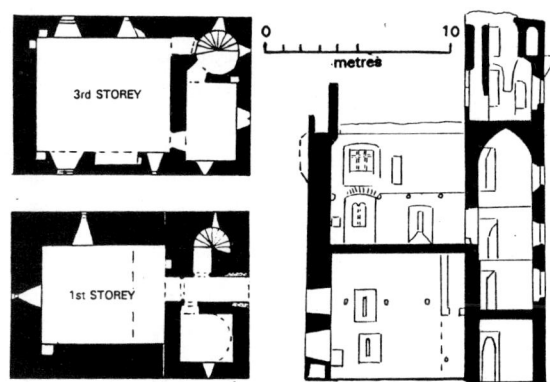

Plans and section of Ballinalacken Castle

BALLINSKELLIGS *Kerry* V4465

A 16th century MacCarthy tower 10m by 8m lies on a shingle promontory by the bay. Just two unvaulted storeys survive but at least two more are assumed to have existed. The entrance has a shot-hole in a jamb and lies in one of the side walls.

BALLYANNAN *Cork* W8672

There are round towers at diagonally opposite corners of the long low stronghouse probably built by Sir John Broderick in c1641. There were two full storeys and attics over a low basement. There are several very high chimney stacks.

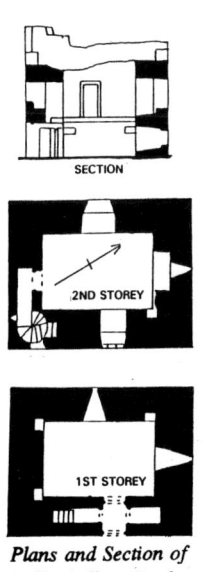

Plans and Section of Ballinskelligs Castle

Ballinskelligs Castle

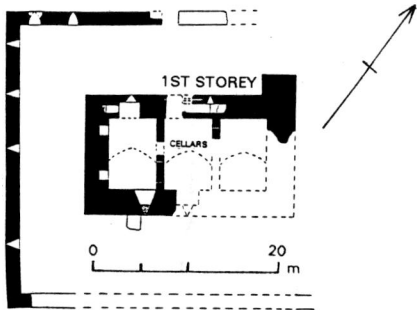

Ballycarbury Castle

Plans of Ballycarbury Castle

BALLYCARBURY *Kerry* V4580

On flat ground near the mouth of the Valencia River lies a huge tower built by MacCarthy Mor probably in the first half of the 15th century. The tower measures 22.7m by 12.9m over walls up to 2.7m thick and contained a hall and chamber side by side above pointed vaults over three compartments with pointed vaults which each contained a cellar with a sleeping loft above. Two of the lofts could only have been reached by ladders and trap-doors from below but the eastern loft was reached by a doorway from a straight flight of stairs rising up from the entrance into the middle cellar. This stair was closed by a door with a drawbar at the NE corner where there is a wing containing small vaulted rooms. and it then continues up in the east wall to reach the hall. A later wall probably replacing an original partition divides off the private room which has a service stair in the west end wall down to the cellar at that end which was presumably reserved for drink. As a security measure the stair ends in an embrasure some way above the cellar floor. The whole of the SE corner has collapsed. Surrounding the tower at a distance of 7 to 8m was a bawn wall 1.5m thick, of which only the western half now remains. There are no bartizans or turrets.

BALLYCULHANE *Limerick* R4654

An ivy-mantled wall about 1.3m thick and 6m high surrounds a bawn 45m long by 40m wide. There are square corner turrets containing tiny vaulted rooms and spiral staircases. On the south and SW are windows and fireplaces of former two storey ranges of apartments. Buildings on the NW side are comparatively modern. There is no sign of a tower house. There is said to have once been a wet moat 9m wide fed from the River Maigue. The castle belonged to the Purcells until the 1650s. After it was stormed by the English in 1581 some 150 women and children were put to death.

BALLYDUFF   *Waterford*   W9799

The three storey stronghouse built by the Earl of Cork in 1628 measures 15m by 9.4m and has a porch facing the small bawn and a stair wing on the other side, making a T-plan. The gables have projecting chimney breasts and are flanked by square bastions on the far corners of the thinly walled bawn which now contains a later farm building.

BALLYGRENNAN   *Limerick*   R6475

A 16th century tower with a vault over the second storey, mullion and transom windows on the two storeys above, and square bartizans at diagonally opposite corners forms about half of the cross wall dividing two bawns about 25m wide. One bawn extends further beyond the end of the tower than the other and both have various ruined outbuildings. The castle was originally held by the Earls of Kildare but by 1583 had been granted to William ffoxe. Although given to others in 1621 it was back in ffoxe hands by 1657, only to be sold to the Evans family soon afterwards.

BALLYGRIFFY   *Clare*   R3384

This small tower not only has an entrance below a tier of six mural rooms but there is a second doorway leading directly onto the foot of the spiral stair, perhaps for a lost later extension. The latter is covered by gunloops in the treads of the stairs above. The lowest mural room has a murder hole covering the other entrance. The top room is at the level of the wall-walk on the four storey main block, within which was an attic.

BALLYMALIS   *Kerry*   V8494

This 16th century tower is traditionally said to have been built by the O'Moriartys or Murrays, although it has also been claimed as a seat of the Ferris family. It was granted in 1677 to Sir Francis Brewster from whom it passed to Alexander Eager. The tower was of four unvaulted storeys with an attic in the roof within the parapet. It measures 14.8m by 9.6m over walls 1.9m thick except for the east wall which is thicker and contains the stair and a tier of chambers. The lord's suite on the third storey has two light windows and bartizans at diagonally opposite corners. The hall above has three light windows. Both these levels have fireplaces in a side wall.

BALLYNACARRIGA   *Cork*   W2951

Randal Hurley's four storey tower is notable for the carvings on the embrasures of the hall windows which include the year 1585, the initials of his wife Catherine Cullinane, a picture of her with three roses for her children, a Crucifixion, and The Instruments of The Passion. This room was subsequently used as church until 1815.

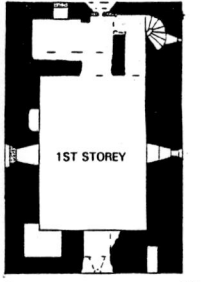
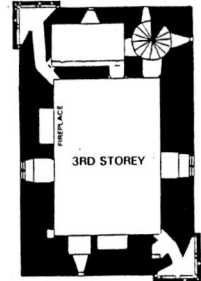
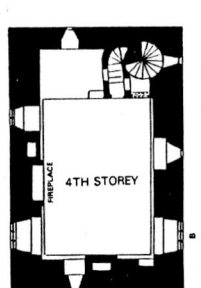

Plans and Drawings of Ballymalis Castle

Ballynahow Castle

Blarney Castle

BALLYNAHOW *Tipperary* S 0860

The 16th century tower of the Purcells is unusually impressive and interesting. It is round externally, 10.4m in diameter and 17m high to the wall-walk off which open four regularly spaced machicolations. There are shot-holes opening off the jambs of embrasures at each of the five storeys. The two lowest rooms under a dome vault are round. The next two rooms are quadrangular with embrasures at the corners and mural chambers beside the staircase just as in a rectangular tower. Finally, above another vault, is the hall. A latrine chamber has a cross-shaped loop, and there are upper windows of two lights both with round and ogival heads.

BALLYNAKILL *Tipperary* S 1087

In the middle of an exceptionally large square bawn is a modestly sized tower house. To it has been added a late 17th century extension with a blind top storey ornamented with ovals and lozenges in the artisan-mannerist style.

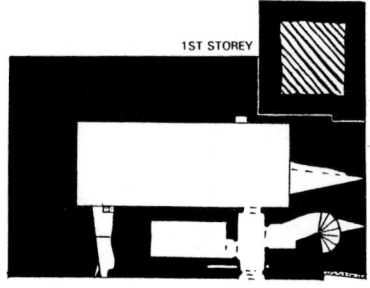

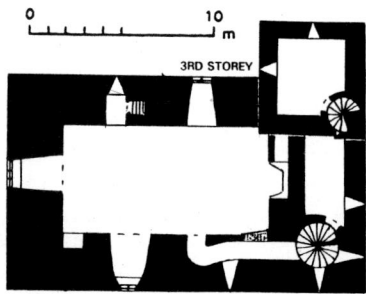

Plans of Blarney Castle

BELVELLY *Cork* W7871

The Hodnets' 24m high tower overlooks Cork Harbour. In 1581 Sir Walter Raleigh tried to obtain a grant of the castle, describing it as broken down to minimise its value. In the 17th century the tower was occupied by the Courthorpes as tenants on a yearly rent of £60. An end wall has six levels although the main block has only four storeys with vaults over the first and third showing signs of wicker construction mats.

BLARNEY *Cork* W6175 A.M.*

The huge tower 19.6m long by 11.6m wide stands on the edge of a cliff in which various rooms have been created, plus a tunnel said to have been used as a means for the garrison to escape when the castle was captured by Cromwellian troops. It had previously been captured in 1643 by Lord Broghill. The tower once bore the date 1446 and the name of its builder Cormac Laidir MacCarthy who lived until 1494. Date stones do not normally occur so early and this one was probably added in the late 16th century when mullioned windows were inserted in the upper storeys and the original parapet of the wall-walk 22.5m above ground was reduced to a stub and the present machicolated parapet added. The famous Blarney stone is one of the lintels carrying the new parapet across the tall pyramidal corbels. Visitors dangle upside down though the machicolation to kiss the underside of this lintel. The MacCarthy of this period was noted for his ability to procrastinate and talk himself out of trouble, professing to be loyal to Elizabeth I but actually doing whatever he wanted, and this was the origin of the gift of eloquence associated with the stone. The tower has five storeys and has walls up to 3.7m thick at the base, making it the most massive of all the Irish tower houses, although the walls are somewhat thinner above the vault over the second storey. It has a thick end wall overlooking the cliff containing a staircase next to the entrance in a side wall and a tier of chambers one of which has a fine oriel window of c1600. The adjoining wing is actually part of a tower about 6m square built before the rest of the structure. So exactly what was built when is a mystery. Perhaps the small tower originally formed part of a four corner-towered structure like Bunratty, or a small court. Its lowest level is solid or has been filled in and its staircase only starts at the level above. The entrance to the main tower has a pistol loop in the jamb, a feature unlikely to be much earlier than 1500. Donagh, 4th Earl of Clancarthy lost his estates after James II's defeat, and in 1701 Blarney was purchased by Sir James Jefferyes, later Governor of Cork. He added a new domestic block which was destroyed by fire in 1820. A descendant built a new house nearby in 1874.

BOURCHIERS *Limerick* R6542

Also known as Castle Doon this is a lofty five storey tower 16.6m long by 10.9m wide lying by a farmyard. It was built by the Earls of Desmond and was confiscated by the English Crown in the 1580s and handed over to Sir George Bourchier whose descendants held it until 1641. A pistol loop commands the entrance. This end was begun first and the main block added later. See plan on page 16. Hidden in scrubs not far away is Black Castle, now just a length of 2.4m thick curtain wall with a gateway in the middle closing off a promontory.

BRITTAS *Limerick* R7351

Beside the Mulkear River are fragments of a 13th century Burke courtyard castle. There is one round corner tower 8m in diameter with a dome vault and a later latrine turret, plus a wall extending to the river and another along the river bank with signs of a domestic range against it. Sir John Burke of Brittas was hanged at Limerick in 1607 for having a priest say mass in his house.

Bunratty Castle

Plan of Bunratty Castle

BUNRATTY   *Clare*   R4562   A.M.*

Robert de Muscegros built an earth and timber castle at Bunratty. In 1277 Edward I granted it to Sir Thomas de Clare who built a stone castle probably similar to that he built at Quin with a small court with round corner towers. This withstood attacks by the Irish in 1285, 1296, 1298, and 1299 but had been burnt twice by 1306. After Richard de Clare was routed and slain at Dysart O'Dea in 1318 his widow abandoned the castle and burnt it. It was restored by James Bellafago but was captured in 1325 and 1331 by adherants of the Earl of Desmond, and finally destroyed by Muirchertach O'Brien, King of Thomond. The English Justiciar Sir Thomas Rokeby built a new castle at Bunratty in 1353 which fell to Murchadh O'Brien two years later.

The present castle was begun c1450 by Maccon MacSioda Macconmara and completed in 1467 by his son Sean Finn. It was taken over by the O'Briens c1500 and remained in their possession with one or two short breaks until 1712. The O'Briens submitted to Henry VIII and were created Earls of Thomond. They made Bunratty into a fine stately home noted for its ornamental grounds and park with three thousand deer. In 1645 Brian, 6th Earl, handed the castle over a Parliamentary force under Admiral William Penn from whom it was captured by Lord Muskerry after a two month siege. It later passed to the Stoddart family and fell into ruin but was restored by Lord Gort who purchased it in 1954. It now forms the focal point of a large folk park.

Hardly anything remains of the large bawn and outbuildings but the tower itself is one of the largest and best preserved Irish tower houses. The main block measures 18.6m by 12.6m over walls mostly 2m thick in which are numerous staircases. The entrance is though the 3m thick north wall into the main hall. Below are cellars, and above is another hall. At the corners are towers about 7m square providing many bedrooms with their own smaller staircases and latrines. On the third storey the SW tower contains a chapel with a three light east window and rich stucco decoration of c1619. Elliptical arches of brick unite the towers at fourth storey level at either end and support a pair of major private rooms added c1600 with six-light mullioned windows. The battlements on the main block and towers are all modern restorations.

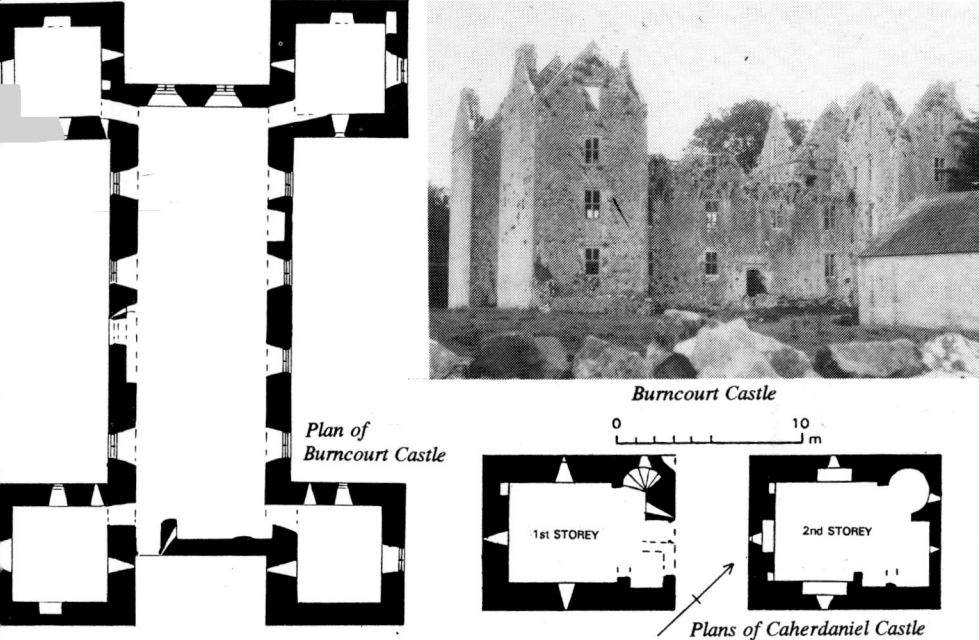

Burncourt Castle

*Plan of
Burncourt Castle*

1st STOREY

2nd STOREY

Plans of Caherdaniel Castle

BURNCOURT   *Tipperary*   R9518

The name is derived from the burning of the stronghouse by Cromwell in 1650 only a few years after it was completed for Sir Richard Everard, who was hanged by Ireton in 1651. It was not restored and a print of 1795 shows as it is now except that the chimney stacks were then complete. By then there was a more modest house at the west end of the bawn and lawns to the north. The ruin has a main block 25m long by 10m wide with a tower 7.5m square at each corner. Both the main entrance on the west and the back door opening out of the kitchen at the south end have pistol loops in the jambs and there are several other gunloops. The main block has pyramidal corbels for machicolations but these were never provided and instead a series of gables with attic windows were raised directly above the outer wall-faces, and the towers given a gable on each of the four sides. The doorway led into a service passage at the south end of the hall. Below was a very low basement with windows at ground level, and there was a storey of state rooms above, bedrooms being provided in the towers which rise one level higher, i.e to five storeys including the basement and attics.

CAHERDANIEL   *Kerry*   V5558

Two unvaulted storeys remain of a tower 10.5m long by 8.2m wide over walls 1.4m thick. A gunloop opening off the stair commands the doorway in the thick end wall.

CAHERMACNAGHTON   *Clare*   M1900

The pre-Norman stone ringfort about 30m in internal diameter has a late medieval two storey gatehouse. It was still in use in 1675 when there was a large house and kitchen and surrounding gardens. The inside ground level has gradually built up to a higher than that outside and has various footings. The O'Davorens ran a law school here.

CAHIR   *Tipperary*   SO525 A.M.*

Some time during the 13th century the Worcester family transferred from the motte at Knockgraffon to a stone castle on a rock in the Suir at Cahir. It comprised a wall about 1.6m thick and 4m high around a court roughly 30m square with a rectangular towers within the northern corners, a larger tower projecting from the southern half of the west side, and a gatehouse with narrow guard rooms flanking a passage and a hall and master bedroom above. In the early 14th century Cahir passed by marriage to the Berminghams. The castle and barony reverted to the English crown after Sir William de Bermingham was executed by Sir Anthony Lucy, the Justiciar in 1332, although in practice both had been overrun and devastated by the O'Briens.

In 1375 Cahir was granted to James Butler, 3rd Earl of Ormond. During the 15th and 16th centuries the castle was gradually rebuilt and improved by the descendants of the 3rd Earl's illegitimate son James who intermarried with the Desmonds and Berminghams. The gateway was converted into a tower house and a new gateway made alongside with a round corner tower to flank it. An outer ward 50m long by 33m wide with two round corner towers was built to the south, although a strip at the northern end was divided off with a thick wall to make a middle ward in the 16th century. The round well tower projecting from the north wall and a block on the east commanding the approach are 17th century.

In 1599 the Earl of Essex captured the castle after a three day siege during which the east wall was breached by cannonfire. Its commander, James, brother of Thomas, 2nd Lord Cahir, escaped by swimming under the adjacent water mill and subsequently reoccupied the castle for a while. Prior to the siege the castle was regarded as one of the strongest in Ireland and the temporary defection of its owner was a matter of grave concern to Elizabeth I's government. The castle was captured by Lord Inchiquin in 1647 after a short siege, and surrendered to Cromwell in 1650 without a siege. It was restored from ruin in the 1840s for Richard Butler, 13th Baron Cahir, the family having lived nearby in the 18th century and then abroad. The inner walls of the west tower and the hall block date from that time. See colour picture on page 86.

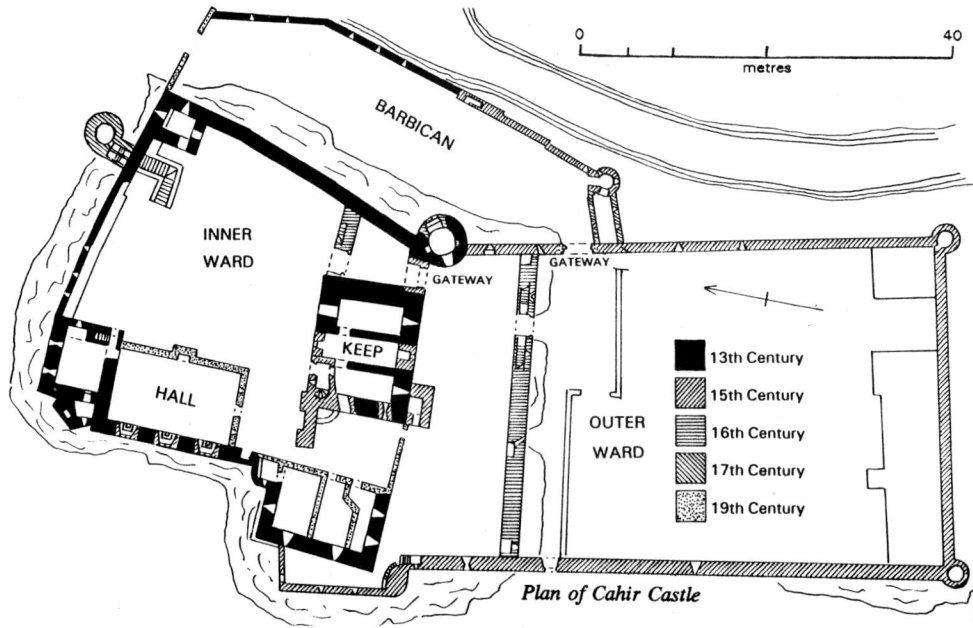

Plan of Cahir Castle

Cahir Castle

CARRICK ON SUIR *Tipperary* S4022 A.M.*

Edmund Butler is said to have built the first castle on this site beside the Suir in 1309. The alternative name Ormonde Castle refers to the Earldom conferred on his son. A new D-shaped bawn 30m long with two substantial five storey towers on the vulnerable straight north side, and possibly a third to the south of which little remains, was built c1450. The rounded south end of the bawn was rebuilt with thinner walls to a nearly rectangular shape later on, perhaps when the fine courtyard house was added against the north front by Thomas Butler, 10th Earl of Ormonde, a courtier of Elizabeth I, having been brought up in England. The house is indeed more English than Irish, lacking defensive features, and having a long gallery extending along the whole of the north side on the upper floor. A chimney breast is dated 1565 and there are a fine series of stucco ceilings and wall decorations with heraldry, monograms, mottos and dates. This part is still roofed although the older part is ruined. In 1649 the castle surrendered to Cromwell just one day after the town was captured. Ormond sent Lord Inchiquin in an unsuccessful attempt to retake it. In the 1650s it was granted to Sir John Reynolds, but in the 1660s the castle was restored to the 12th Earl. The last occupant apart from caretakers was a Waterford wine merchant as a tenant in the 1780s. Plan p102.

Elizabethan house, Carrick on Suir

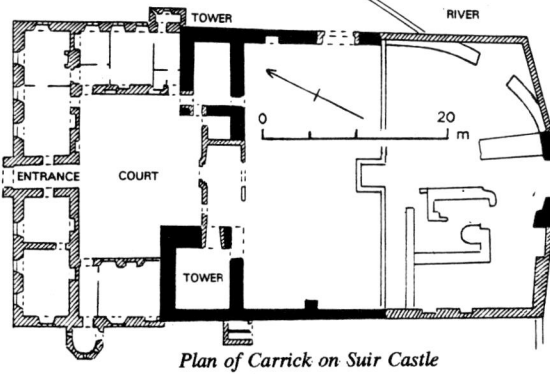

Plan of Carrick on Suir Castle

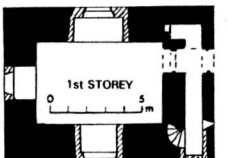

Carrigacunna Castle

Plans of Carrigacunna Castle

CARRIGACUNNA *Cork* W6699

The tower stands empty but still roofed beside a much later house. There are minor alterations such as added fireplaces and inserted windows on each of the four storeys except the second. The three light mullioned windows on the third storey are original.

CARRIGADROHID *Cork* W 4172

The interior of this 16th century MacCarthy castle on a rock in the River Lee can be seen from a window facing an adjacent bridge. Roger Boyle, Lord Broghill, besieged the castle in 1650. He hanged the Bishop of Ross within sight of the walls when he refused to exhort the defenders to surrender. It was eventually captured by a ruse.

CARRIGAFOYLE *Kerry* Q9947 A.M.

By the Shannon estuary, and with its entrance directly opening to the water, is a large tower 17.9m long by 9.7m wide built in the late 15th century by the O'Conors of Kerry. There were five storeys with vaults over the second and fourth. There is the usual thick end wall containing a tier of chambers although the oven beside the foot of the wide spiral stair is an unusual feature. The tower is protected to landward by a water girt square bawn with round turrets, one of which contained a dovecote. Beyond was an outer bawn with square corner turrets and between the two bawns was a dock for boats. In March 1580 the Italian Engineer Captain Julian with 15 Irish and 16 Spaniards held the castle for the rebel Earl of Desmond against an English force led by Sir William Pelham. It fell in just two days after artillery was brought up by sea, and the bawn was breached and taken by storm. The garrison were hanged and the Earl of Desmond's plate stored in the castle sent to Queen Elizabeth. The O'Conors recovered the castle during Hugh O'Neill's rebellion but surrendered it to Sir George Carew in 1600. It was then granted to Sir Charles Wilmot. It was further damaged during the war of 1649-52 and artillery fire has caused the upper parts of the landward end of the tower to collapse. Entry is now through the stump of this wall.

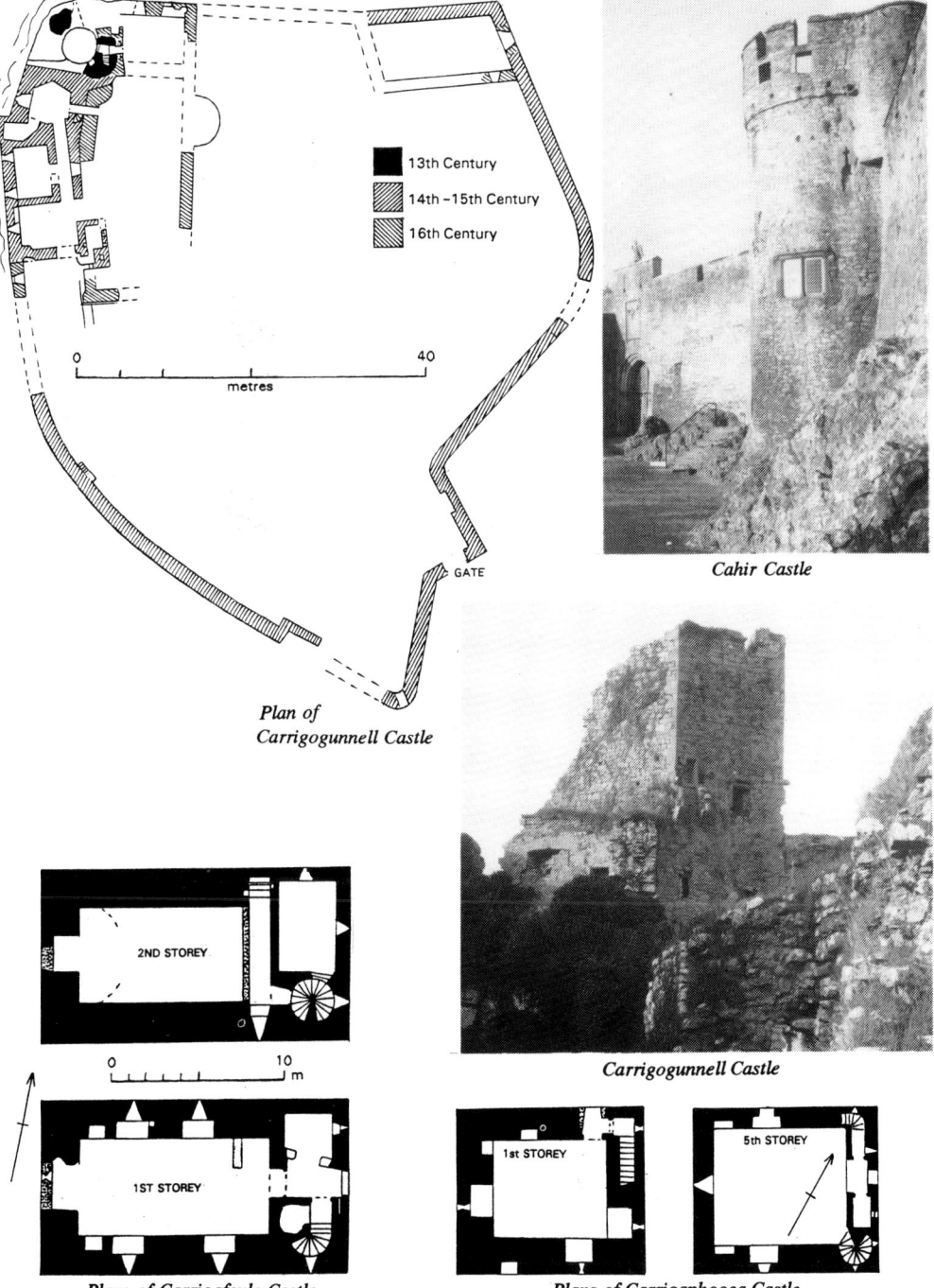

13th Century

14th – 15th Century

16th Century

0   40
metres

GATE

*Plan of
Carrigogunnell Castle*

Cahir Castle

Carrigogunnell Castle

2ND STOREY

0   10
                     m

1ST STOREY

Plans of Carrigafoyle Castle

1st STOREY

5th STOREY

Plans of Carrigaphooca Castle

CARRIGAHOLT   *Clare*   Q8552   A.M.

The MacMahons, Lords of Corcabascin, built this well preserved tower and bawn in the early 16th century. The tower has pistol loops and internal machicolations. The turret on the side of the bawn facing the pier is modern. Teige Caech Macmahon was unsuccessfully besieged here by Sir Conyers Clifford in 1598, but a few months later it was captured by the Earl of Thomond after a four day siege. In breach of the surrender terms he hanged the garrison and handed it over to his brother Donal. The latter inserted several new windows and the fifth storey fireplace dated 1603. The castle was captured by Ludlow in 1651 and only restored to the O'Briens in 1666. William III confiscated the 57,000 acre estate of Donal's grandson the 3rd Lord Clare and in 1691 Carrigaholt went to the Earl of Albemarle. He sold it almost immediately to the Burtons, who held the castle up to the present century.

CARRIGAPHOOCA   *Cork*   W2974

The five storey tower conspicuously placed on a high rock measures 10.7m by 9.2m and has straight flights of steps and a lack of fireplaces thought to indicate an early 15th century date. There are square top turrets on diagonally opposite corners. It was built by the MacCarthys of Drishane. Teig MacCarthy took refuge here in 1601 after the Battle of Kinsale but O'Sullivan Bere captured and sacked the castle.

CARRIGOGUNNELL   *Limerick*   R5050   A.M.

The castle lies on a volcanic crag overlooking the Shannon estuary. A very ruined round tower 10m in diameter in the north corner is probably 13th century and represents either a keep or a corner tower of a square courtyard castle. The hexagonal room west of it is perhaps 14th century and beyond is a later hall block with two cellars and a passage on the ground floor. East of the round tower is a four storey apartment block of the 16th century when a small inner court was created in front of the ranges. A large heart-shaped outer enclosure about 75m in each direction with a 15th century wall extends to the south and east away from the estuary. There are no flanking towers but the gateway lies in a projection near the rounded south corner and there are remains of another range of apartments among bushes at the east corner. In 1536 Mahon O'Brien surrendered the castle to Lord Deputy Grey. It later passed to Donough O'Brien, and was eventually sold to Michael Boyle, subsequently Archbishop of Dublin. In 1691 a Jacobite garrison of 150 men surrendered the castle to William III's forces and shortly afterwards General Ginckell had it blown up. See plan p103.

CASHEL   *Tipperary*   S0741   A.M.*

The Rock of Cashel bore a fortress from early times and was the seat of Brian Boru, crowned King of Ireland in 977. In 1101 Muircheartach O'Brien handed it over to the church. The famous Cormac's Chapel was built c1127-34, and the cathedral alongside it was gradually erected from east to west during the 13th century. The nave was, or was intended to be, longer, but was eventually closed off at the west end by a grim 22m high residential tower, probably by Risteard O'Hedigan, Archbishop from 1406 to 1440, who built the Hall of the Vicars Choral on the south side of the close. The tower measures 12.6m by 8.8m. There were three storeys below a vault and a hall above approached either by a long flight of stairs in the west wall or from a mural passage on the nave north wall. There was another room and an attic above, perhaps as the result of later alterations. The upper parts of the south wall fell during a storm in 1847. After the Rock was stormed by Lord Inchiquin's forces in 1647 twenty ecclesiastics were killed in the castle by being smothered in fire.

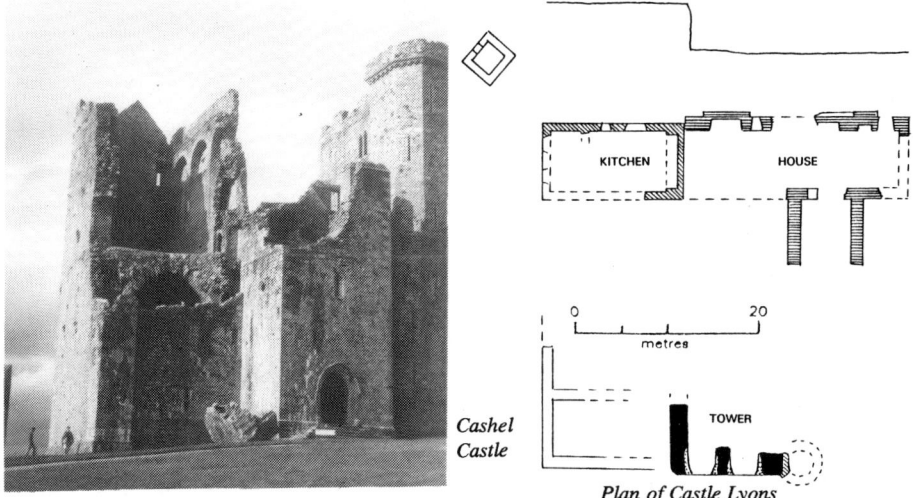

Cashel Castle

Plan of Castle Lyons

CASTLE CONNELL   *Limerick*   R6563

The original de Burgo castle on the rock was destroyed in 1261 by King Conor O'Brien of Thomond. In 1275 it passed to the de Clares who may have been responsible for the present layout of the shattered ruins, a court 48m by 30m with round towers on the western corners. It was later returned to the de Burgos, or Burkes as they styled themselves in later years. The castle was surrendered to Cromwellian forces in 1651, and to supporters of William III in 1690. General Ginkell had it blown up the following year after it had been temporarily retaken by forces loyal to James II.

CASTLE GRACE   *Tipperary*   S0415

Beside the River Tar are remains of a late 13th century de Bermingham castle with walls 1.4m thick around a court about 30m by 23m. The only side which is complete has round towers 5.5m and 5m in diameter at each end with crossloops, and seems to have had a hall built against it. The other corner towers seem to have been square.

CASTLE LYONS   *Cork*   W8494

Castle Lyons was the seat of Lord Barrymore and was accidentally burnt in 1771. On one side of a court is half of what appears to be a massive tower house with a round stair turret later added and big new windows inserted. On the other side is a long range of buildings comprising a stronghouse of four storeys and an attic, and a large later kitchen at one end, both parts having very large fireplaces.

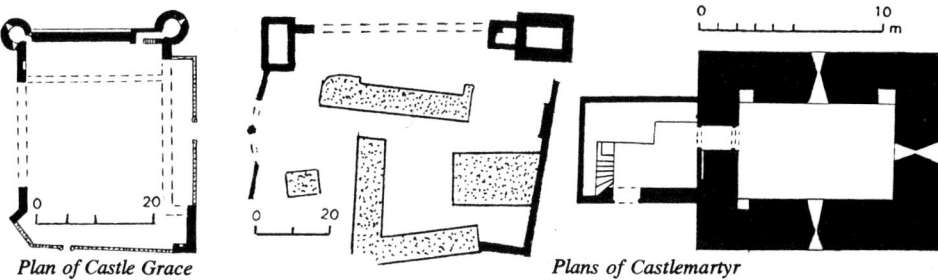

Plan of Castle Grace   *Plans of Castlemartyr*

Plan of Clonshire Castle

Castle Matrix   Doonagore Castle

Plan of Conna Castle

CASTLEMARTYR   *Cork*   W9673

This mid 15th century castle was the seat of the Earl of Desmond's seneschal of the barony of Imokilly. It had a large quadrangular bawn 75m by 43m, now fragmentary and with the interior cluttered with farm buildings. There is a large rectangular tower at the north corner now only two storeys high, and at the east corner is an even larger (13m by 10.4m) five storey tower house entered through a tiny forecourt. The basement has three lockers and three double splayed loops. The staircase starts at a higher level. There are later mullion and transom windows in the uppermost storey.

CASTLE MATRIX   *Limerick*   R3040

In 1487 James, 9th Earl of Desmond was murdered here by his servants on the instigation of his brother. Edmund Spenser and Walter Raleigh occupied the castle in 1580. It was granted to the Southwells who added a wing in 1610. The Irish captured the castle in 1641, and the Cromwellians took it in 1651. The tower has four storeys in the main block and seven in the thick end wall. It is 18m high and measures 13.2m by 10.6m. It was repaired in the 19th century and again in 1970.

CASTLE MORE   *Cork*   W5693

Two walls remain in a very fragmentary state of a 13th century hall-house built by the de Cogans. A later medieval wing 6.3m wide projects 6.8m beyond one end. The castle is also known as Barrett's Castle after the family who held it in 1604-89.

CLONSHIRE   *Limerick*   R4445

The original four storey tower measures 9m by 7m. The basement vault blocks the original stair and may have been inserted when a wing containing a new entrance and spiral staircase with a gunloop between the two was added in the 16th century. This part has a caphouse higher than the main block. Another wing, lower than the main block and only having three storeys, was added at the other end at later on.

CONNA   *Cork*   W9494

The Earl of Desmond built this five storey tower on a rock above the Bride c1500. It measures 13.9m by 10.2m and has a fragment of a bawn and a thinly walled extension of much later date. James I granted it to Richard Boyle after the death of the "Sugan" Earl of Desmond, who was born in the castle. It was captured by Lord Castlehaven in 1645 but is said to have held against Cromwellian troops in 1650, although three daughters of the occupant were killed when it was burnt in 1653.

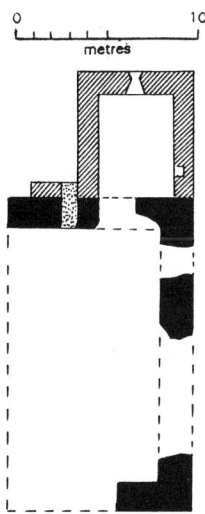

Plan of Castle More

Coppingers Court

COPPINGERS COURT *Cork* W2636

The stronghouse is named after Sir Walter Coppinger, a leading Cork merchant, who built it c1620-40. On the south side of a thinly walled bawn 30m by 28m with traces of former outbuildings is a block 22.2m by 8m over walls 1m thick. There are two large square wings on the corners facing the bawn, and a narrower staircase wing in the middle of the other side where there is a vertical joint in the wall which is hard to explain. There are three fireplaces at ground level for a kitchen and offices. Above were two storeys of staterooms and attic rooms for servants in the roof. There are remains of machicolated parapets on the east and west sides of the wings and on the north and south walls of the main block but no other defensive features.

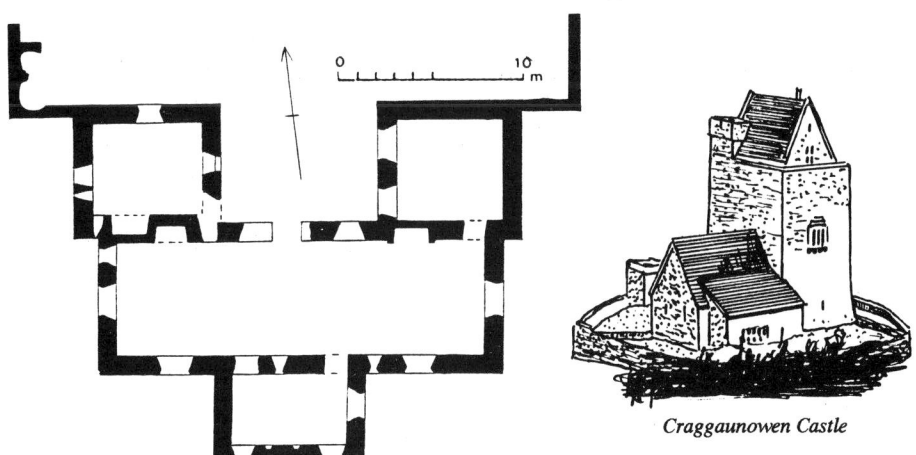

Craggaunowen Castle

Plan of Coppingers Court

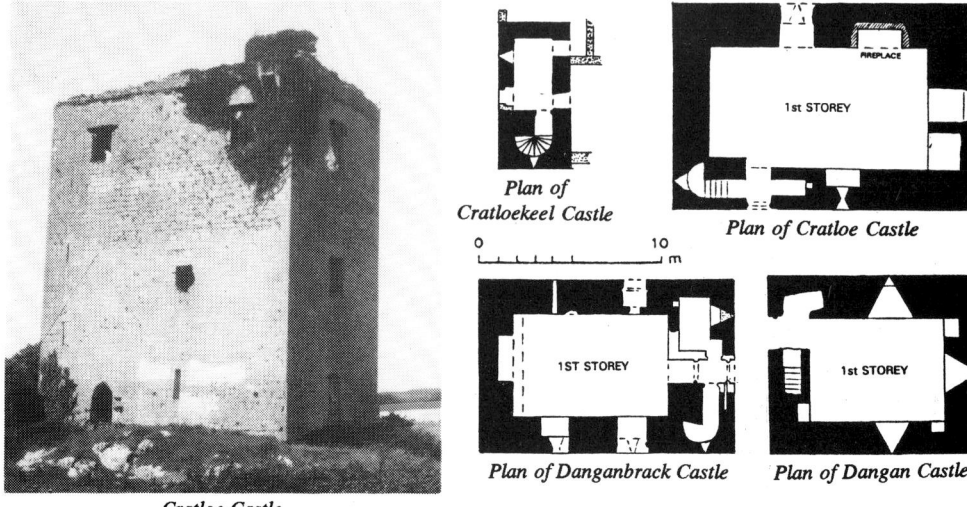

Plan of Cratloekeel Castle

Plan of Cratloe Castle

Plan of Danganbrack Castle

Plan of Dangan Castle

Cratloe Castle

CRAGGAUNOWEN *Clare* R 4675 A.M.*

A rock beside a small lake bears a polygonal bawn with a rock cut ditch on the landward side. In the middle stands a tower built c1550 by John MacSheeda. It was later held by the O'Hartigans and Mulchonrys and was confiscated and slighted in the 1650s. The tower was restored in the 19th century and again in the 1960s when it was made into a museum and an exhibition crannog was created in the adjacent lake.

CRATLOE *Clare* R5259

With external dimensions of 16.5m by 11.0m this Macnamara tower of c1500 is one of the largest plain rectangular towers in Ireland. It contained four storeys with the second and third vaulted. Mural chambers are provided in an end wall 2.2m thick like the other walls at basement level but with an internal arch to carry double the thickness higher up. Part of the cellar was made into a kitchen with a large fireplace in the 17th century, and, using the same stack, is another fireplace higher up. Nearby is Cratloekeel, a ruined house adjoining a thick end wall of a tower containing four rooms under a vault. The intended main body does not seem to have been added.

DANGAN *Clare* R2864

This ivy-clad tower on a high rock had vaults over the second and third of four storeys. A straight stair leads from the entrance to a spiral stair in the NW corner. A second storey wall chamber could only be reached by a hatch from above. The cellar has three loops and three lockers. The rooms above have fireplaces in the west wall.

DANGANBRACK *Clare* R4375

This MacNamara tower 14m long by 9.2m wide was probably originally built c1500 but if so was remodelled c1600 as the basement has a kitchen fireplace at the far end and at the summit are four gables flush with the outer walls. So there was no wall-walk although reached off the attic room above five full storeys were open fighting positions in the form of square bartizans with pyramidal corbels on two diagonally opposite corners, and round bartizans with double stepped corbels on the others.

DE CLARE'S HOUSE   *Clare*   R2792

Beside the River Fergus at Killinaboy is a is a bawn 31m long by 24m wide with a wall 1.2m thick with a gateway facing north, a postern towards the river opposite, and a small turret containing chambers in the SE corner. The whole of the west end was filled with a modest unfortified house. No connections with the De Clares are known.

DOONAGORE   *Clare*   M0696

In the 1970s this round tower house high above Doolin was restored and given a new parapet and conical roof and the wall of the small bawn was heavily patched up. There are four storeys with a pointed vault over the second. The staircases follow the curvature of the walls. Latrines are collected together on the side outside the bawn. The castle was alternately held by the MacClancys and the O'Briens.

DOONMACFELIM   *Clare*   R0797

This ruined O'Brien tower with very high quality stonework beside Doolin village now only partly stands three storeys high. It measures 10.6m by 8.8m and has only a small basement because of the thick walls, although there are big embrasures containing loops. The storey above was divided into two rooms.

DRISHANE   *Cork*   W2892   A.M.

The lofty round cornered tower low lying in the grounds of a convent was built c1450 by Dermot MacCarthy, Lord of Munster. It was garrisoned against the Irish in 1641. Additions made about that time have fireplaces with a W monogram for the Wallis family, owners until the late 19th century. The castle was garrisoned in the Fenian rising of 1867. The top stage was added by Lady Beaumont in the 19th century.

DROMANEEN   *Cork*   W5097

The O'Callaghans built an L-plan stronghouse with mullioned windows overlooking the Blackwater in c1600 and then added a six-acre bawn entered through an adjoining wing. After the rebellion of 1641 the castle was given to Sir Richard Kyrle, and was sold to Richard Newman of Cork. Dillon Newman repaired the castle and it was garrisoned during the conflicts of 1689-92 but was abandoned soon afterwards.

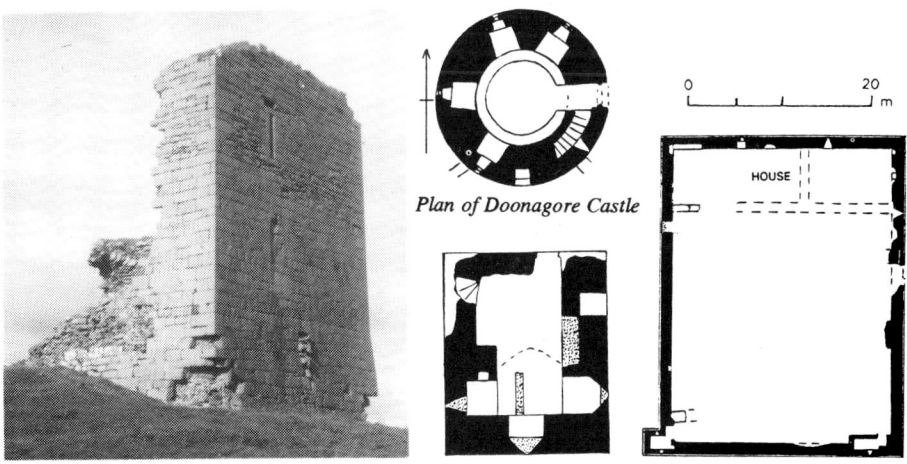

Doonmacfelim Castle   *Plan of Doonagore Castle*   *Plan of Doonmacfelim Castle*   *Plan of De Clare's House*

DUNBOY   *Cork*   V6644

Excavations in 1967-73 around the stump of a 15th century tower built by Donal O'Sullivan Beare found footings of a square wing added to one corner and a narrow bawn to the west, south and east with a salient angled wall. Immediately outside that were earthwork defences probably built just prior to when the castle was captured and slighted by Carew in 1602. To the south and east extended a large outer bawn.

DUNDEADY   *Cork*   W3432

On a rock by the neck of the promontory known at Dundeady Island are fragments of a thin wall around an irregularly shaped bawn. Within are a modern house, a barn, and a small L-shaped building with the main body 9m long by just 5m wide.

DUNHILL   *Waterford*   S5001

Dramatically placed on a rock are the Power family's 15th century tower 10.5m by 9.6m and a tiny shovel shaped bawn just 19m by 12m with low sections of walling 1.5m thick on two sides. Above the segmental vault over the basement sleeping loft the walls are reduced in thickness from 2.1m to 1.1m, perhaps evidence of rebuilding.

DUNMANUS   *Cork*   V8533

The tower measures 9.4m by 8.6m and had three storeys below a pointed vault and a lofty hall with two light windows above. Clasping the southern corner is a square wing 5.5m square. In the SW wall next to the wing is a tier of latrines.

FAUNAROOSKA   *Clare*   M1405

This castle guarded a hill track called the Green Road high up on the west side of the Burren. It comprises a very ruined bawn about 25m long by 20m wide with a round tower 7m in diameter in the southern corner. The tower had four storeys but in recent years it has mostly collapsed to seaward, burying the basement and vaulted loft above with debris. Gunloops are the only surviving features of interest. The castle was held by Fernandus MacFelim in 1641. It was later given to James Aylmer and Henry Ivers.

Faunarooska Castle

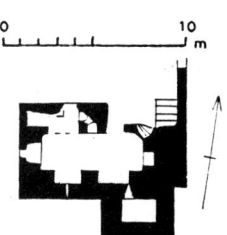

Plan of Dundeady Castle

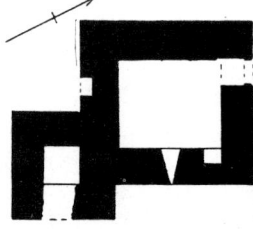

Plan of Dunmanus Castle

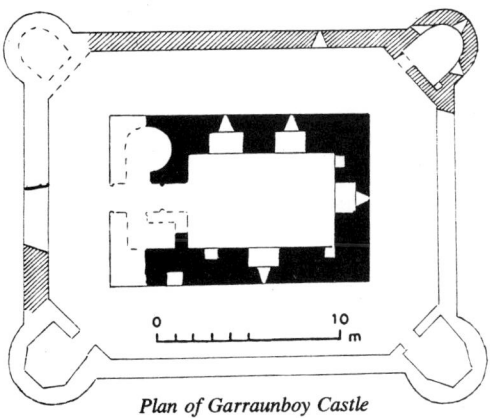

Plan of Garraunboy Castle

Gallarus Castle

GALLARUS   *Kerry*   Q3905

North of the famous Gallarus oratory is a 16th century tower built by the Knight of Kerry. Later, after the fifth storey above the vault fell or was removed, it was used as a barn and a wider opening, now blocked, made into the basement from the entrance lobby. Above the lobby are narrow chambers but there is no sign of staircase. Two of the basement loops are splayed both inwards and outwards.

GARRAUNBOY   *Limerick*   R4345

The outer wall of the thick end wall of a five storey tower 14m long by 9m wide has fallen although the rest still stands high. The fourth storey is vaulted. Closely surrounding the tower are remains of a small rectangular bawn with four round corner turrets between 4m and 5m in diameter. One has a vault and three gunloops.

GLANWORTH   *Cork*   R7505   A.M.

The seat of the Roche family on a rock was destroyed by Ireton's artillery in 1649. The original 13th century castle comprised a rectangular keep 12.7m by 10.8m still surviving two storeys high standing free in an irregularly shaped courtyard with a rectangular gatehouse with a passage flanked by guardrooms on the vulnerable west side. In the 15th century the court was extended westwards beyond the gatehouse which was converted into a tower house with an added latrine block, the only part still standing high, on the west side. The bawn wall was then also mostly rebuilt. It has a square SW corner turret and row of openings on the east side for a vanished outbuilding. The thinly walled round turrets with gunloops on the NW, NE, and SE corners are 16th century additions. There have been recent excavations and repairs.

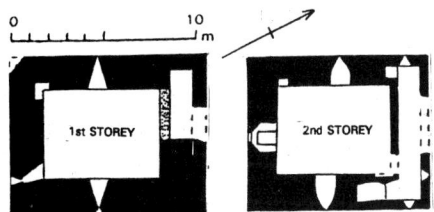

Plans of Gallarus Castle

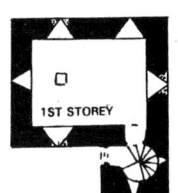

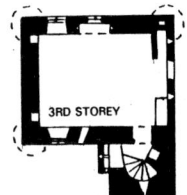

Plans of Gleninagh Castle

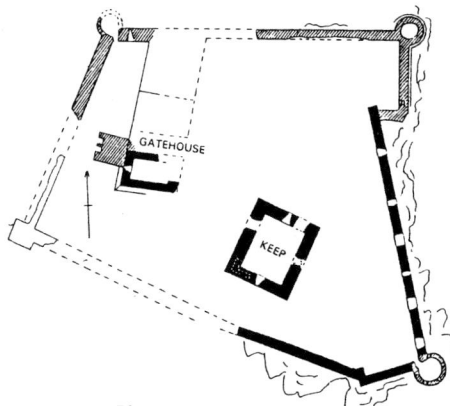

Plan of Glenogra Castle

Gleninagh Castle

Plan of Glanworth Castle

GLENINAGH   *Clare*   M1910 A.M.

The O'Loughlins occupied this tower until 1840, hence its good state of preservation. It is an L-planned 16th century building 8.5m long by 6.7m wide over walls 1.1m thick and has a spiral staircase in a wing. The entrance lies at its foot and is covered by machicolations high above. The other three corners have round bartizans. Above a subterranean pit prison are four full storeys and there was an attic in the roof which has gables flush with the outer walls. Evidence of slightly later alterations or a change in design during construction are the fireplaces created out of former window embrasures in the end wall of the second storey and a side wall of the fourth storey.

GLENOGRA   *Limerick*   R5942

Of a castle built c1400-20 by the Earl of Desmond there remain a massive octagonal tower 13m in diameter with a dome vault and staircases following the wall contours, and the lower part of a 3m thick wall connecting it to a similar tower. There seems to. have been a rectangular projection between the two. The bawn would have been about 40m square and was perhaps intended to have two more such towers although it is possible that the castle was modelled on that newly built at Newport in Gwent by the Staffords where there are two large octagonal towers facing the river. A thin wall of much later date has replaced the original wall on the south and east and extends 20m further to the west than the original enclosure did.

GLENQUIN *Limerick* R2526

This six storey tower is said to have been built by the O'Hallinans who were wiped out by the O'Briens. It was surrendered to the English in 1569, and granted firstly in 1587 to Captain Hungerford, and then in 1599 to Captain Collum of Glengoume. In the 1840s it was restored for use by the Duke of Devonshire's agent. Two storeys are vaulted. One of the ground floor doorways is a later insertion.

GLIN *Limerick* R1347

Only a single plain damaged tower remains of the seat of the Knights of Glin, a branch of the Munster Geraldines who held land here for seven centuries, and who later built a mansion nearby. One of them was killed defending the castle against Sir George Carew in 1600. A sketch of about that time shows a rectangular bawn with a tower house in one corner and rectangular towers in the other corners.

GORTMAKELLIS *Tipperary* S0942

The tower measures 10m by 7.8m and has four storeys with a pointed vault over the second. A third storey window has a pair of eliptical headed lights. There was an attic in the gables which are flush with the outer end walls, although there were open wall-walks along the sides.

GOURDEEN *Tipperary* R8979

Beside a stream is what appears at first sight to be an early hall house 16.9m long by 11.4m wide over walls 1.8m thick above a plinth and three unvaulted storeys. However the second storey fireplace and the niche for a wooden spiral stair suggest that it is actually an unusual type of late 16th century stronghouse.

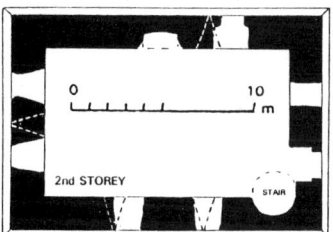

Plan of Gourdeen Castle

Plans of Gortmakellis Castle

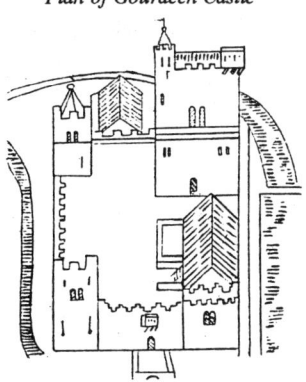

Old sketch of Glin Castle

Inchiquin Castle

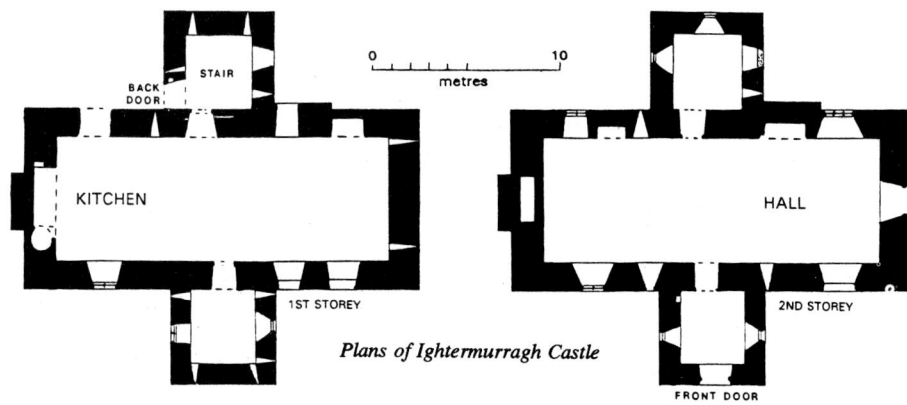

Plans of Ightermurragh Castle

IGHTERMURRAGH *Cork* W9973

This is an impressive four storey stronghouse now lacking the parapet to the wall-walk. It measures 21.8m by 9.6m over walls 1.6m thick. A second storey fireplace is dated 1641. There is a projecting breast at one end to contain the kitchen fireplace at ground level. There are wings with gunports in the middle of each side wall, one containing a wooden tread staircase with the back door at its foot, and the other having the front door reached by a flight of wooden steps in front.

INCHIQUIN *Cork* X0475

A huge round keep stands two storeys high. It measures 9m in diameter inside at ground level where the walls are 4.5m thick. Above the battered plinth and an offset the wall thickness is reduced to 2.5m. The basement has three loops and remains of a dome vault. The hall above has a fireplace, latrine, two windows, one with seats in the embrasure, and a jamb of the entrance doorway.

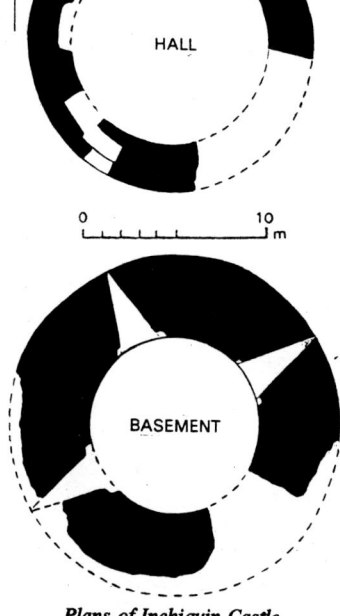

Ightermurragh Castle

Plans of Inchiquin Castle

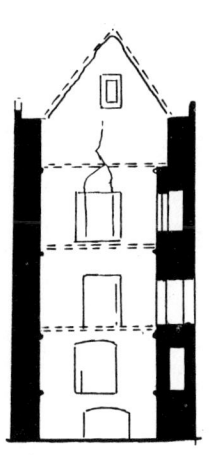

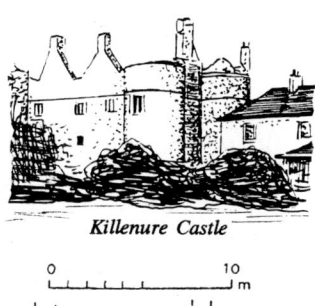

Killenure Castle

Kilcash Castle

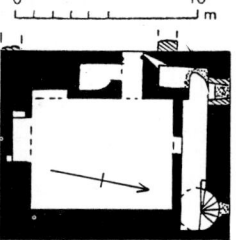

Plan and section of Kilcash Castle

KANTURK   *Cork*   W3802

This impressive stronghouse with corbels for a continuous machicolated parapet was under construction for Dermot MacDonagh MacCarthy at the time of Battle of Kinsale in 1601. It seems to have been left incomplete either because of the aftermath of the battle, Dermot's inability to borrow any more money, or because the Privy Council began to have doubts about the building's purpose and ordered the work to be stopped. Bold mouldings divide the storeys externally. There were four with three light mullioned windows in the main block, and five with two light windows in the four corner towers. There are several fine fireplaces.

KILBOLANE   *Cork*   R4221

The Cogans are thought to have built this square moated castle with round corner towers in the 16th century. It passed to The Earl of Desmond but was confiscated in the 1580s and eventually granted to Sir William Power in 1613.

KILCASH   *Tipperary*   S3427

This late Butler tower has high ivy mantled walls of a later block to the west and fragments of a bawn to the north. There are no vaults to any of the six storeys, the uppermost of which was an attic within the roof. There is a round bartizan on the SE corner. The basement shows signs of later alterations with a passage leading out of the cellar to a spiral stair in the NE corner but the entrance facing the later wing must be original as it is covered by a shot-hole in the jamb and a machicolation high above.

KILLENURE   *Tipperary*   S0044

Except for one of the four round corner towers the O'Dwyers' stronghouse has been a ruin since the time of the antiquarian Austin Cooper who made a sketch of it in 1793 showing also his humble house nearby. Above a low basement with small loops and the doorway were two storeys of living rooms with two and three light windows and an attic with small windows in the numerous gables on the sides and ends. The fancy windows in one of the corner towers were inserted in the 18th century.

The Old Head of Kinsale

KILLILEA *Tipperary* R9094

This four storey O'Connor castle with openings varying from a small round hole to a crossloop and mullioned windows of two and three lights once bore the date 1601. It is on an unusual plan with two unequal rectangles overlapping corner to corner with a wide square newel stair at the joint. There are round bartizans and a machicolation over the doorway at the foot of the stair. The brick vaults are 19th century insertions.

KILMALLOCK *Limerick* R6128

Part of the basement of the four storey tower 18m high called King John's Castle is now a public passageway. It was granted to Henry Billingsley in 1588 and to Thomas Browne in 1604. Lord Castlehaven's forces used the tower as an arsenal in 1645, and in 1651 it was used as a military hospital. In the 19th century it contained a forge.

KINSALE *Cork* W6451 & W6341

The small three storey tower with a finely decorated doorway in the town is called the Desmond Castle or The French Prison because during the 17th and 18th centuries, when Kinsale was an important naval base, it was used to incarcerate foreign prisoners. The huge Charles Fort of 1677 3km to the south lies on the site of a de Barry Og castle. There are ruined 19th century barracks within. Still further south is the Old Head of Kinsale, a headland of several acres isolated by the de Courcys in the 15th century with a 135m long curtain wall, now much reduced, and ditch across the neck. The wall has two rectangular flanking turrets and beside the gateway in the middle is a tower 8.2m by 6.4m still mostly standing 16m high. It had a lofty hall over a pointed vault, and a high basement and two much lower storeys below.

KNAPPOGUE *Clare* R1234 A.M.*

Medieval banquets are staged in the impressive restored 16th century tower with a lower extension in front added by the Earl of Dunboyne in the mid 19th century.

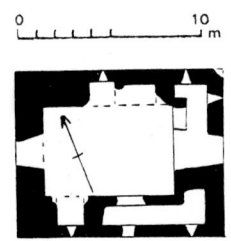

Plan of Knockgraffon Castle

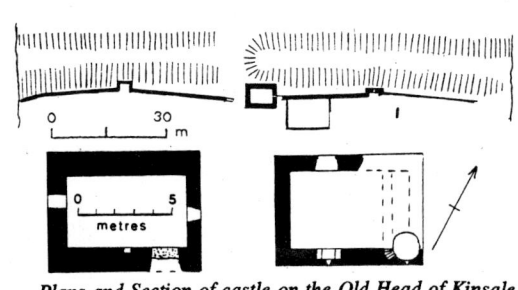

Plans and Section of castle on the Old Head of Kinsale

Leamaneh Castle

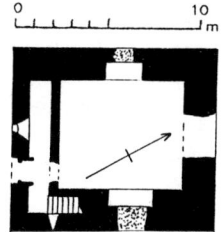

Plan of Lackeen Castle

Killilea Castle

KNOCKGRAFFON   *Tipperary*   S0529

Above the River Suir is a high motte with a summit 20m across having a bean shaped bailey 40m by 70m to the NW. It was built during a raid against Donal Mor O Brien, King of Thomond in 1192, and given to William de Braose, but later regranted to Philip of Worcester. On the east side of the bailey is a fragment of a later stone building 5.6m wide. Not far away is a very ruined church with a large central tower and north transept which appear to have been later made into a stronghouse. In a field beyond it is a 16th century Butler tower 11.5m by 8.7m with shot-holes in the jambs of the entrance doorway on the east. A long straight stair in the south wall rises to the base of a spiral stair in the SW corner. There are round bartizans on the NW and SE corners. See colour picture of motte on page 86.

KNOCKKELLY   *Tipperary*   S2308

The tiers of mullioned windows in the tower betray its late date. It now serves as a byre. The large surrounding bawn has big corner towers. In the 18th century the Everard owners evicted the Keatings for non payment of rent.

LACKEEN   *Tipperary*   M9504

The basement of the four storey tower is now used as a barn. The second storey has a fine fireplace and the third has a window with tracery and a vault. The castle belonged to Brian Ua Cinneide Fionn who died in 1588. It was confiscated by Cromwell in 1653. The bawn surrounding the tower has a round headed doorway.

LEAMANEH   *Clare*   R2494   A.M.

The castle is first mentioned in 1550 when it was granted to Donough O'Brien. He was hanged by the English in 1582. It has a thick end wall of c1500-30 with a wide spiral staircase, an entrance passage with rebates and drawbar holes for inner and outer doors, and a tier of chambers with pistol holes, angle loops at third storey level and a window of twin cusped lights at the sixth storey. The intended main body was never built and a century elapsed before a stronghouse of four storeys and an attic was grafted on to create a building 24.1m long by 10.5m wide. The house has its own entrance flanked by four-light mullion and transom windows. There were offices and a kitchen on the ground floor and living rooms above. At the far end from the older part is a bartizan on one corner and wing on the opposite side with a wall-walk. In front was a bawn with a gateway which was removed to Dromoland in the 19th century. It was dated 1643 with an inscription recording its erection for Conor O'Brien and his wife Maire Ni Mahon. Legends abound about Maire Ni Mahon. After her first husband was mortally wounded in the battle of Inchicronan in 1651 she saved her lands for her son by marrying a Cromwellian soldier. She is said to have kicked him out of an upper window after he was rude about her first husband. See plan on page 16.

LIMERICK   *Limerick*   R5858   A.M.*

Limerick was the chief seat of the O'Briens descended from Brian Boru until captured in 1194 by Raymond le Gros. King John (1199-1216) began the rectangular court 66m by 54m beside the Shannon with curtain walls as much as 4m thick on the most vulnerable side, four round corner towers up to 14m in diameter, and a gateway on the north side flanked by towers 10m in diameter. There is also a rectangular tower on the river front, where the domestic buildings probably were. The upper parts of this side have been rebuilt and in the early 17th century the SE tower was replaced by a large spear-head shaped bastion and the other towers were reduced in height and fitted with thick upper vaults to bear heavy artillery. Most of this bastion and the east wall have gone and been replaced by a modern museum building contrasting starkly with the older remains. The castle was surrendered to the O'Briens and MacNamaras in 1369 but was recovered soon afterwards and held for the English Crown by the citizens of the town. It was captured by the Irish in 1641, the Cromwellians in 1651, and the Williamites in 1691. A large new visitor centre quite out of character with the rest of the building now occupies much of the bailey. In the town are remains of two semi-fortified houses built in the early 17th century by the Fanning and Burke families respectively. The latter has a series of bold machicolations, more decorative than functional. See the plan of the castle on page 8 and the colour picture on page 85.

LISCANNOR   *Clare*   R0688

The thick end wall built first still stands six storeys high but the lower and later main block is more damaged. The castle was built by the O'Connors but was granted to the O'Briens in 1582. From 1712 the Earl of Thomond leased it to the FitzGeralds.

LISCARROLL   *Cork*   R4512

The de Barrys late 13th century castle comprises a rectangular court 61m by 44m with four corner towers 8m in diameter above deeply battered plinths, a rectangular gatehouse 12m by 7m on the south side, and a smaller rectangular tower in the middle of the north side. These all stand fairly complete except for breaches in the south wall and the loss of the outer parts of the SE tower, which contained the well. The vaulted gatehouse passage with a portcullis groove was blocked at either end when it was made into a tower house in the 15th century, but part of the blocking has been since removed. In the 1620s the castle went to Sir Philip Percival from whom it was forcibly taken by Lord Castlehaven in 1642. It was returned to the Percivals in the 1650s.

LISMORE   *Waterford*   X0599

Incorporated in the 19th century mansion of the Dukes of Devonshire are parts of the seat of the Bishops of Lismore given to Sir Walter Raleigh in 1589 and sold by him to the Earl of Cork in 1602. His family successfully held it against the Confederate Catholics in 1641 and 1643, but Lismore was captured by Lord Castlehaven in 1645.

LISNACULLIN   *Limerick*   R3343

The four storey tower built c1460-80 by the MacSheehies has a square wing clasping one corner and containing small rooms, a spiral stair very awkwardly reached by a dog leg passage from the main block, and latrines. Probably it is a later addition and it has a second stair carried on a squinch arch over one of the re-entrant angles. Fragments of a polygonal bawn about 30m by 23m also remain with an outbuilding and a square turret in the corner furthest from the main tower. The castle was confiscated after the 1579 Desmond rebellion and given to Thomas Caune. In 1620 it went to Donagh O'Brien, and in 1655 was held by Sir Edward Fitzgerald.

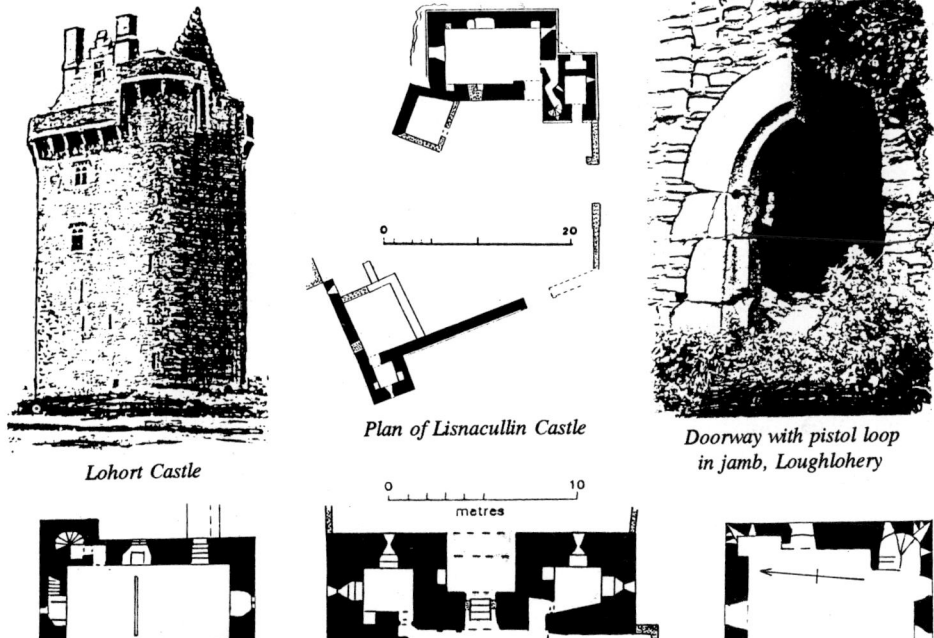

Lohort Castle

Plan of Lisnacullin Castle

Doorway with pistol loop
in jamb, Loughlohery

Gatehouse Plan, Liscarroll

Plan of Listowell Castle

Plan of Loughlohery Castle

LISTOWELL Kerry Q9924

In the garden of a house in the town square is one end of a 15th century castle built by the McGilligans. It was taken over by Fitzmaurice in 1582, and in 1600 was surrendered to Sir Charles Wilmot, who slaughtered the garrison. The main block was 9.6m wide over walls 2m thick and had corner towers about 6m square of which only two now remain, with double splayed loops at basement level.

LOHORT Cork R4602

This impressive six storey tower with rounded corners is said to have been built in the late 15th century by MacDonagh MacCarthy but the continuous machicolated parapet which continues at a higher level over the staircase corner must be an addition of about a century later. Sir Hardess Waller bombarded and captured the castle for Cromwell in 1650. The Earl of Egmont had the tower repaired in 1750, and it was restored and some of the windows renewed in 1876. It is now a ruin again.

LOUGHLOHERY Tipperary S0824

This 16th century tower measures 11.4m by 9.5m and has four storeys with the second storey vaulted. There was also an attic in the roof which had gables on all four sides. There are round bartizans on two diagonally opposite corners. The hall was on the third storey where there are four angle loops with pistol loops on either side. The fourth storey was divided into two rooms forming a suite for the owner.

LOUGHMOE   *Tipperary*   S1367   A.M.

The round cornered 15th century tower 16m long by 11.8m wide and 17m high to the wall-walk is a fine specimen despite the south wall being partly defaced. There are four storeys with vaults over the cellar and third storey and the ends are carried up to contain fifth storey rooms at wall-walk level, the east end being thickened above hall level by means of an arcade. There are or were machicolated sections in the middle of each side. The second storey contain the lord's room and has a fine 17th century fireplace with the initials of one of the Purcells, the last of whom, Colonel Nicholas, died in 1722. There are rooms in the end walls, that at fourth storey level at the west end being the full width of the tower and having angle loops, whilst the SE corner contains a prison high up. In the early 17th century a 26m long mansion of four storeys with large upper mullion and transom windows was added to the north side. Beside the tower the mansion has a porch which faced the former bawn to the east and which has shot holes in the outer doorway jamb and arch. A large fireplace at ground level adjoins it. Clasping the NW corner is a large five storey wing which seems to have been divided into two rooms at each level. The wall-walks of the mansion have parapets with the middle part of each merlon made into a semi-circle.

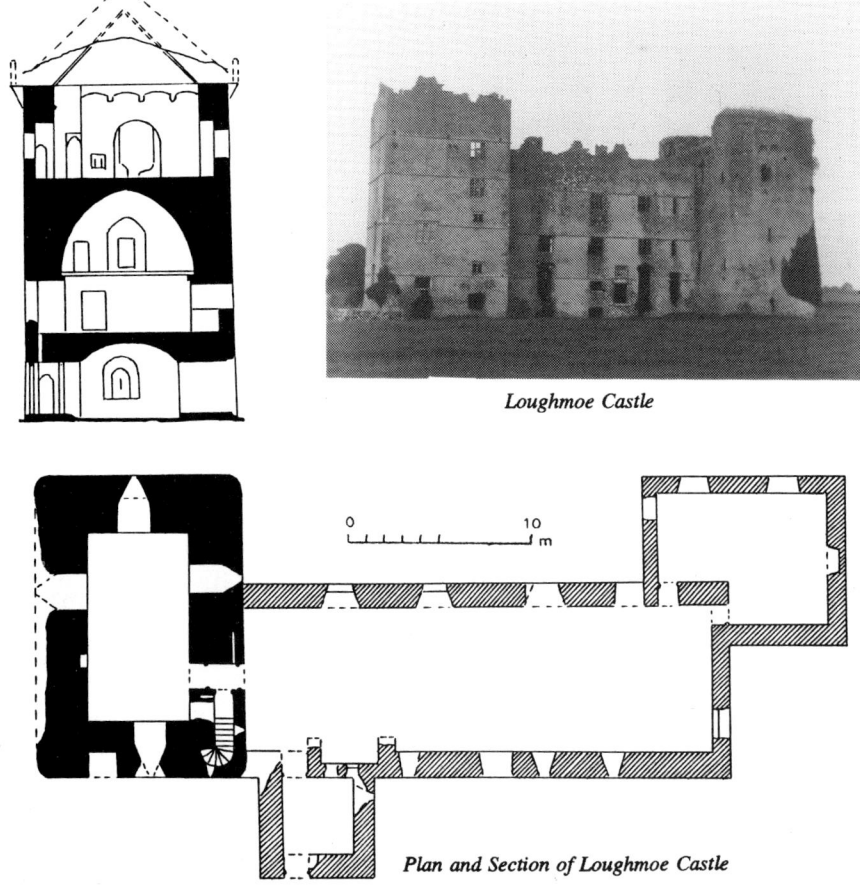

Loughmoe Castle

Plan and Section of Loughmoe Castle

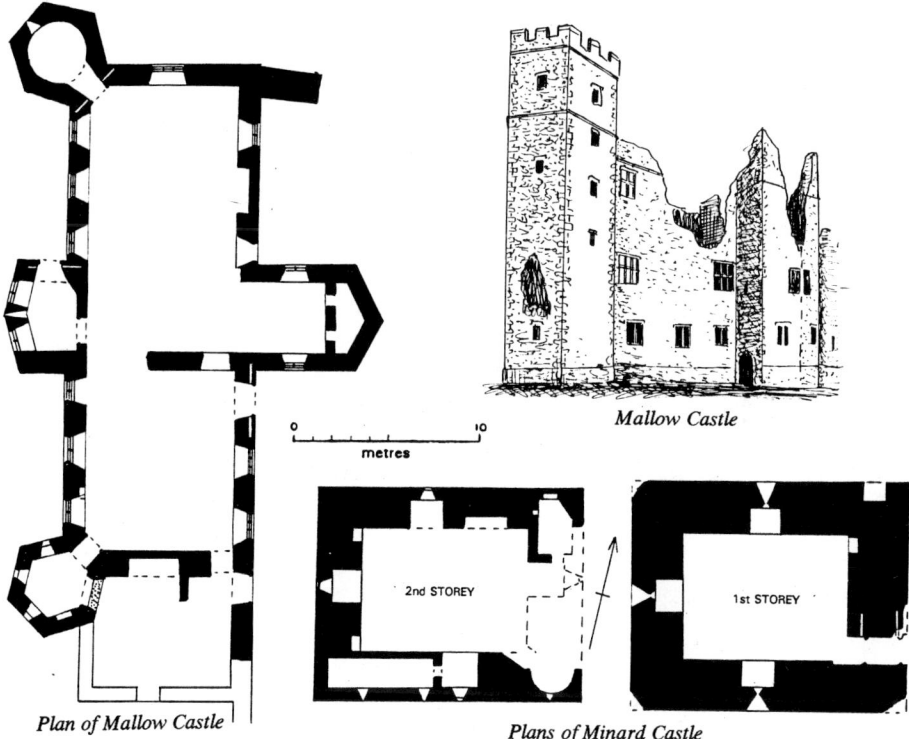

Mallow Castle

metres

Plan of Mallow Castle

2nd STOREY

1st STOREY

Plans of Minard Castle

MALLOW *Cork* W5698 A.M.

Only a fragment remains of a 13th century Roche castle on a promontory which was later held by the Geraldines. The stronghouse on the neck was built either by Sir Thomas Norreys or his daughter and her Jephson husband after the town was burnt in 1598. It measures 27.2m by 10.6m and has hexagonal turrets, one containing a stair, on the corners facing the field, a five sided porch in the middle, and a deeper five sided wing containing the main stair in the middle of the other side. There are pistol holes below the mullion-and-transom windows. Only the turrets and wings had open battlements which were of the English single stepped type. A lower extension at the north end contained a kitchen. Mallow held out against Lord Mountgarret in 1642 but was captured by Lord Castlehaven in 1645. It was burnt by the Jacobites in 1689 and the Jephsons made themselves a more modest house out of the original stable block.

MINARD *Kerry* V5598

The basement of this large tower 15m by 12m has walls 2.5m to 3.3m thick containing an entrance passage with rebates and draw bar holes for two doors and three square embrasures with loops splayed outwards. The staircase only started at the storey above, a living room with a loop in a square embrasure in each wall, a fireplace, and mural chambers in the NE and SW corners, so perhaps there was a second entrance there. The third storey is vaulted and has a chamber in the NW corner with a rare two-light angle loop. The thinner walled hall above the vault is destroyed.

MOCOLLOP *Waterford* W9499

The round tower 10.2m in diameter with a staircase curving up within the wall and a dome vault over the 4th storey probably existed by 1462 when the 6th Earl of Desmond died here. The tower lies on one side of a thinly walled rectangular bawn with a large building at one end and a smaller building and a rectangular flanker at the other end. Another flanker lies on the other side of the tower. In 1642 Mocollop was surrendered by the Boyles to the Confederate Catholics but it was abandoned and in 1645 was occupied by Lord Castlehaven. It was captured in 1647 by Lord Inchiquin, and in 1650 the Maunsells held it against Cromwellian troops.

MONANIMY *Cork* W9965

This is a peculiar building about 10m square of three storeys. Much of it is early 17th century but the basement may be partly older and has a blocked doorway. Beside this an outside flight of steps leads to an upper entrance covered by a loop from a tiny room in a round turret on the corner which is clearly a later addition. On the diagonally opposite corner is a boldly projecting square turret. The staircase seems to have been of wood and only had a partition between it and the rooms. At the summit there was only a wall-walk on the side containing the entrance, plus a bartizan on a far corner.

MONKSTOWN *Cork* W7666

The impressive stronghouse was built for the Archdekin family in the 1630s. It was in use as the club-house of a golf club until fairly recently, but is now ruined. Towers about 7m square of four storeys plus a fifth in the four-gabled roofs lie at the corners of a rectangular main block with a large kitchen fireplace opposite the entrance doorway. Mouldings mark the divisions between storeys. The towers have many shot-holes and each has a square bartizan on pyramidal corbels on the outermost corner.

Monkstown Castle

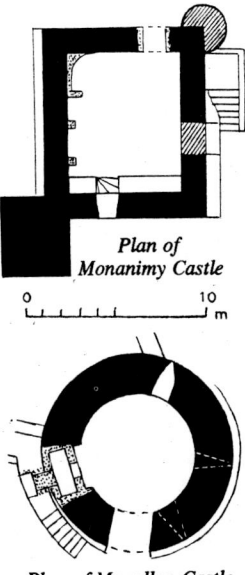

Plan of Monanimy Castle

0   10 m

Plan of Mocollop Castle

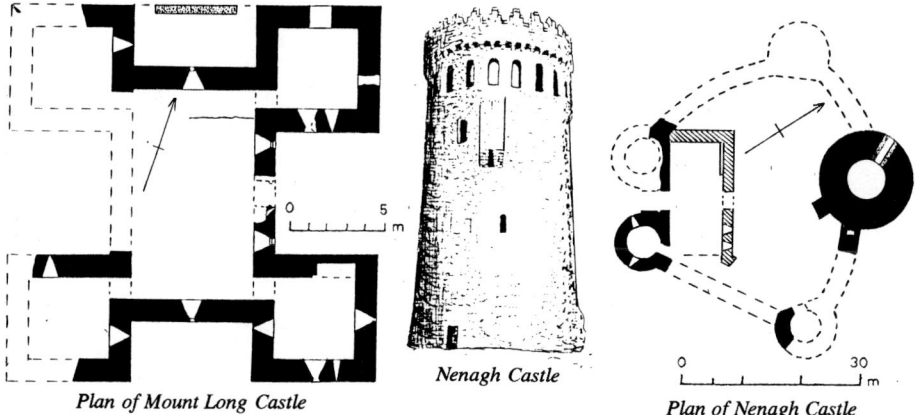

Plan of Mount Long Castle

Nenagh Castle

Plan of Nenagh Castle

MOUNT LONG   *Cork*   W6753

This early 17th century building is the twin of the stronghouse at Monkstown, being about the same size and shape and having the same horizontal mouldings and small mullioned windows in tiers. The eastern towers retain their arrangement of four gables at the top but the western towers have mostly fallen.

MOYCARKEY   *Tipperary*   S1554

The tower measures 11.3m by 8.1m and is unusual in that the thick end wall only contains rooms from the fourth storey level upwards. Below are straight stairs and latrines, and a straight stair in a side wall leads down to the entrance and cellar where there are two recesses below the thick end wall. One corner retains a round bartizan. The tower lies in the middle of a rectangular bawn 53m by 44m with a fragmentary wall 1.5m thick flanked at diagonally opposite corners by round turrets 5.8m in diameter with staircases following the wall curvature and numerous gunloops.

NENAGH   *Tipperary*   R8679   A.M.

Theobald Walter's castle of c1200-20 comprised a round keep 16m in diameter with walls up to 4.6m thick standing at one corner of a pentagonal court 37m across with round towers up to 10m in diameter at the other corners. The curtain is destroyed and only one of the two southern towers between which was the gateway, and a fragment of the eastern tower remain although there is rather more surviving of a rectangular block probably containing a hall which was built across the back of the gateway c1300. The fine keep is well preserved and was heightened to 30m by the addition of a folly top storey c1860. Originally it rose about 22m to the wall walk and was entered at the second of four storeys. A spiral stair rises from there to the hall and chamber above which both have original fireplaces. From the hall a dog leg passage lead out of a window embrasure to the wall-walk on the NW curtain. A similar passage above leads to a latrine in a corbelled out projection. Theobald Walter's descendants the Butlers abandoned Nenagh to the O'Briens in the late 14th century, but in 1533 Sir Piers Butler, later Earl of Ormond, recovered it. The castle was burnt by the O'Carrolls in 1548. It was captured by Eoghan Rua O'Neill in 1648 but was recaptured by Murrough O'Brien and then surrendered to Ireton in 1650 after a short siege. The O'Carrolls seized Nenagh in 1689 but Ginkell captured the castle for William III after a siege lasting just one day and the defences were then slighted.

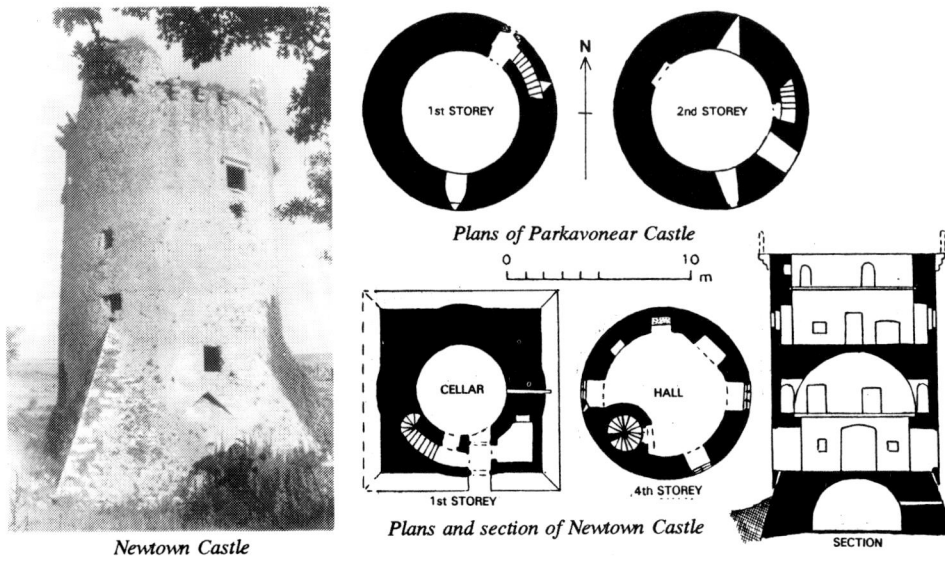

Plans of Parkavonear Castle

Newtown Castle

Plans and section of Newtown Castle

NEWCASTLE WEST   *Limerick*   R2833

In and around a modern residence are relics of a castle of the Earls of Desmond granted in 1591 to Sir William Courtenay, taken by the "Sugan" Earl of Desmond in 1598, and recaptured in 1599. After a four month siege in 1641 it was surrendered to the Confederate Catholics and burnt. There are round and rectangular towers, parts of the curtains, moats, and two 15th century halls, one with a vaulted basement.

NEWTOWN   *Clare*   M2206

This 15m high tower with dome vaults over the first and third of five storeys has a cylindrical superstructure 9m in diameter rising above a massive square pyramidal base. At the join of the two shapes are triangular recesses in the apex of which are shotholes in the sills of second storey windows commanding the whole of the base. There are several other pistol holes higher up and corbels for four machicolation at the summit, one commanding the entrance. The hall on the fourth storey has mullioned windows with hoodmoulds. The staircase projects into this thinly walled room.

PARKAVONEAR   *Kerry*   V9493   A.M.

Near Aghadoe Cathedral is a plain round tower 10.6m in diameter standing in a square enclosure which had a wall and moat. It is thought to be an Irish copy of a 13th century Norman keep. There are now just two storeys connected by a stair following the curvature of the 2.1m thick wall. The doorway at the foot of the stair may be an insertion as there is an upper entrance near the head of the stair. The hall it leads into has a shallow fireplace and just two narrow loops. The cellar below has one loop only.

POOKEENEE   *Kerry*   Q8642

Immediately within the ditch cutting off the neck of a large promontory fort are remains of later medieval stone defences. There are fragments of a tower about 12m by 10.5m over walls 2.5m thick with a wall running west from it to a small chamber.

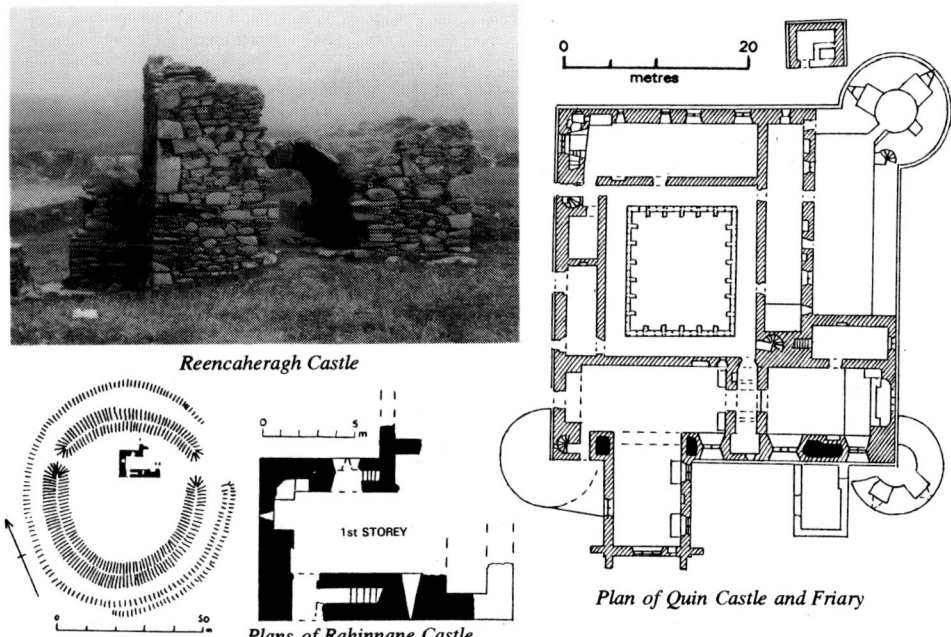

Reencaheragh Castle

1st STOREY

Plans of Rahinnane Castle

Plan of Quin Castle and Friary

QUIN   *Clare*   R4275   A.M.

In 1280 Thomas de Clare built at Quin a court 33m square enclosed by a wall 3m thick with round corner towers up to 12m in diameter. In 1286 the garrison killed an Irish chief called O'Liddy and in revenge Cuvea Macnamara captured and destroyed the castle in 1288. By 1350 a church had been built on top of the ruins, although it was mostly rebuilt in the 1430s when Sioda Cam Macnamara founded a Franciscan Friary here. The gateway, internal buildings, and one corner tower have vanished, and only an outline remains of another but the other towers and the wall between them remain east of the friary buildings. The thick south wall of the church probably also contains original work through which many 15th century openings have been pierced.

RAHEEN   *Cork*   W1933

Only one end of this 16th century tower still stands to the original height of four storeys with an attic in the roof. It had the lower walls sloped back to central recesses commanded by pistol holes in the sills of third storey windows. The vault shows traces of the wickerwork mat upon which it was constructed. See page 17.

RAHINNANE   *Kerry*   Q3703

Inside a ringfort about 50m in diameter with an impressively steep rampart and ditch are ruins of an L-shaped tower built probably in the 16th century by the Knight of Kerry, captured by Sir Charles Wilmot in 1602, and dismantled in c1650. The destroyed wing adjoined a thick end wall of the main block 13.9m long by 8.6m wide. The entrance and main staircase are in the south side wall, and there is a narrower service stair on the other side. The second storey was vaulted. Above was a hall where the walls were thinner and need arcades to return them to a sufficient thickness to carry a wall-walk.

RATHGORMUCK *Waterford* S3418

Beside a modern house is a ruined three storey tower measuring 8.2m by 7.5m with a small wing projecting from the SW corner. The basement vault does not extend to the south end wall so there were perhaps mural chambers there with a staircase in the SE corner. Entry is now by means of a breach in the north end wall.

RATHMORE *Limerick* R5743

The tower measures 10.7m by 8.8m and has four storeys below a vault and a lofty hall above. A thick end wall contains a latrine at ground level, five chambers, and a wider sixth chamber with its inner wall carried on an arch over one end of the hall.

RATHURLES *Tipperary* R9280

Hidden amongst shrubs near the ruined church is the stump of a 16th century round tower house 12m in diameter over walls 2.9m thick now broken down above the second storey dome vault. The doorway has a shot-hole in the jamb. The passage from it leads only to the staircase and a double turn has to be made to reach the cellar.

REENCAHERAGH *Kerry* V3573

A headland near Bray Head on Valencia Island is closed off by a low wall 1.5m thick and 34m long. Near the east end is a gatehouse 4.5m deep by 6.7m wide with tiny rooms on either side of a passage 2m wide plus a stair on one side. Little remains of the room above and the inner arch of the passage has gone. About 15m behind the gatehouse are foundations of a house 11.5m long by 6.5m wide with two doorways opposite each other and the west end of the sidewalls.

Rathgormuck Castle

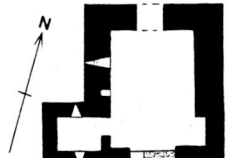

Plan of Rathgormuck Castle

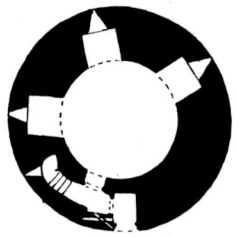

Plan of Rathurles Castle

0   10 m

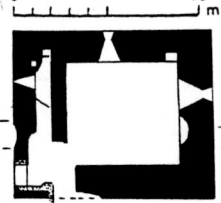

Plan of Rathmore Castle

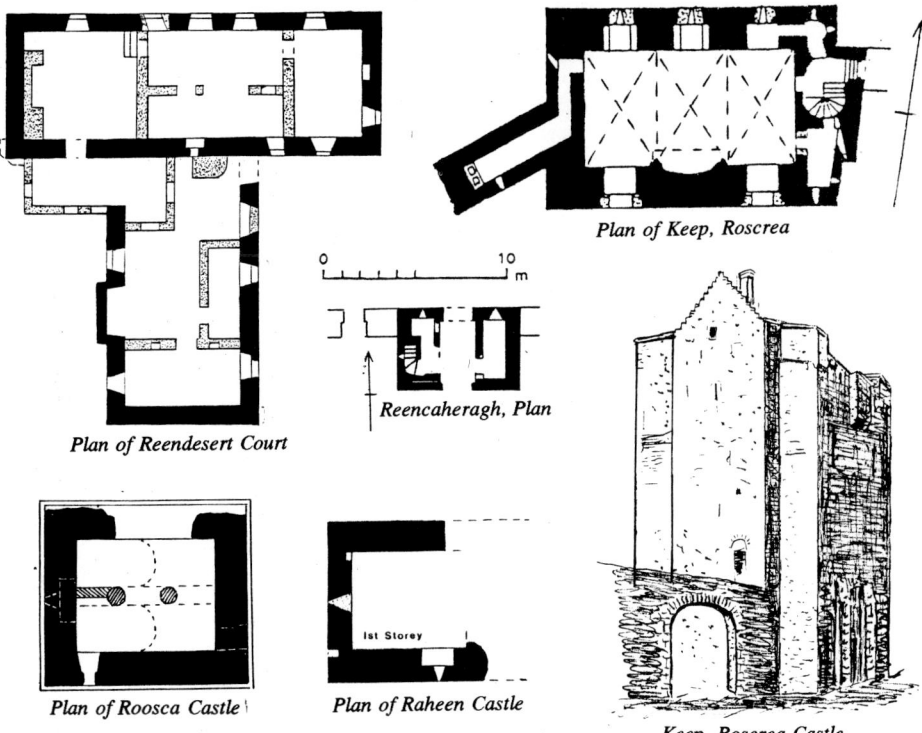

Plan of Keep, Roscrea

Plan of Reendesert Court

Reencaheragh, Plan

Plan of Roosca Castle

Plan of Raheen Castle

Keep, Roscrea Castle

REENDESERT   *Cork*   W0054

The T-shaped stronghouse of O'Sullivan Beare has been much altered internally but retains a wide kitchen fireplace in the main stem and bartizans on two of the corners which are square but with the outer angle canted off. There were three storeys plus attics in the roof. Most of it is ruined although one end of the cross wing is roofed.

ROOSCA   *Tipperary*   S0619

The tower measures about 11m by 9.6m above a damaged plinth and may be 14th century as it lacks the mural chambers and passages normal later on. The two octagonal piers in the basement to carry slightly pointed vaults are later insertions.

ROSCREA   *Tipperary*   S1489   A.M.

King John built a wooden castle here in 1213, probably on the same site as the present mid 13th century D-shaped bailey with two round flanking towers up to 10m in diameter. The wall is breached on the south where there is a much more recent building. On the north is a rectangular tower measuring 16.3m by 10.3m built c1280. It originally contained the gateway passage but this was blocked when it was later converted into a tower house. The upper parts were then much altered but the hall over the gate retains an original rib vault in three bays and a fine fireplace. Roscrea was held by the Bishops of Killaloe for much of the 13th century until there was an exchange of lands with King Edward I. From 1315 until 1689 it was held by the Butler Earls of Ormonde. See Plan on Page 9.

ROSS   *Kerry*   V9589   A.M.*

This famous and often illustrated ruin lies on Ross Island, a promontory in Lough Leane. It consists of a gutted but almost complete 16th century tower inside a square bawn with round corner towers. The tower has chambers in a thick end wall and square bartizans on two diagonally opposite corners. These have only one machicolation slot on each face instead of the usual two. A ruined 17th century block with mullioned windows adjoins it. The castle formed the chief seat of O'Donaghue Mor until it was acquired by MacCarthy Mor after the Desmond rebellion. Soon afterwards it went to an English planter named Browne. In 1652 Lord Muskerry held the castle against a Cromwellian force of 1,500 foot and 700 horse under Ludlow. It fell after floating batteries were brought up to bombard it from the lough, thus fulfilling an ancient tradition that it would remain impregnable until attacked by water.

SEVEN HEADS   *Cork*   W4836

Most of the width of the neck of a promontory is closed by a small tower 6m by 5m now destroyed above a vault carried on two pointed ribs over the second storey. There are doorways opposite each other at the east end at ground level and there seems to have been a wider gateway in the short length of adjacent curtain walling.

SHANID   *Limerick*   R2545

The original principal seat of the Desmond FitzGeralds comprised a multi-sided tower keep 12.6 in diameter and round inside probably added slightly later to an oval court with a wall 1.5m thick on top of a natural motte 11m high. A bailey on one side shows no evidence of stone walls. Only low fragments remain of the shell wall probably built c1200-10 by Thomas Fitz-Maurice, but part of the tower keep stands to the height of the wall-walk 11.5m above ground. Shanid was captured by Hugh O'Donnell in 1601.

Plan of Smithstown Castle

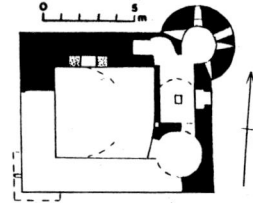

Plan of Shippool Castle

Ross Castle

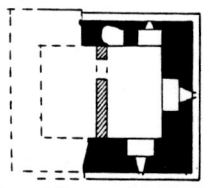

Plan of Shanmuckinish Castle

SHANMUCKINISH   *Clare*   M2610

On one side of the neck of a small coastal promontory occupied by a modern house stands the southern half of a tower 7.8m wide by about 10m long above a plinth. There is a thin later crosswall. There were vaults over the second and third storeys with chambers in the haunches of the latter. The top room has a three light mullion and transom window. The summit has corbels for sections of machicolated parapet.

SHIPPOOL   *Cork*   W5755

The tower doorway with a shot-hole in the jamb opens directly to the Bandon River on the west side. The east wall contained a spiral stair and a tier of rooms with latrines in the north wall and was flanked by a round turret with gunloops on the NE corner. On this side the ground is level with the third storey which was covered by a pointed vault. There was a square bartizan on the fallen SW corner at this level.

SMERWICK   *Kerry*   Q3508

On a cliff on Dingle peninsular are two small enclosures with a rock cut ditch between them and two bastions to landward. This was the fort of Dun an Oir built by Italians and Spaniards under James Fitzmaurice who landed in the bay below in September 1580. Seven weeks later the fort was bombarded for three days by Lord Deputy Grey and Admiral Winter until the 600 men crowded within surrendered and were all slaughtered except for their officers. Also taken were the Jesuits Laurence Moore, Oliver Plunket, and William Wollick who were tortured, mutilated, and then hanged.

SMITHSTOWN   *Clare*   R1594

The tower measures 12.5m by 8.2m and lies by a stream. It has four storeys with vaults over the second and fourth. The hall over the top vault has been destroyed. The third storey has a fine fireplace and angle loops, off one of which are shot-holes. On the second storey an L-plan room is tucked in behind the usual thick end wall room.

SPRINGFIELD   *Limerick*   R3523

The roofless but well preserved four storey 16th century tower has four gables and two round bartizans at diagonally opposite corners. A pistol hole guards the doorway. After Sir John Fitzgerald fled to France following the Treaty of Limerick in 1691 Springfield went to the FitzMaurices and later passed to the Deanes, Lords Muskerry.

TEMPLEMORE   *Tipperary*   S1171

The lake protected two sides of a courtyard about 50m by 40m. Fragments of the 1.5m thick curtain wall adjoin a massive early three storey keep 16.5m by 11m projecting from the most vulnerable corner. The basement vault, the attic, and probably also the buttresses at one end are later medieval additions.

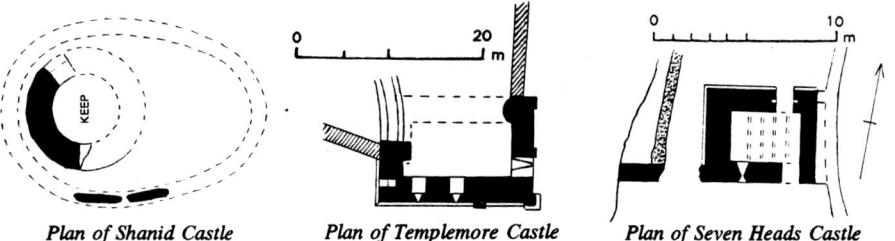

Plan of Shanid Castle   *Plan of Templemore Castle*   *Plan of Seven Heads Castle*

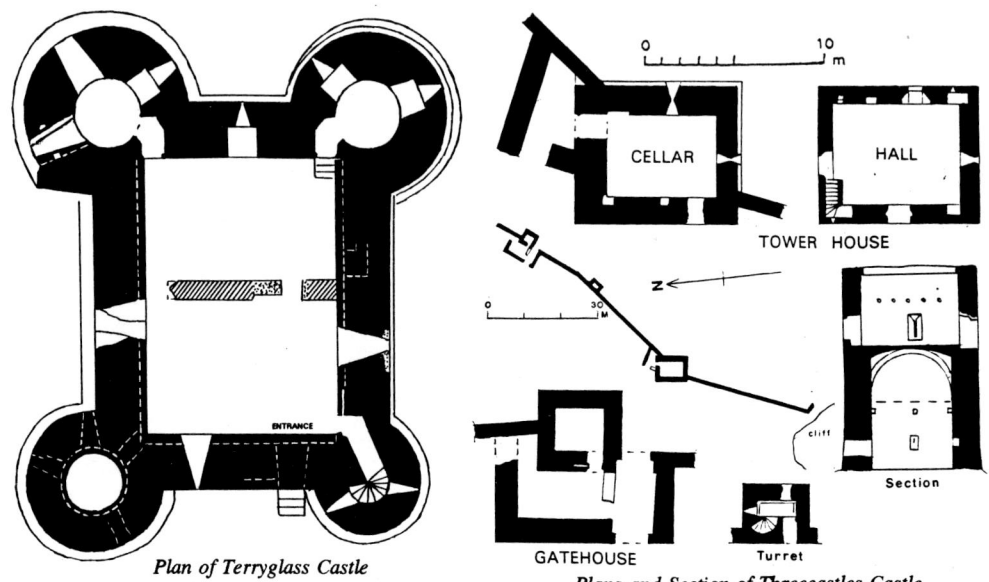

Plan of Terryglass Castle

Plans and Section of Threecastles Castle

TERRYGLASS   *Tipperary*   R 8601   A.M.

Terryglass was a Butler seat from the 13th century until at least the 1640s. In the village are three sides of a bawn about 28m square with the wall-walk and parapet remaining on a wall 1.2m thick. Only one corner with a round bartizan remains of a stronghouse which formed the fourth side. Not far away lies a 13th century keep of great interest despite being ruined to second storey level. Above plinths rising as much as 4m high it measures 20.5m by 16.3m over walls up to 2.8m thick. The basement has a loop in each wall and has a later crosswall although there are no signs of vaulting and the next floor was carried on an offset of the side walls. There are round towers at the corners, two of them being about 9m in diameter. A third has rooms lacking access to the interior about the same size as those in the other towers but is smaller because the walls are thinner. The fourth tower contains a spiral staircase reached by a round headed doorway and beside which is the entrance. There is the base of a second stair leading up from the second storey in an adjacent side wall.

THREECASTLES   *Cork*   V7426

A lake occupies half of the width of the neck of a large rocky headland. In the 15th century a four storey tower with a vault half way up and measuring 9m by 7.4m was built on the highest point of the other half of the neck. Subsequently curtain walls 0.8m thick were built to connect it with the cliff and lake, the latter section having two rectangular turrets. Beside the turret by the lake was the gateway, originally just an arch, although an internal gate building was added on later.

TICKINCOR   *Waterford*   S2424

Adjoining a modern farmhouse is a ruined stronghouse with a staircase wing projecting from the middle of the east side. There was a low basement, two main storeys, and a top storey partly in the roof which had gables not only on the end walls but in pairs on the side walls also, and open lookout points on the corners.

Threecastles Castle

Tullow Castle

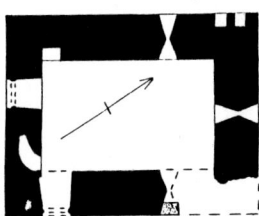

Plan of Timoleague Castle

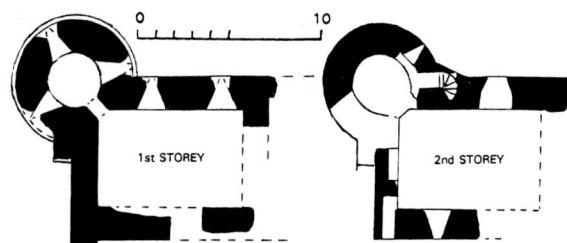

Plan of Tullow Castle

TIMOLEAGUE *Cork* W4644

Only two storeys remain of a large tower 14m by 11m with walls up to 2.5m thick in the basement which has double splayed loops. There are separate entrances to each storey in the east wall. From the second storey a stair in the west wall led up.

TULLOW *Tipperary* S1972

This tower is unusual in having a round tower 6.2m in diameter on one corner. It has a spiral stair serving the upper storeys carried on a round squinch arch above the re-entrant angle with the main block side wall and a dome vault over the fourth storey. There were no vaults in the main block which had three main storeys and an attic in the roof. The end wall adjoining the tower contains fireplaces, that at third storey level being a 17th century insertion, and has at second storey level a doorway which led out to the wall-walk on the bawn wall 1.4m thick by 3.6m high. The other end wall, which perhaps contained the main stair and a tier of chambers has fallen.

TWOMILEBORRIS *Tipperary* S1958

The tower measures 13.2m by 10.4m and contained three storeys below a vault and a hall above. The end walls are continued up to contain rooms and serve as gables and there are bartizans on two diagonally opposite corners. At the lower levels there are long mural rooms in one end wall and straight flights of steps in a side wall.

WATERFORD *Waterford*
S6112 A.M.*

The keep-like Reginald's Tower probably dating from the 13th century and now serving as a museum is the largest of several round towers and other fragments surviving from the city walls. It is over 13m in diameter and 17.5m high with walls over 3m thick. The blocked stair curving within the wall is probably original but the upper doorway and adjacent spiral staircase may be later medieval insertions. The tower had four storeys (one is now only a gallery) and has a plain parapet on a projecting course.

Reginald's Tower, Waterford

Plan of Reginald's Tower

Clarecastle, Co Clare

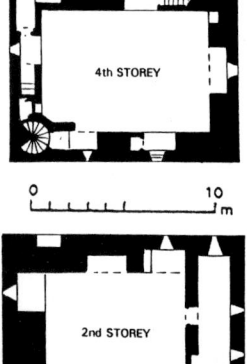

4th STOREY

0   10
     m

2nd STOREY

Plans of Twomileborris Castle

Springfield Castle

Ballymalis Castle

Tickincor Castle

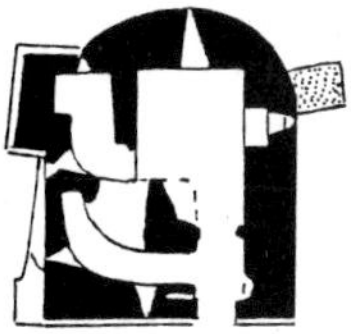

MAP OF CASTLES OF MUNSTER

*Court Castle,
Co Limerick
(R4753)*

Fireplace, Kilcash

GLENINAGH
SHANMUCKINISH
NEWTOWN
FAUNAROOSKA
BALLINALACKEN
DOONMACFELIM
DOONAGORE
CAHERMACNAGHTON
LEAMANEH
DE CLARE'S HOUSE
SMITHSTOWN
LISCANNOR
BALLYGRIFFY
CLARE
DANGANBRACK
CRAGGAUNOWEN
CLARECASTLE QUIN
KNAPPOGUE
DANGAN
BUNRATTY
CRATLOE
LIMERICK
CARRIGAHOLT
ASKEATON CARRIGOGUNNELL
GLIN BALLYCULHANE
SHANID ADARE
CARRIGAFOYLE CLONSHIRE GARRAUNBOY
POOKEENEE
LISNACULLIN RATHMORE
BALLINGARRY LISTOWEL CASTLE MATRIX
NEWCASTLE WEST
SPRINGFIELD
GLENQUIN
KILBOLANE
KERRY
KANTURK

LACKEEN
TERRYGLASS
KILLILEA ROSCREA
RATHURLES BALLYNAKILL
NENAGH GOURDEEN TULLOW
TIPPERARY TEMPLEMORE
LOUGHMOE
CASTLE CONNELL
BALLYNAHOW
TWOMILEBORRIS
MOYCARKEY
KILLENURE
BRITTAS GORTMAKELLIS
GOLDEN KNOCKKELLY
BOURCHIERS CASHEL
GLENOGRA KILCASH
BALLYGRENNAN KNOCKGRAFFON
KILMALLOCK LOUGHLOHERY
LIMERICK CAHIR TICKINCOR
BURNCOURT ROOSCA CARRICK ON SUIR
ARDFINNAN RATHGORMUCK
LISCARROLL CASTLE GRACE **WATERFORD** WATERFORD

RWICK
GALLARUS
AHINNANE
MINARD BALLYMALIS
PARKAVONEAR
ROSS DRISHANE
CORK
BALLYCARBURY
REENCAHERAGH
BALLINSKELLIGS
CAHERDANIEL ARDEA
REENDESERT
DUNBOY
DUNMANUS
THREECASTLES

LOHORT
DROMANEEN MONANIMY GLANWORTH
MALLOW MOCOLLOP BALLYDUFF
CARRIGACUNNA CASTLE MORE LISMORE
CASTLE LYONS CONNA
CARRIGAPHOOCA BLARNEY CASTLEMARTYR INCHIQUIN
BELVELLY IGHTERMURRAGH
CARRIGADROHID BALLYANNAN
MONKSTOWN
BALLEA
SHIPPOOL
BALLNACARRIGA
TIMOLEAGUE KINSALE
COPPINGERS COURT SEVEN HEADS
RAHEEN
DUNDEADY

Kilsheelan Motte, Co Tipparary

GAZETTEER OF CASTLES OF ULSTER

ARDGLASS *Down* J5637 A.M.*

There are no less than five fortified merchants' houses at Ardglass. Jordan's Castle is a four storey tower of c1450 with a staircase turret and latrine turret both projecting from the north side with a machicolation between them and and a second machicolation at right angles covering the doorway. It is named after Jordan de Saukeville, whose castle here was visited by King John in 1210, or the Jordan family, one of whom was blockaded here by the O'Neills for three years until relieved by Lord Deputy Mountjoy in 1601. The tower was restored from ruin by a Mr Biggar in c1920. Margaret's Castle is similar in form but less well preserved. There the doorway is protected by an internal machicolation. King's Castle and Cowd Castle are plain rectangles lacking features of interest and now only two storeys high. The latter measures just 5.8m by 5.4m externally. Horn Castle was no less than 29.4m long by 8m wide. It seems to have been an embattled warehouse with living accommodation at one end, where there is a projecting turret. Remains of it are embedded in the building of 1790 called Ardglass Castle now forming a clubhouse for a golf course.

AUDLEY'S *Down* J5851 A.M.*

The Audleys were here from the 13th century until they sold up to a neighbour, Bernard Ward, in 1646. Their 15th century tower lies on or near the site of a motte and stands in the north corner of a bawn 28m by 20m inside a wall 1m thick, now reduced to its base. The tower measures 9.1m by 7.7m and contained a basement, a vaulted hall, and a bedroom with a total height to the top of the parapet of 11m. Turrets projecting 2m towards the court contain the stair and latrines serving the upper storeys. Joining them at the top is an arch with a machicolation over the doorway. The turret tops are missing but a third turret on the west corner remains complete.

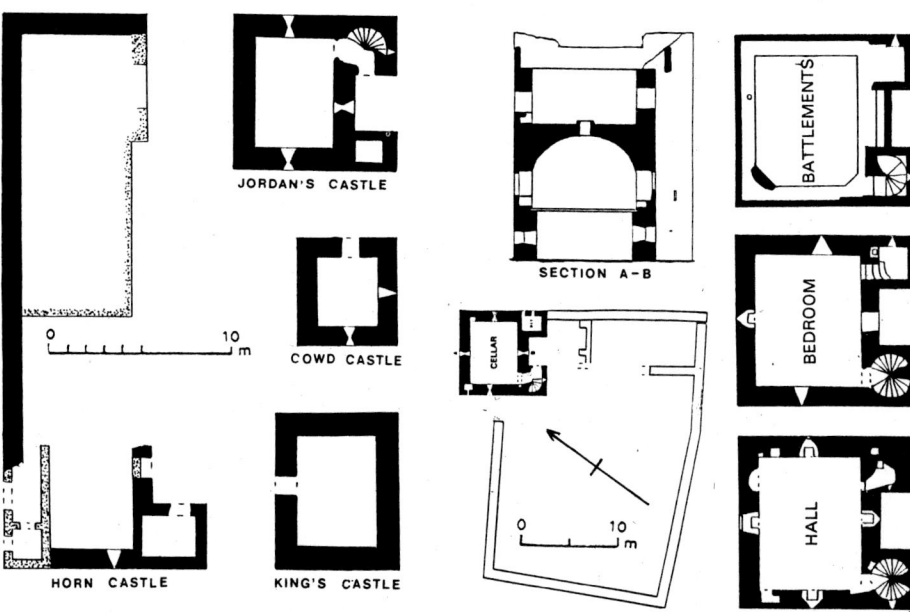

Plans of Castles at Ardglass

Plans of Audley's Castle

Augher or Spur Royal Castle

Ballygalley Castle

AUGHENTAINE   *Tyrone*   H4652

Sir William Stewart's stronghouse of c1620 was probably not restored after being burnt by Sir Phelim O'Neill in 1641, although it stood almost complete until the south wall collapsed in 1935. A wing 6.8m wide near the middle of the north side of the main block 15.6m long by 6.6m wide contained the main stair. Access from the hall and drawing room to the bedrooms above was by a stair corbelled out over the western re-entrant angle.

AUGHER (SPUR ROYAL)   *Tyrone*   H5654

The name Spur Royal refers to the remarkable plan of the three storey embattled tower built in 1610 by Sir Thomas Ridgeway, a square of 9m with a triangular bay in the middle of each side, giving a shape like an eight pointed riding spur. A machicolation opening off the parapet defends the entrance. Only one round flanker remains of the bawn. The castle held out against Sir Phelim O'Neill in 1641 but was burnt in 1689 and dismantled by order of the Irish Parliament. It lay ruinous until 1827 when the tower was restored, new basement windows inserted, and a house built alongside.

BALLYGALLEY   *Antrim*   D3708

This building, now a hotel, is a typically Scottish type L-plan tower built by James Shaw of Greenock in 1625. The main block contains two vaulted cellars, a hall, and two bedrooms side by side and attics in the roof with dormer windows and conical roofed round bartizans. Some windows have been rebuilt. The wing contains the spiral staircase and rises a stage higher with a stair corbelled out over the re-entrant angle.

BALLYKELLY   *Londonderry*   C6322

The Fishmongers' Company built a bawn with a 3.6m high wall here c1615 to protect the house of their agent Mr Higgins. It was later leased to the Hamiltons and the Beresfords. The latter family c1730 replaced a corner flanker with a house called Walworth. Three other flankers survive, two being two storey round towers, and the other a polygonal salient bastion. The Fishmongers' regained possession in 1820.

BALLYREAGH   *Donegal*   C8539

In the late 1960s the local authority removed nearly 17m of walling 1.2m thick and 4m high with musket loops on the inner edge of a ditch isolating a promontory rising 15m above the sea. The castle belonged to the McHenrys. The garrison fled when Lord Deputy Sir John Perrot approached the site with heavy artillery in 1584.

BELLAGHY   *Londonderry*   H9396

The house now called Bellaghy Castle is a late 17th century building but one round and two rectangular flankers are said to survive of a bawn built by the Vintners' Company c1615-20. A report of 1622 mentions a house with two round towers of brick with dome roofs. It was not repaired after being burnt by the MacDonnells in the rebellion of 1641.

BELTRIM   *Tyrone*   H4886

The garden wall of the 18th and 19th century house above the River Owenkillew includes two round flankers and a turret with later windows of the house and bawn built in the early 17th century by William Hamilton.

BENBURB   *Tyrone*   H8152

Sean O'Neill "The Proud" had his chief seat at Benburb. It was burnt in 1566 but was restored and used by Turlough O'Neill until 1573. Materials were plundered from it for the new English fort at Blackwatertown. In 1615 Sir Richard Wingfield built a bawn on a cliff 36m above the river. It has a loopholed wall 4.8m high with square flanking towers with mullion and transom windows on the northern corners. There is a small round stair turret at the SE corner. A flanker at the SW corner has been replaced by a 19th century house. Benburb was sacked by the O'Neills in 1641.

BRACKFIELD   *Londonderry*   C5110

The 18.6m square bawn built by the Skinners Company c1615 is well preserved although the gateway has been widened and only the outer wall with two fireplace recesses remains of the house. The wall is 0.8m thick, 3m high and has 3.6m high round bastions 4.5m in diameter at diagonally opposite corners. One has partly fallen.

BUNCRANA   *Donegal*   C3531

The O'Dohertys' three storey tower of c1330-50 measures 9.8m by 8.7m. and has a low-lying site beside a stream. Straight slab-roofed stairs in the north and east walls connect the unvaulted rooms which are now inaccessible as the lower openings are all blocked up. The existing top storey and the parapets and harled gables date from 1602 when Hugh Boy O'Doherty refurbished the castle to form a base for the Spanish troops expected in support of the Catholic rebellion against Elizabeth I. Her troops burnt the castle but it was repaired and in 1608 was granted to Sir Arthur Chichester. It was leased to the Vaughans who inserted larger upper windows and fireplaces and lived in the tower until 1718 when Sir John Vaughan demolished the bawn wall to provide materials for building a new mansion on the hill above.

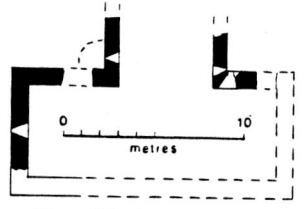

Plan of Aughentaine Castle

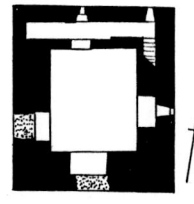

Plan of Buncrana Castle

Benburb Castle

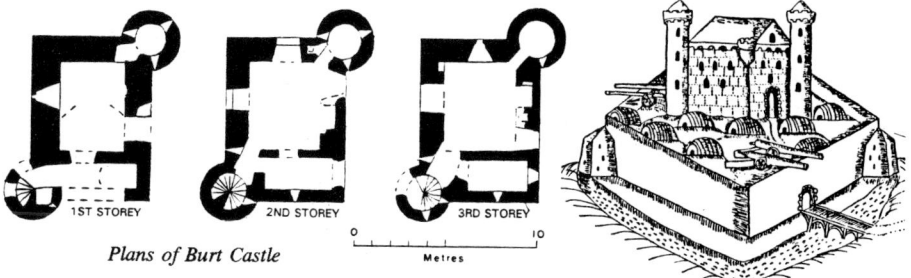

Plans of Burt Castle

Old sketch of Burt Castle

BURT *Donegal* C3119

The earliest mention of this castle is in a grant of land to Sir John Doherty in 1587 and it was probably then newly built. It was captured by Sir Henry Docwra in 1601 and is depicted on a map of that year as an embattled tower of three storeys plus an attic standing amidst several beehive huts within a square bawn surrounded by a dry ditch crossed by a bridge and flanked at diagonally opposite corners by casemates with musketry loops. The bawn has vanished but the tower stands almost to full height and measures 8.7m by 6.5m over walls 1.5m thick. There are turrets 3.2m in diameter at diagonally opposite corners. One contains the staircase adjacent to a tier of small chambers over the entrance. There are pistol loops but no vaults. The castle was besieged by the English in 1607, taken after the rebellion of 1608, and was maintained as a garrisoned house and bawn until at least the 1690s.

CARRICKABRAGHY *Donegal* C4053

A map of 1690 depicts here an oval bawn of which only slight traces now survive with seven round flanking turrets around a square tower of which two unvaulted storeys remain. It measures just 5.6m by 5.0m externally and has adjoining it parts of a later round turret 5m in diameter beyond which was the bawn gateway. It was here that Sir Cahir O'Doherty planned his revolt of 1608.

Carrickabraghy Castle

Plans of
Carrickabraghy
Castle

CARRICKFERGUS   *Antrim*   J4187   A.M.*

In the 1180s John de Courcy, an adventurer from Somerset who conquered most of eastern Ulster, began building a polygonal curtain wall around a court 44m long by 26m wide on the end of the rocky promontory. Shortly afterwards work began on a four storey tower keep about 16.5m square and 27m high at the north end of the court. The twin barrel vaulted cellars were originally only reached from the hall above. The south corners have projections to help house the staircase adjacent to the original entrance and tiers of latrines. Both projections die into the wallface below the summit,, where these corners rise as low turrets. In 1204 de Courcy was defeated at Carrickfergus by Hugh de Lacy, who became Earl of Ulster. He completed the keep and added on the north and east sides a narrow and thinly walled new court with a small boldly projecting square tower facing east, and a polygonal tower facing north, with a gateway between them. The latter, plus the adjoining walls, were reduced to their footings c1700 and were only uncovered again in the 1950s. Of about the same period are footings of a hall in the inner ward. In 1210 King John captured the castle and it was then retained as a state fortress, prison, and administrative centre until 1928 when it was transferred to the Ministry of Finance for preservation.

In c1225-45 Henry III had the remainder of the rock enclosed to form an outer ward 40m wide with one small square flanking tower on the west side. The north end was closed off by a gatehouse with twin fully round towers about 12m in diameter flanking a passageway. The latter was remodelled c1320 probably because of damage caused during the long siege of 1315-16 by Edward Bruce and was given a new vault, portcullis grooves and internal and external machicolations. In front was a pit crossed by a removable bridge. An upper room in the eastern tower is known as the chapel on account of the fine two-light window of c1200 reset within it from elsewhere in the castle. Carrickfergus was often inadequately garrisoned and maintained during the late medieval period and was captured and damaged by Niall Nor O'Neill in 1384.

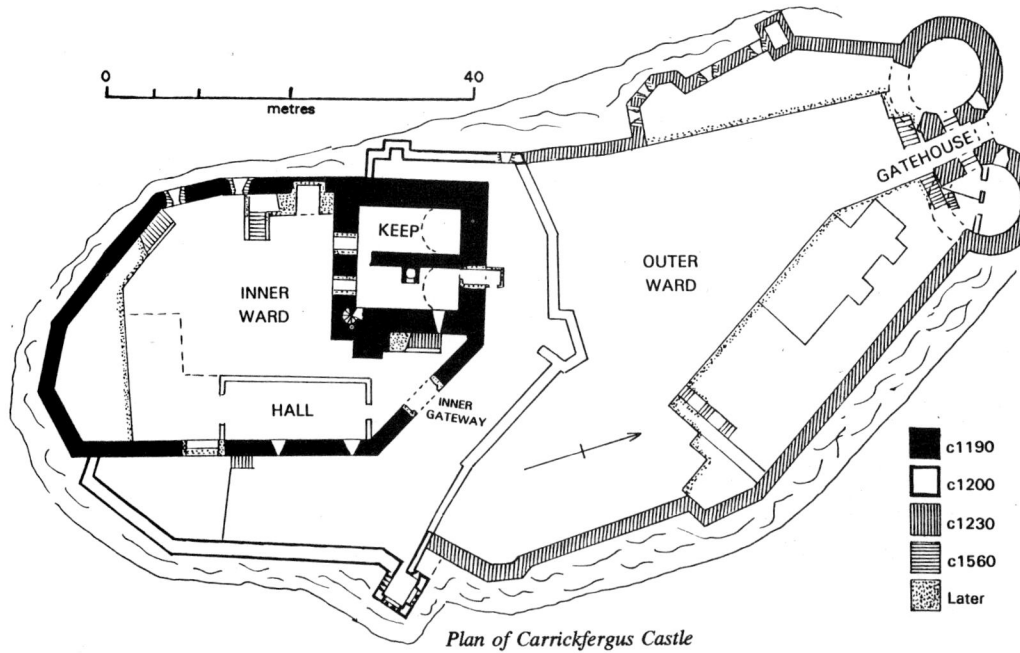

Plan of Carrickfergus Castle

Carrickfergus Castle

Gatehouse Window

In the 1560s Carrickfergus Castle was remodelled for defence by artillery. Wide mouthed ports were inserted in the walls and the lower rooms of the gatehouse towers were filled up with earth to provide a solid floor for mounting cannon. The inner parts of the towers were pulled down to provide easier access for these and the outer wall-head lowered and made suitable for an upper battery. In 1575 Somhairle Buidhe MacDonnell overthrew the castle garrison in revenge for the burning of 600 defenceless Scots by the Earl of Essex, and in 1597 the MacDonnells ambushed and beheaded the castle governor. Con O'Neill, chief of Clannaboye, escaped from imprisonment in the castle in 1602 using a rope smuggled in by his wife in a cheese.

William III landed beside the castle in June 1690 after the Duke of Schomberg had captured it from James II's forces. It was then left to decay until in January 1754 a 15m length of the curtain at the south end fell down. This breach was still open in 1760 when Commodore Thurot landed 800 French troops from three ships and assaulted the castle. The garrison of 230 men, mostly raw recruits, and five officers repelled three assaults even though they ran out of bullets and had to fire their tunic buttons and then use bayonets, bricks and stones. Eventually, with no hope of relief, they surrendered and marched out with the honours of war, having delayed Thurot enough for him to be defeated and killed by the Royal Navy off the Isle of Man on his way home. The breach was subsequently filled with a huge solid gun platform and several others were created elsewhere along the defences. Anti-submarine guns defending the lough were mounted on these platforms in the 1914-18 war and the keep basement was used as an air raid shelter in 1939-45.

Carrickfergus was the chief port of Ulster in the medieval period and many of the wealthier merchants built themselves tower houses like those of Ardglass, and Carlingford. Nothing survives of any of them but a late 16th century sketch shows no less than twelve, including two almost adjoining and one which was round in plan.

CASTLE ARCHDALE   *Fermanagh*   H1649

In the wooded demesne of the house of 1773 are fragments of a stronghouse and bawn built by John Archdale in 1615, wrecked by Rory Maguire in 1641, and burnt in 1689. The house had two storeys and attics, was 21.4m long and had a staircase wing projecting on the north side where the ground sloped away. On the other side a bawn extended 19.4m to a gateway with an inscription above it. This is now leaning and held up with buttresses. Three flankers mentioned by Pynnar in 1619 have gone.

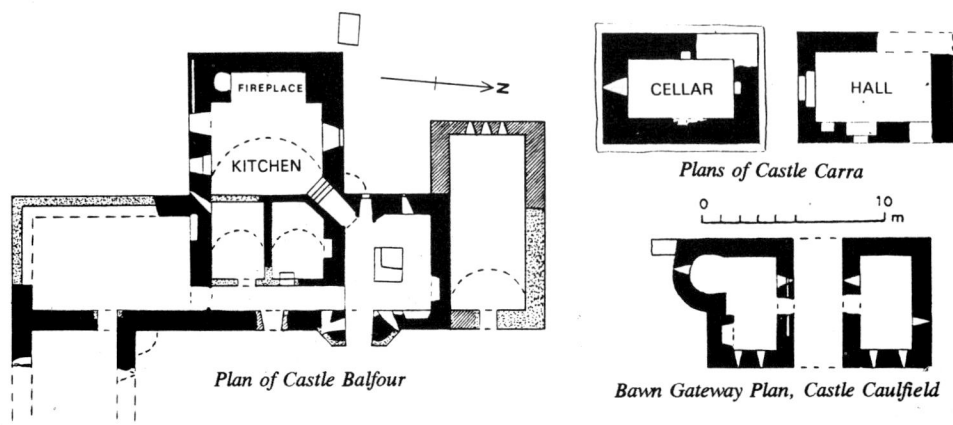

Plan of Castle Balfour

Plans of Castle Carra

Bawn Gateway Plan, Castle Caulfield

CASTLE BALFOUR *Fermanagh* H3634 A.M.

Sir James Balfour's stronghouse of 1618 has a wing facing a low cliff on the west, and originally had a bawn 21m square on the flat east side. The wing and adjoining part of the main block contained the hall above a kitchen with a big fireplace and two small cellars reached off a passage, all of them vaulted. North of them the main block contained a wide scale-and-platt staircase leading up from an entrance in a canted bay. The main block continues to the south and has a spiral stair in a turret corbelled out in the angle between it and another wing to the east. A similar stair led off the main staircase to serve the bedrooms over the hall. The castle was refortified by Ludlow in 1652. It was burnt in 1689, but was restored and inhabited until c1820.

CASTLE CALDWELL *Fermanagh* H0261

Much of the present heavily overgrown ruin dates from the 1790s but the west front has a pair of two storey 17th century flankers bristling with gunports. The house was originally called Rossbeg and was built by Sir Francis Blennerhasset in 1612. It was renamed after being sold in 1671 to Sir James Caldwell, an Enniskillen merchant created a baronet in 1683. In the early 19th century it passed by marriage to the Bloomfields, who were in residence until a fire c1905.

CASTLE CARRA *Antrim* D2533

Two unvaulted storeys remain of this early 16th century MacDonnell tower, said to have been the scene where they murdered Sean The Proud O'Neill of Tyrone in 1567. It measures 8.5m by 6m over walls 1.4m thick above a substantial battered base. The stair, if there was one, must have been in the destroyed corner.

CASTLE CAULFIELD *Tyrone* H7563 A.M.

All that remains of the O'Donellys' 16th century bawn is the gatehouse with small guard rooms either side of a passage 6.9m long by 2.7m wide with three murder holes in the vault. The west guard room has a fireplace and had a timber stair in a round turret to a lost upper storey. The gate adjoins the survivor of two large wings of Sir Toby Caulfield's three storey stronghouse of 1611-19 described by Pynnar as the "fairest building in the North". Most of the mullion and transom windows have been torn out and the openings blocked up and fireplaces in projecting breasts have been similarly treated. Patrick O'Donelly burnt the house in 1641. It was restored in the 1660s by the Caulfields, then Viscounts Charlemont, but was ruined again by c1760.

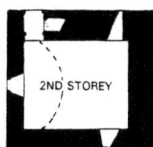

Plans of Castle Ward

Plan of Castle Chichester

CASTLE CHICHESTER *Antrim* J4892

The plain three storey tower built by Sir Moses Hill c1604 is roughly a cube of 8.4m. It cannot be entered as the windows of the lowest two storeys and the doorway with a machicolation above have all been blocked up in recent times.

CASTLEDERG *Tyrone* H2684

Only the east gable of the stronghouse and the loopholed north wall with two square flankers remain of the bawn 34.5m long by 30m wide built by Sir John Davies c1612. The flankers, plus a second enclosure to the south, were added slightly later. It withstood attacks by Sir Phelim O'Neill in 1641 but the damage then done to it was never repaired.

Castle Ward

CASTLE WARD *Down* J5750

This derelict but otherwise complete tower lies among the service buildings of an 18th century mansion now administered by the National Trust. The tower was built in 1610 by Nicholas Ward, a Cheshire man who obtained a government position in Ireland late in Elizabeth I's reign. It measures 8.6m by 7.8m and rises almost 15m to the top of the double stepped battlements. A brick arch has been made into the basement. The original entrance, a gothic arch with the pock marking more usual in Connacht and Munster and protected by a machicolation from the parapet, is at the level of the vaulted loft forming the second storey. From there straight stairs lead up to the hall and bedroom. Access down to the cellar could only have been by means of a ladder.

CHARLEMONT *Armagh* H8655

This fort was begun during Lord Mountjoy's campaign of 1602 against Hugh O'Neill. It was completed in 1624, but was extended in 1673, and the surviving gateway is probably late 18th century. It bears the arms of the Caulfields who lived in a fine three storey house with canted bay windows within the fort, and took their later title from it. The fort was captured by Sir Phelim O'Neill in 1641 and it was not recaptured until the Cromwellian commander Venables took it in 1650. Williamite forces led by the Duke of Schomberg stormed the fort in 1690. It continued to hold a garrison until 1858. The house and a later barrack block were demolished in 1922 after being burnt.

CLOUGH *Antrim* H3405

The de Mandevilles motte and bailey castle on a basalt outcrop was later refortified in stone by the MacQuillans. It passed to the Mac Donnells, and was rebuilt in the early 17th century as a Plantation stronghouse. It was captured by the Catholics in 1641 and destroyed during the Cromwellian campaign of 1650. Few traces remain.

CLOUGH   *Down*   J4120   A.M.

On the summit 24m diameter summit of the fine motte, which has a worn bean shaped bailey platform 20m by 34m to the south and a ditch with a counterscarp, is a tiny two storey late 13th century tower just 6.8m by 4.1m over walls 0.9m thick. In the 17th century it was extended by a wing 3.4m deep with two double splayed loopholes. Coins of King John's reign were found on the top during excavations.

CLOUGHOUGHTER   *Cavan*   H8655

The O'Reillys built this round keep on a crannog perhaps in the 13th century. They later transferred to Tullymongan Castle. The northern part stands high and has a round arched entrance formerly defended by a wooden brattice in a gap in the stone parapet and holes for three wooden floors. Here in 1641 Bishop Bedell was imprisoned by the rebel Irish Catholics whose General Eoghan Rua O'Neill died at the castle in 1649.

CORRATRASNA   *Fermanagh*   H2730

The ruined gables and footings of the side walls remain of a two storey stronghouse probably built by the Balfours c1610. It measures 10.8m by 4.8m inside and has fireplaces at each level and gunloops on the upper storey.

CREVENISH   *Fermanagh*   H1662

At the NW corner of Thomas Blennerhasset's three storey stronghouse of c1615 is a tower with gunloops and an acute outermost angle. There are slight remains of a second such tower embedded in farm buildings to the NE and it is likely that there were once a full set of four, those by the house being of four storeys, and those on the bawn wall being just of two or three storeys. In 1641 Crevenish was the home of Lady Deborah Blennerhasset and her second husband Captain Rory Maguire who destroyed many of his Protestant neighbours' houses in the Catholic revolt that year.

CROM   *Fermanagh*   H3624

In the garden adjoining the house of 1834 are ruins of two towers, one square and the other round, plus other traces of a stronghouse begun in 1611 by Michael Balfour. According to the surveyor Captain Pynnar the bawn was 61 feet square with a wall 12 feet high. It was sold to Sir Stephen Butler in 1619, and to Abraham Crichton of Aghalane c1660. In 1689 the castle was twice besieged by the Jacobites. It accidentally caught fire in 1764 whilst the Crichtons were at a neighbouring house.

CURRAN (OLDERFLETE)   *Down*   D4102   A.M.

There were originally three towers guarding Larne harbour. Two of them were called Curran and Olderflete and there is confusion as to which one has survived. The basement of the three storey tower 10.6m square over walls 2m thick was later subdivided and given barrel vaults and an oven. Some of the double splayed loops were blocked in the process. The entrance gave onto the foot of a straight stair in one of two walls now destroyed down to their foundations.

DALWAYS   *Antrim*   J4491

The bawn is named after John Dalloway, who built it in 1609. The house has been replaced by a clutter of farm buildings but the bawn wall 0.9m thick and 5m high enclosing a rectangle 33m by 40m is one of the best preserved in Ulster. Three of the corners have ruined flankers 5.5m in diameter, two of which have three storeys of rooms with renewed mullioned windows which were connected by wooden stairs in square diagonally placed turrets on the inside. There is a ring above the entrance.

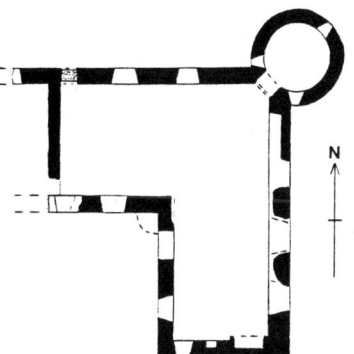

Plan of Derrywoone Castle

Clough Castle, Co Down

DERRYWOONE *Tyrone* H3784

This L-plan house of three storeys plus attics dates from c1625. The main block, which contains a kitchen at ground level, originally extended beyond the crosswall now forming the west end. There are no other crosswalls, vaults, or pistol holes, despite the provision of a round tower on the outermost angle. A stair leading from the hall and drawing room to the bedrooms is corbelled out over the re-entrant angle.

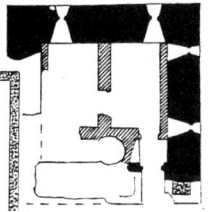

Plan of Curran Castle

Dalway's Bawn

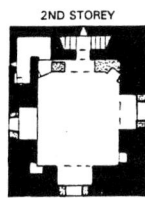

Keep, Doe Castle

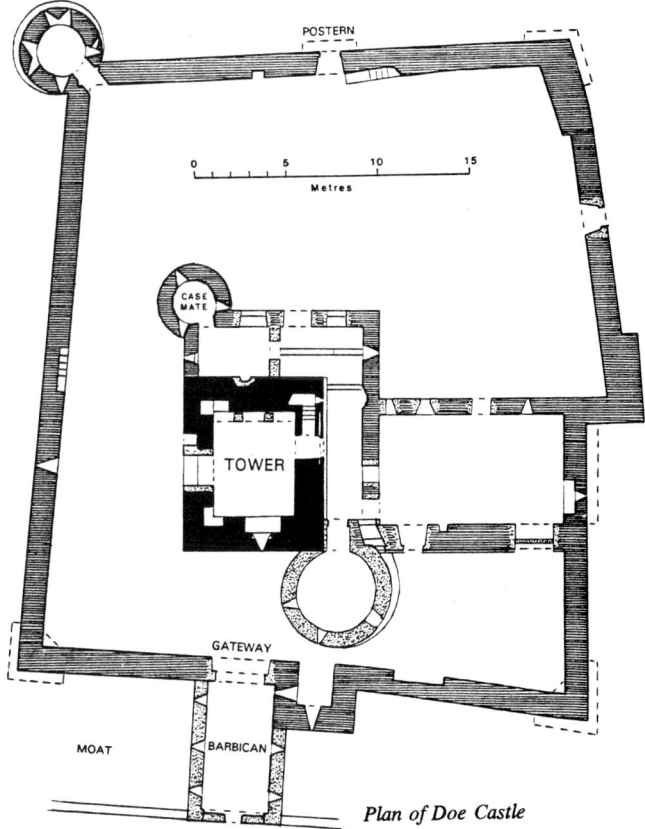

Plan of Doe Castle

DOE *Donegal* B0832 A.M.

This is the most interesting and complete of the tower-and-bawn type castles of the native Irish chiefs of Ulster. The tower, 9.2m by 7.6m over walls 1.6m thick, rising through four unvaulted storeys connected by straight stairs in the north and east walls to a level wall-head (originally there was a gabled attic) 16.5m above ground, is thought to have been built by the Quin family c1520-35. It is first mentioned in 1544 in connection with the struggles between the sons of MacSweeney of Tuatha. This family added the narrow building which extends around the south and east sides of the tower with a beehive slab-roofed casemate at the NE corner with musket loops. An apartment 10m long by 5.7m wide on the south side, presumably a hall block, connects with a curtain wall 1.3m thick probably of c1570-80 surrounding the tower. This bawn wall, although somewhat rebuilt in the 17th and 19th centuries has a rectangular turret beside the rebuilt gateway in the middle of the west side and at the NE corner a steeply battered round turret 4.5m in diameter bristling with musket loops. At the other three corners and in the middle of the south and east sides are machicolations (the latter protects a postern facing the sea), and straight flights of steps on the east and north lead up to the wall walk.

Doe Castle was taken over for the English Crown c1600 by Eoghan Og MacSweeney. He resisted attacks by his brother Rory and Red Hugh O'Donnell. The castle was granted to Rory O'Donnell c1603, but was recaptured by the MacSweeneys in 1606. In 1608 it was taken by Sir Cahir O'Doherty and used as a base for an attack on Derry. The MacSweeneys were back in possession from 1641 until Sir Charles Coote took the place by a surprise attack in 1650. Colonel Myles MacSweeney was defeated by Coote after he weakened his army by detaching 1,400 men from his Catholic army in an attempt to recapture the castle. Doe contained a royal garrison during Charles II's reign, but the MacSweeneys captured it in support of James II in 1689, only to be dispossessed soon afterwards. The castle lay in ruins during the 18th century but in the early 1800s was restored as a residence for Captain George Vaughan Harte whose arms appear over the inner doorway. Many of the features of the tower and the adjoining apartments, and perhaps all of the round tower added to the tower house SW corner, plus parts of the bawn, especially the parapet, date from this period. It remained occupied until c1900.

Doe Castle

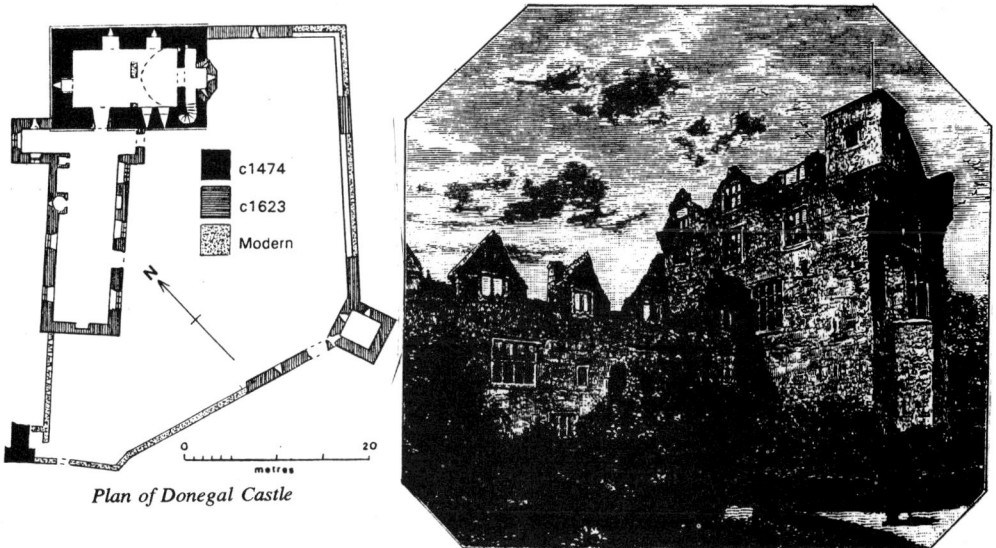

Plan of Donegal Castle

Donegal Castle

DONEGAL   *Donegal*   G9377   A.M.*

Donegal was the chief seat of the O'Donnells, originally Kings of Tyrconnell. Hugh O'Donnell and Nuala O'Brien are thought to have begun the large tower house in the 1470s. It measures 16.6m by 10.6m over walls 2.3m thick. The vaulted basement was entered through a narrow lobby in the thick SE wall off which led a spiral stair. Of the 1560s are the doorway from the stair to the hall above with ferns in the spandrels of the four-centred arch, and a similarly designed fireplace now hanging in space. In 1591 the English occupied the town and fortified the friary and in 1595 Red Hugh O'Donnell is said to have burnt the castle to prevent it being occupied. In 1603 James I recognised Red Hugh O'Donnell as Earl of Tyrconnell but the latter found his position untenable and he fled to Spain in 1607. Sir Basil Brooke was then granted the Friary, and in 1616 he was given a lease, later converted to ownership, of the town and derelict castle. He restored the castle, remodelling the upper parts of the tower, adding a pleasant adjoining three storey manor house with a wing facing the field, and rebuilding the bawn. The latter is much ruined but preserves two loopholes, and the gateway with an adjoining square tower. The original tower doorway was blocked by the base of a bay window opening off the hall and a new doorway was forced through towards the entrance passage of the manor house, on the other side of which was a kitchen. The tower hall was given a splendid new fireplace c1625 with the arms of Sir Basil and his wife Anne Leycester. The two upper storeys were entirely rebuilt with three light mullion-and-transom windows matching those of the manor house. The top storey was within the multi-gabled roof and has two rather ugly square bartizans at the SE end. The tower and house are now being re-roofed by the Irish Board of Works.

DOWNPATRICK   *Down*   J4845   A.M.

This was the seat of Rory Mac Donlevy, King of Ulster, which John de Courcy took in a surprise attack in 1177. An attempt at recapture was crushed with heavy losses. The large pear shaped bailey 165m long by 120m wide with a huge rampart on the landward SE side may represent the original fort but the large motte must be the work of de Courcy. It has its own ditch and is somewhat collapsed on the NW side.

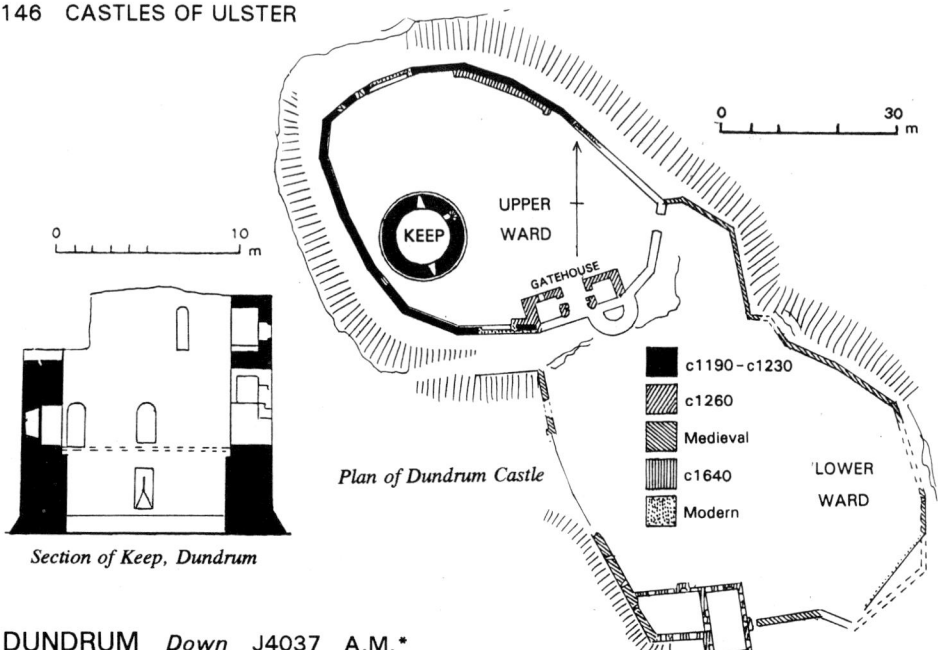

UPPER WARD

KEEP

GATEHOUSE

Plan of Dundrum Castle

c1190–c1230

c1260

Medieval

c1640

Modern

LOWER WARD

Section of Keep, Dundrum

DUNDRUM *Down* J4037 A.M.*

The 1m thick wall of the oval upper ward 56m long by 40m wide was probably built by John de Courcy in the 1190s. He was dispossessed by Hugh de Lacy in 1204 but attempted to recover the castle by force in 1205. King John captured the castle in 1210. The four storey round tower keep 14m high by 14.6m diameter over walls 2m thick above the plinth probably dates from immediately after the castle was granted to Hugh de Lacy, Earl of Ulster in 1227. The original entrance was at hall level from which a spiral stair led down but a new doorway into the basement was made during 15th century remodelling of the topmost storey. Expenditure recorded in the 1260s may refer to the building of the gatehouse which has twin square guard chambers flanking a passage. In front of the eastern part was a half-round tower. There was no twin because the entrance was approached at an oblique angle from the west around the rock face. The wall of the outer bailey extending down the hillside for 67m to the SE is thin except on the vulnerable west side where it has its own entrance. It could be of any period from the late 13th century to the end of the medieval era. The castle was said to be ruinous in 1333 and was taken over by a native Irish family, the Magennises. It was captured from them by Lord Grey in 1538. Felim Magennis surrendered it to the English Crown in 1610, and in 1636 it was granted to Sir Francis Blundell, who built the L-shaped house in the SW corner of the lower ward. The Magennises recovered the castle during the revolt of 1641 but it was slighted by the Cromwellians in 1652. See colour pictures on page 87.

DUNGANNON *Tyrone* H8062

In the 13th century the O'Neills moved from the drystone fort of the Grianan above Derry to Dungannon which became the centre of their kingdom of Tyrone. They eventually built a castle which was captured c1498 by the 8th Earl of Kildare and demolished in 1590 by the O'Donnells. In 1607 Dungannon was granted to Sir Arthur Chichester who removed what was left of the old castle and built a bawn 36m square with four flankers. It was captured by the O'Neills in 1641, and was destroyed in 1646. A round tower of Thomas Knox Harrington's mansion of c1790 lies on the site.

DUNGIVEN   *Londonderry*   C6908   A.M.

Nothing remains of the principal castle of the O'Kanes (O'Cahans) at Dungiven. James I's bawn, originally called The King's House and later granted to the Skinners' Company, is the largest of its type in Ireland, being 60m long by 48m wide. Half of the east wall 0.8m thick and 4m high with a modern gateway, and part of the west wall and square NW flanker remain. Upper firing embrasures were served by a platform on arches, the last remains of which were removed in 1972. A house of 1839 lies on the south side. In 1982 excavations at the nearby priory revealed footings of a second house and bawn built by Sir Edward Doddington before 1611. He built a house beside the church tower with a wing facing west and a bawn to the east, where the cloister lay. The house was captured in 1641 by the Irish and later burnt down accidentally.

DUNLUCE   *Antrim*   C9041   A.M.*

The castle has a very strong site on a rock which is pierced by a natural cave at sea level in which galleys could be concealed. Two round towers about 9m in diameter on the east side and the 1.8m thick landward facing south wall are evidently relics of a castle built c1300 by Richard de Burgh, Earl of Ulster, or one of his followers although it is not mentioned in any records until the early 16th century when it was the seat of the MacQuillans. The towers have doorways at ground level and stairs curving round with the walls to reach the upper storeys. The northern tower overlies a souterrain or rock cut hiding place of the Early Christian period, proof of early usage of the site.

The castle passed to Somhairle Buidhe MacDonnell who surrendered it to Sean The Proud O'Neill in 1565, but recovered it when the latter was murdered in 1567. The English Lord Deputy, Sir John Perrot, besieged and captured the castle in 1584 doing great damage to it with "a culverin and two shakers of brass". The landward facing wall was mostly rebuilt after the siege, being provided with two large cannon ports with an open loggia behind, and a new gatehouse with a passageway flanked by a long guard room and conical roofed bartizans on the outer corners was built at the SW corner. The large unfortified outer court providing extra accommodation, offices, and outbuildings on the mainland may also be as early as this period.

Dunluce Castle

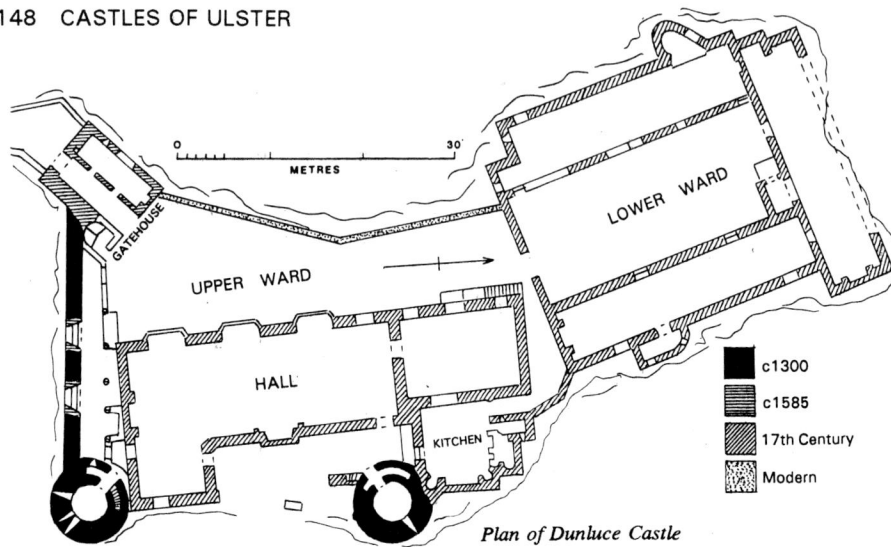

Plan of Dunluce Castle

Somhairle's son Sir Randal remained loyal to the English Crown and was rewarded with large estates and titles, notably that of Earl of Antrim granted in 1620. At Dunluce he built a huge new hall 28m long by 10m wide with three westward facing bay windows in the main courtyard. A buttery adjoins to the north with a kitchen east of it in a wing and there is a balancing SE wing at the other end of the hall. Further north a lower yard was created with long ranges of offices, workshops, and lodgings on the west, east, and north sides. It was probably the north wall of the latter that collapsed in 1639, killing several of the servants. The castle was besieged by the rebel Irish in 1641 and in 1642 the Scottish Covenanter General Monroe arrested the 2nd Earl of Antrim whilst being entertained here, and carried him off to Carrickfergus. The castle was subsequently little used. A new house further inland was begun at the insistence of the 2nd Earl's wife, who disliked the noise of the sea. It may never have been used and little or nothing of it remains. See colour picture on page 88.

DUNSEVERICK *Antrim* C9844

Occupying the narrow neck of a small coastal promontory with footings of a thin breastwork around a bawn 13m long is a ruined 16th century tower measuring 6.7m by 6.0m over walls 1.3m thick. It was held by the O'Kanes under the MacQuillans, and was captured in 1565 by Sean The Proud O'Neill. Giolla O'Kane was executed in 1653 by the Cromwellians and his castle was dismantled and not used again.

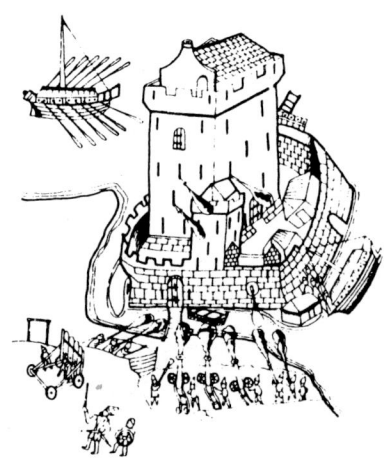

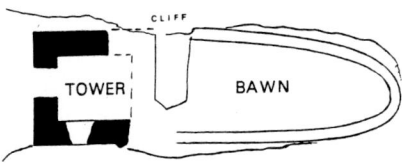

Plan of Dunseverick Castle

Old Sketch of Enniskillen Castle

Water Gate, Enniskillen

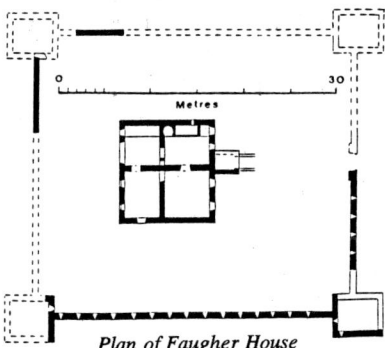

Plan of Faugher House

ENNISKILLEN   *Fermanagh*   H2144   A.M.*

A drawing made by a soldier during the siege of 1595 when Captain John Dowdall captured the castle shows a bawn beside the River Erne with a large four storey tower house with an attic inside the battlements on the east side and a smaller tower flanking the gateway on the north. All that remains of the castle at it then stood, which is thought to have been built by Hugh Maguire "The Hospitable" c1415-20 to help consolidate the Maguire hold on Fermanagh, is part of the massively walled basement of the tower house. It is first mentioned in 1439 when the chief of the clan was taken prisoner here. The Maguires recaptured the castle in 1595, and lost it once more before the water-borne attack of 1602 by Niall Garbh O'Donnell during which it was wrecked. In 1607 Enniskillen was granted to Captain William Cole who built a new stronghouse on what was left of the tower house, and rebuilt the bawn wall to a height of 7.8m with a wall-walk and flankers. The family lived alongside the castle in a timber framed house. In c1615-20 he added the so-called Watergate, a rectangular tower containing a well and having a pair of lofty conical roofed round bartizans corbelled out from the outer face, in which there is now no sign of a gateway. Cole was knighted in 1618 and managed to hold out against Rory Maguire in 1641. The castle also held out against James II's Lord Lieutenant Tyrconnell in 1690. The castle was refurbished as a barracks from 1796, the main block being mostly rebuilt and much of the bawn wall removed.

FAUGHER (WRAY CASTLE)   *Donegal*   C0535

Tirlogh Oge O'Boyle's house and bawn of c1611 were confiscated after the 1641 rebellion and given to Sir John Stephens and Hugh Hamill. They acquired an alternative name of Wray Castle after being sold in 1700 to William Wray of Ards. A nearly square unfortified house of three low storeys divided by crosswalls into four unequal parts with part of a porch remaining on the south side lies in the middle of a rectangular bawn 34m by 29m with a loopholed wall 0.7m thick and 2.9m high. The wall is fragmentary except on the west side and has traces of four rectangular corner flankers each measuring about 5.5m by 5.0m.

FAVOUR ROYAL   *Tyrone*   H6354

Defaced ivy-mantled walls 0.9m thick with four round flankers 4.2m diameter with five musket loops remain of George Ridgeway's 24m square bawn of 1611. It passed to his brother Thomas and was later transferred to Sir James Erskine, the name commemorating Charles I's charter ratifying the agreement. It was abandoned in 1670. See plan on page 21.

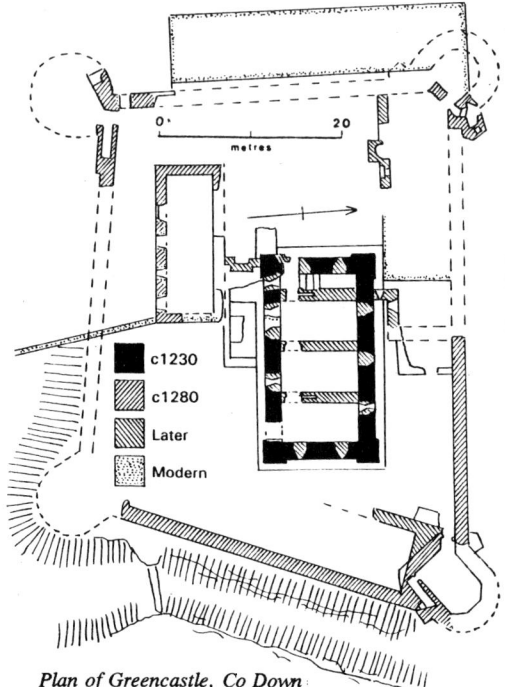

Interior of the Keep, Greencastle, Co Down   *Plan of Greencastle, Co Down*

GREENCASTLE *Down* J2861 A.M.*

The mound of the timber earliest castle here lies near the end of the peninsular. The keep was probably built by Henry III c1220-40. Repairs to it are recorded in 1252 and 1260. It was probably when the castle was restored after being wrecked by the local Irish in the latter year that the stone walled court about 47m by 37m with D-shaped corner towers and a rock cut ditch was added around the keep. The Crown entrusted the keeping of Greencastle to the de Burgh Earls of Ulster. It was the original home of Elizabeth, second wife of Robert Bruce, King of Scotland, although that did not prevent Edward Bruce from capturing and wrecking the castle in 1316. It was wrecked again by the Magennis family in 1375. The FitzGerald Earls of Kildare were later keepers until their downfall in 1534. By 1547 it was in a decayed condition but it was later granted to the Baganals by whom the castle was remodelled as a residence.

The whole of the SE corner tower and most of the adjacent walls have vanished and only fragments and foundations partly muddled up with farm buildings remain of the rest of the outer defences. One outbuilding south of the keep is still roofed but is much rebuilt. The roofless keep survives almost complete. It measures 21.3m by 11.9m over walls 1.8m thick. The basement was originally a single dark room reached only from the hall above but was given crosswalls, vaults, double splayed loops, and a new entrance with a gunloop in the 16th century. The hall probably originally had a private bedroom divided off at the east end where there is a latrine in one corner. The big fireplace, the wide straight stair down to the basement, and the very large window openings are all 16th century. A spiral stair by the original westward facing entrance leads to the battlements where the clasping buttresses of the corners continue up as turrets. See pictures on pages 8 and 88.

Greencastle, Co Donegal

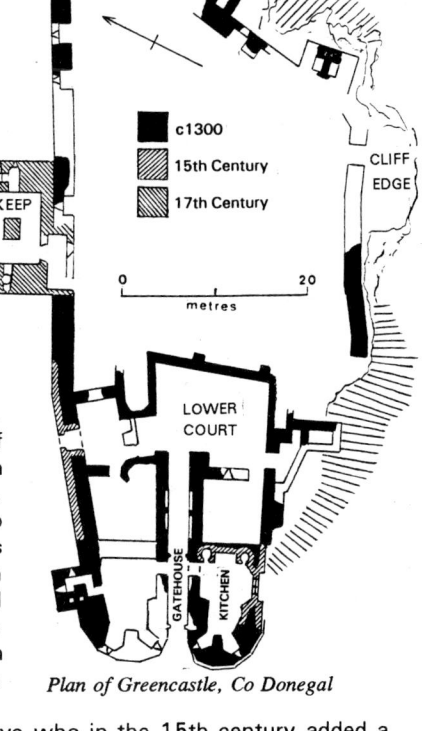

TOWER

c1300

15th Century

17th Century

CLIFF EDGE

KEEP

0   20

metres

LOWER COURT

GATEHOUSE

KITCHEN

GREENCASTLE *Donegal* H6540

This building, also called Northburg or Newcastle, was begun in 1305 by Richard de Burgo, Earl of Ulster to subdue the O'Neills and O'Donnells. In 1316 the castle was captured by Edward Bruce, brother of Robert, King of Scotland. It reverted to the Earl after Bruce, then King of Ireland, was killed in 1318. Richard's grandson William captured his kinsman Walter Burke in 1332 and starved him to death in Greencastle. In revenge the Burkes murdered Earl William at Belfast in 1333. As a direct result of this Norman influence in western Ulster declined considerably.

Plan of Greencastle, Co Donegal

Greencastle was taken over by the O'Dohertys who in the 15th century added a large tower house which greatly strengthened the landward side. In 1555 the castle was wrecked by Calbhach O'Donnell who ravaged the Inishowen peninsular with Scottish auxiliaries after quarrelling with his father. It was not properly repaired until after 1608 when the castle was captured from the O'Dohertys and granted to Sir Arthur Chichester. It was garrisoned until at least the 1690s. A new fort to the east took over its former role of protecting the narrow entrance to Lough Foyle in 1812.

The castle has an irregularly shaped court 30m wide protected by cliffs to the south and east and extending 59m from the back of a gatehouse with twin polygonal fronted towers to the straight inner wall, now only footings, of a large polygonal NE tower of irregular plan. A square latrine turret lies on the north side of the gatehouse and there is another at the SE corner of the court. All the parts are very ruined. Behind the gatehouse, which seems to have contained the main apartments, were service rooms and a small lower court. In the 17th century a new kitchen was created in the room flanking the south side of the entrance passage, which has a vaulted basement below it, and a low parapet replaced a part of the outer wall of the NE tower which had fallen or been destroyed. The tower house built over and against the north curtain wall facing flat ground measures 14m by 13m over walls 3.2m thick. There is a large square central pier to help support the floor of the upper storey which has embrasures giving access to a latrine and a well. The entrance was at this level.

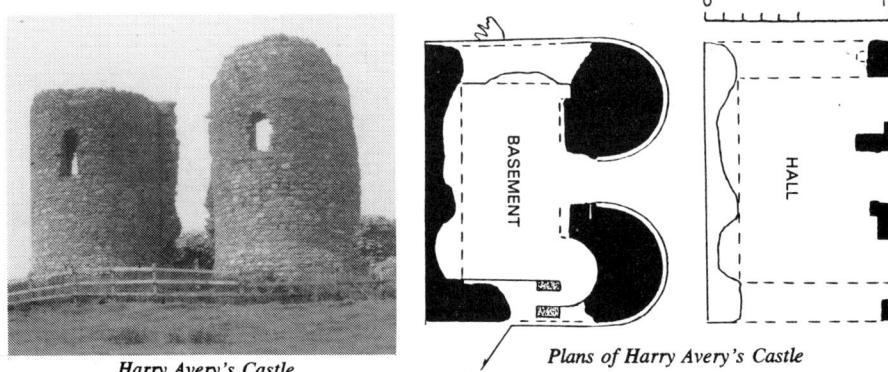

Harry Avery's Castle

Plans of Harry Avery's Castle

HARRY AVERY'S   *Tyrone*   H3985   A.M.

The name is corrupted from that of the builder, Henry Aimbredh O'Neill, who died in 1392. Foundations of a polygonal court about 35m across crown a knoll. On one side is what looks like a twin-round towered gatehouse 15m wide with walls 2m thick. However the entrance led simply into a dead end basement with a solid wall against the knoll and only a narrow mural stair led to the courtyard and the hall above. The towers have square rooms with windows at hall level, but are solid below. There was probably a third storey above. The castle was dismantled by the English for the sake of its materials in 1609.

INCH   *Donegal*   C3222

On a rock on the south side of Inch island stands the east half of a tower and footings of a bawn built in the 1430s by Neachtan O'Donnell with the consent of his father-in-law O'Doherty of Inishowen. In 1454 the Tyrconnell lordship was disputed by two O'Donnell cousins. O'Doherty imprisoned one of them, Donnell, in Inch Castle. The other cousin, Rory, was killed by a stone thrown from the battlements when he attacked the castle. Donnell thus became lord of Tyrconnell, but was killed by Rory's brother Turlough in 1456. The castle was already ruinous by 1600 when the English devastated the island and was not restored. The tower is 9.8m wide and was probably about 14m long. A crosswall divides the vaulted basement which had sleeping lofts above the cellars. Straight stairs in the north and east walls lead to the upper storeys.

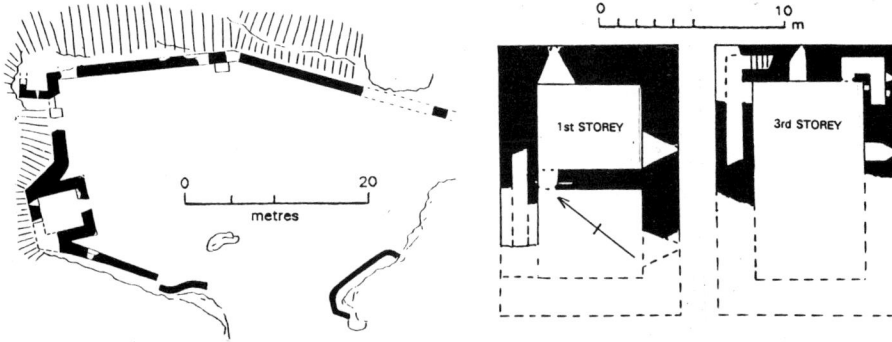

Plan of Kinbane Castle

Plans of Inch Castle

KILBARRON *Donegal* G8365

On a promontory with sheer sides 15m above the sea are slight remains of an irregularly shaped bawn 45m long by 33m wide entered through the eastern part of the basement of a tower 16.5m long by 11m wide occupying half of the neck. The rest of the basement was further subdivided and there is a projecting latrine turret at the SW corner. The castle was built in the 15th century by the O'Sgingins, hereditary historiographers of Tyrconnell. Both office and castle later passed to the O'Clerys, of which the most famous was Michael, main author of the Annals of the Four Masters.

KILCLIEF *Down* J6046

In 1441 John Cely, Bishop of Down since 1412, was deprived of his living for living in adultery in the tower. It has four storeys and measures 10.2m by 8m. Projecting from the east wall are a stair turret and a latrine turret which are joined at the top by an arch behind which is a machicolation protecting the entrance. The turret tops above the arch are restored. The west corners are also carried up as turrets, and the upper storeys have chimney breasts corbelled out of the outer walls and two light windows.

KILLYLEAGH *Down* J5253

The SW tower is said to be a relic of a late 13th century stone castle built on the site of a motte. The Mandevilles held Killyleagh from at least the 1330s until ousted by the Clannaboy O'Neills in the 16th century. In 1561 Elizabeth I granted the castle along with the barony of Dufferin to the Whytes of Dublin. They sold the castle in 1610 to Sir James Hamilton who built the core of the present house including the entrance protected by a machicolation and the bailey wall. The castle was badly damaged in 1648 when it was besieged and captured by General Monck for Cromwell. Henry Hamilton, 2nd Earl of Clanbrassil, restored the castle in 1666 when the main block was extended eastward, the SE tower added, and the bailey wall given a new parapet and square towers at either end of the south side. The subterranean dome and access passage of the bailey well also date from this period. The castle later became derelict but was restored in 1850-62 in a Rhineland style with grandiose roofs and dormers.

KINBANE *Antrim* D0944

In 1558 Colla Dubh Mac Donnell, elder brother of Somhairle Buidhe, died in his castle of Kinbane begun in 1547. A tower 6.5m square with just a single room over a basement and gables to east and west but open battlements on the other sides, plus a second smaller and more ruined tower to the west command the approach to an irregularly shaped court over 40m long by 24m wide on the neck of the headland.

Killyleagh Castle

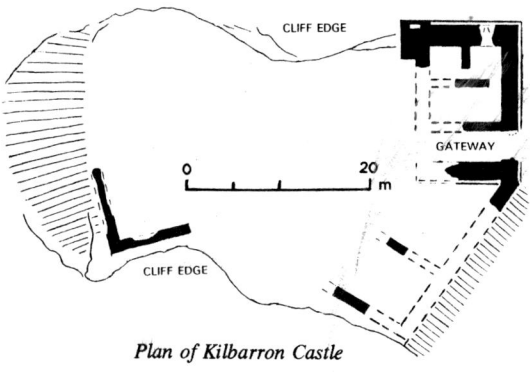

Plan of Kilbarron Castle

MACHUGH *Tyrone* H3684

A crannog bears the remains of a late 15th century tower 6m high measuring just 4.5m by 3.5m inside walls 0.9m thick with a doorway, one window, and a stepped square-corbelled roof. There are traces of a bawn to the south and east.

MAHEE *Down* J5264

A tower 12.8m by 6.7m built in 1570 by a Captain Browne guards the causeway approach to Mahee Island. The basement contained a cellar vaulted longitudinally and a smaller chamber vaulted in the other direction which may have formed a boat store or a gateway passage onto the island. A stair from the cellar leads to the hall, and a second stair in the diagonally opposite corner then leads up to a third storey probably divided into two bedrooms. The south corner and most of the adjoining sides are gone.

MONEA *Fermanagh* H1649 A.M.

The stronghouse was built c1615-18 by Malcolm Hamilton, Rector of Devenish and Chancellor of Down, and the bawn was added just prior to his elevation to the see of Cashel in 1623. It was captured during the 1641 rising but survived the war of 1688-90 when it was the home of Gustavus Hamilton, Governor of Enniskillen, and remained occupied until an accidental fire in the mid 18th century. The design of the building reflects the Scottish origin of the builder. Lying on the south side of a bawn 32m by 28m with remains of round flankers on the northern corners and footings of a barn on the west is a stronghouse 17.4m long by 8.9m wide with a pair of round towers at the west end. One contained the main stair and the entrance which is flanked by a gunloop in the other tower and connected with a passage leading past cellars for wine and food to the kitchen at the east end. The wine cellar and kitchen both have service stairs to the hall, east of which was the drawing room, placed to enjoy heat rising from the kitchen. On the third storey were three main bedrooms, two of which were reached by a continuation of the stair up from the kitchen. Only one of the two conical roofed round bartizans at the east end survives. The roof was thatched, contrary to the usual Scottish practice of slate or tile roofing. At this level there are square diagonally set caphouses corbelled out over the towers. An earlier crannog lies in the adjacent lough. See plan on page 21.

MONGAVLIN *Donegal* C3506

The rectangular stronghouse 15m long by 7.4m wide built by Sir John Stewart c1620 was used by James II as a base during the siege of Derry. It remained inhabited until the mid 19th century but is now very ruined. The gable walls 1.2m thick retain corbelling for three of the round corner bartizans and various fireplaces. The basement had a kitchen at the south end with a drawing room above opening off the main hall. Above was a storey of main bedrooms and there were servants' rooms in the attic. There were no vaults. The lower windows have marks of former iron protective grilles.

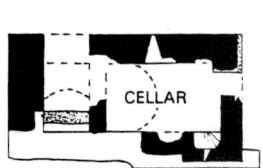
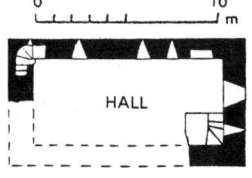

Plans of Mahee Castle

Plan of Mongavelin Castle

MOUNTJOY *Tyrone* H9069 A.M.

This was a government fort begun at the end of Elizabeth I's reign rather than a private stronghouse and was named after her Viceroy Lord Mountjoy. It was captured by Sir Phelim O'Neill's forces in 1641, burnt in 1642, restored by the English the same year, but vacated and burnt by them in 1644. It was granted to the Earl of Dartmouth in 1683 and was garrisoned throughout William III's reign. The outworks have gone but the main block stands two storeys high. It originally measured 6m square inside and has four corner towers 3.6m square inside but with the outer walls carried to a salient angle so that each tower flanks the outer faces of the next two with gunports.

MOYRY *Armagh* J5715

The small ruined three storey tower with rounded corners standing in a corner of a now fragmentary bawn was built in 1601 by Lord Mountjoy to command the road from Dundalk in Co Louth to Newry.

NARROW WATER *Down* J1319 A.M.*

This castle protecting the entrance to a long narrow arm of Carlingford Lough is thought to have been built by the English c1560 but soon passed to the Magennises of Iveagh. After James II's defeat in 1691 it was confiscated and granted to the Halls. A tower 11.2m by 10.1m over walls 2m thick with three storeys and an attic within the wall-walk, off which is a machicolation defending the entrance, stands within a quadrangular bawn roughly 36m square with a wall 0.6m thick, 2m high in the inside, but rather more on the outside where it rises from the shore. The wall has a projection towards the lough on the south side and a modern gateway on the north side.

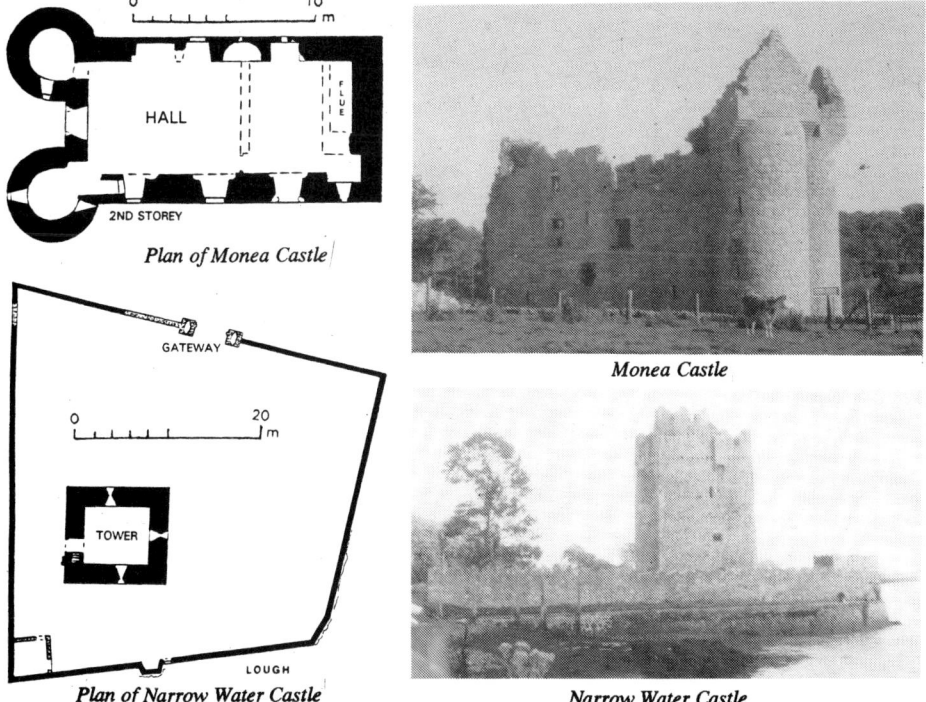

Plan of Monea Castle

Monea Castle

Plan of Narrow Water Castle

Narrow Water Castle

PORTAFERRY   *Down*   J5951

Above the harbour is a ruined 16th century tower of three unvaulted storeys with a stair wing projecting on the south side. The east corner has fallen. A machicolation defends the entrance. The tower is now being repaired. It belonged to the Savages.

PORTORA   *Fermanagh*   H2245

Despite damage caused by an explosion made by boys of Portora School in 1859 and gales of 1894 three quarters of Sir William Cole's bawn of c1615 remains complete. It measures 21.5m by 17.9m inside walls 0.9m thick with a round gunlooped flanker 4.8m in diameter at each corner. Little remains of the house 6.8m wide occupying the western third of the bawn apart from a large fireplace, presumably that of the kitchen.

QUOILE   *Down*   J5047   A.M.

This ruined 16th century tower 10.8m by 8.1m has recently been repaired and made safe following the collapse of one of the upper corners. The basement is divided into two vaulted cellars with numerous gunloops. From the entrance a straight stair in the east wall leads to the second storey, also subdivided, from which a stair in the north wall rises to the main room on the third storey which had wooden lintelled windows.

RAPHOE   *Donegal*   C2603

Bishop John Leslie's palace of the 1630s is a block 16m square with a partly destroyed spine wall thickened to contain a huge kitchen fireplace at ground level. There are four boldly projecting corner towers nearly square but with the outermost angle acute in which are a few pistol loops. The palace was besieged by the rebel Irish in 1641, captured by Cromwellian forces in 1650, and plundered by James II's troops in 1688. Large new windows were inserted in the mid 18th century, and a brick vault was inserted in the base of one of the towers to create a strongroom or ice-house. William Bisset, the last Bishop, added the embattled fourth storey with bartizans on the outermost corners. Shortly after the Protestant diocese was united with Derry in 1835 the palace was burnt down by a would-be tenant in the hope of obtaining a cheaper lease of the lands.

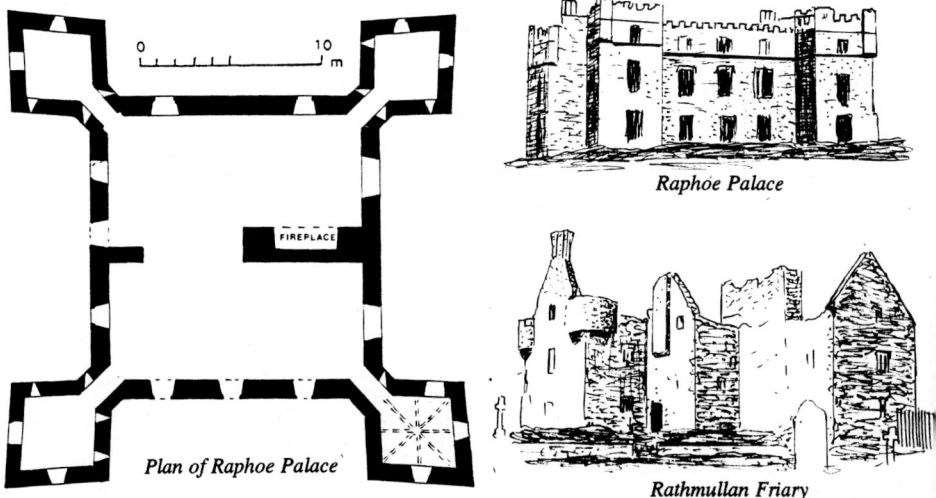

Raphoe Palace

Plan of Raphoe Palace

Rathmullan Friary

Plans of Ringhaddy Castle

Plan of Quoile Castle   Plan of Red Bay Castle

Ringhaddy Castle

RATHMULLAN   *Donegal*   C3027

A 16th century military map shows to the SW of the friary a now vanished castle which was captured by the O'Donnells in 1516. In 1587 Red Hugh O'Donnell was captured here by the English when he was lured aboard a ship to sample wines. In 1603 the friary was granted by James I to Sir James Fullerton who allowed Sir Ralph Bingley to use the building as a barracks. In 1617 it was obtained by Andrew Knox, Protestant Bishop of Raphoe, and the nave and south transept of the church were converted into an L-shaped three storey stronghouse, round bartizans being added to the nave west gable. The east end was retained unaltered as a chapel, and the thin original central tower still divides it off. A projection between the nave and transept contained a wooden scale and platt staircase and has over the entrance a stone with the bishop's initials, the date 1618, and a machicolation above.

RED BAY   *Antrim*   D2426

A Bissett motte above the coast road bears fragments of a tower of three low storeys about 12.6m long by 7.8m wide with a crudely built bawn roughly 12m square to the west. An outer bawn lay on the site of the bailey. The site was refortified by Sir James Mac Donnell in 1561 but was ravaged by Sean The Proud O'Neill in 1565. So the ruins are may be what Somhairle Buidhe Mac Donnell built from 1568 onwards. The castle was dismantled in 1597 by his elder son James, but the younger son Randal restored it in 1604. It was destroyed by the garrison of Carrickfergus in 1652.

RINGHADDY   *Down*   J5459

Ringhaddy belonged to the Mandevilles from the 13th century to the 16th when it passed to the Whytes, from whom it went to the Hamiltons in the 17th century. It has a motte and a ruined 15th century castle in the form of a block 11.5m by 8.3m with square projecting turrets at diagonally opposite corners containing the now broken down spiral stair and the latrines. The cellar vault was either never built or has been removed. The walls above are slightly thicker than below, suggesting rebuilding or a change in design. The hall has a big fireplace and several altered windows. There were bedrooms above and then attics within gabled roofs rising direct from the outer walls although battlements with open wall-walks must have been intended originally.

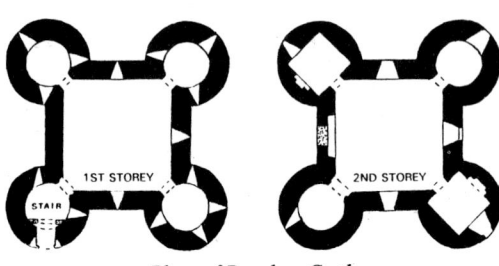

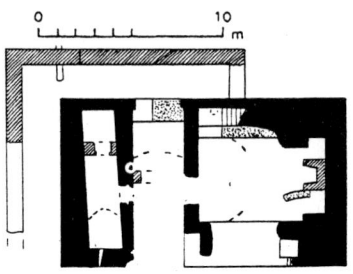

Plans of Roughan Castle   *Plan of Skettrick Castle*

ROUGHAN   *Tyrone*   H8268

Sir Andrew Stewart's ruined stronghouse of 1618 now lies on the lawn of a later house. It later belonged to Sir Phelim O'Neill who was captured on a nearby crannog in 1653 and hanged in Dublin. The house measures 6m square inside walls 1m thick and has four round corner towers, one of which the west one contained the entrance and staircase. The south tower contains a vaulted strongroom. It and the north tower contain rectangular rooms with fireplaces on the second and third storeys. The third storey is distinguished by moulded string courses at top and bottom and an arch connects the south and east towers at that level. The south tower has a scar of the former adjoining bawn wall.

SALTERSTOWN   *Londonderry*   H9582

One of the unusually large 8.3m diameter flankers set at diagonally opposite corners is mostly destroyed. Otherwise the loopholed bawn wall built by the Salters's Company of London c1615 to guard a port on Lough Neagh survives intact apart from the entrance. The inner wall of the house is destroyed. It was later made a T-plan by adding on a wing, probably for a timber scale-and-platt stair, on the outer side.

SEAFIN   *Down*   J2239

On a hillock opposite an earlier motte are remains of a stone castle built in 1252 by the English Justiciar Maurice Fitzgerald. It was captured and wrecked by Brian O'Neill of Tyrone in 1253 and not restored until after his death at the battle of Down in 1260. It was probably later occupied by the Magennis family.

SKETTRICK   *Down*   J5363

The MacQuillans' tower by the causeway approach to Skettrick Island was seized by the Clannaboy O'Neills but was returned by Henry O'Neill in 1470. Access to the island was by a 2.7m wide passageway through the base of the tower with a narrow vaulted guardroom on one side and a kitchen, now lacking its vault, on the other. A mural stair in the wall facing the island led up to two upper storeys, now very ruined because the wall facing the causeway which contained their latrines has fallen. In the 16th century the passageway was blocked, a small bawn of which parts remain was built around the tower and the inner end of the guard room walled off as a prison.

STRANGFORD   *Down*   J5950   A.M.*

A squat 16th century tower 7.5m square over walls 1m thick guards the ferry port. There are three storeys without vaults and there was probably once an attic within the battlements. A machicolation at the top defends the entrance. There are no stone stairs and communication between the storeys was by wooden steps and hatchways.

TERMON   *Donegal*   G1066

This castle was built c1615 by James MacGrath, son of a Catholic Bishop of Down, who adopted Protestantism in 1567 and held the Archbishopric of Cashel from 1571 to 1603. It has lain in ruins since Colonel Henry Ireton demolished much of the landward facing sides of the tower and bawn with cannonfire in 1650. The tower measures 11.7m by 9.4m over steeply battered walls 2.0m thick as the base. A round turret contains a stair connecting the three upper storeys, the upper two of which have two and three light windows. The turret base is solid and access from the entrance in an end wall to the foot of the main stair was by a timber stair within the cellar. None of the storeys is vaulted. At the summit are square machicolated bartizans on pyramidal corbels and stepped battlements. The bawn is 27m wide and extends 19m north of the tower. The east side extends down to enclose the tower doorway. The loopholed wall is 0.9m thick and has round flankers on the north corners.

TULLY   *Fermanagh*   H1357   A.M.

Sir John Hume's stronghouse has been ruined since Christmas Day 1641 when Rory Maguire captured it and slaughtered most of those within. The house is T-shaped with a wing containing the entrance and a former scale-and-platt stair on the south side. It is 15m long by 7m wide and contains a vaulted basement with a huge kitchen fireplace at the east end, a hall above with the drawing room over the kitchen, and then there were a series of bedrooms in the roof. The bawn to the south, described by Pynnar in 1619 as 100ft square with a 14ft high wall with four rectangular flankers, is very ruined except for the NE flanker. The bawn has recently been excavated and cleared.

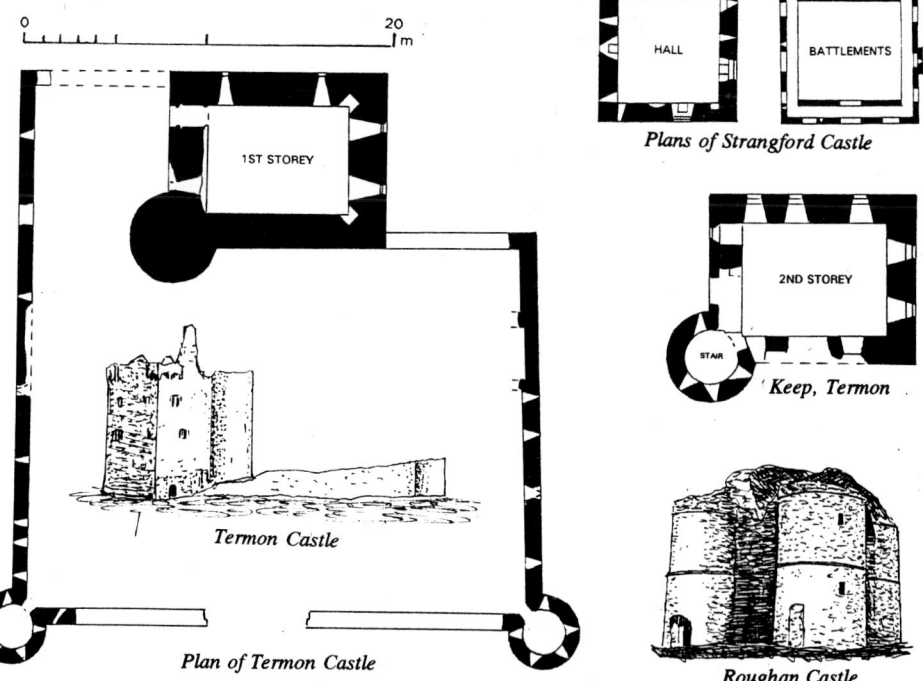

Plans of Strangford Castle

Keep, Termon

Termon Castle

Plan of Termon Castle

Roughan Castle

WALSHESTOWN *Down* J5450

This 16th century tower 7.8m by 6.8m has four storeys, a low pitched roof, and stepped battlements with square turrets rising above diagonally opposite corners. From the entrance a straight stair leads to the hall, and then a spiral stair leads to the bedrooms and roof. Part of a loopholed bawn wall 2.5m high lies around the tower.

MAP OF CASTLES OF ULSTER

FURTHER READING

Irish Castles and Castellated Houses, Harold Leask, 1941
Houses of Ireland, Brian de Breffny and Rosemary Ffoliott, 1975
The architecture of Ireland, Maurice Craig, 1982
Historic Monuments of Northern Ireland, H.M.S.O., 1983
Castles of County Cork, James N. Healy, 1988
Ancient Castles of Limerick, Thomas Johnston Westropp
The Shell Guide to Ireland, Lord Killanin and Michael Duignan, 1969
North West Ulster, Alastair Rowan, 1979 (first volume of Buildings of Ireland series)
Guide to the National Monuments of Ireland, Peter Harbison, 1970
Journals of the archaeological societies of Cork, Galway, Kerry, Kildare, Louth, Ulster
Journals of the Royal Society of Antiquaries of Ireland and the Royal Irish Academy
Archaeological Journal, Medieval Archaeology. Guide pamphlets exist for: Ardglass, Audleys, Carrickfergus, Dundrum, Dungiven, Dunluce, Enniskillen, Greencastle, Monea. Aughanure, Cahir, Carrick-on-Suir, Cashel, Dublin, Kilkenny, Portumna, Parke's.